# ESSENTIALS OF MODERN RESEARCH METHODS IN HEALTH, PHYSICAL EDUCATION, AND RECREATION

Kris E. Berg

Richard W. Latin

*School of Health, Physical Education, and Recreation*
*University of Nebraska at Omaha*

PRENTICE HALL, ENGLEWOOD CLIFFS, NEW JERSEY 07632

*Library of Congress Cataloging-in-Publication Data*

BERG, KRIS E., [date]
   Essentials of modern research methods in health, physical education, and recreation
KRIS E. BERG and RICHARD W. LATIN

      p.   cm,
      Includes bibliographical references and index.
      ISBN 0-13-644014-2
      1. Research—Methodology.   2. Technical writing.   3. Medical
sciences—Research—Methodology.   4. Physical education and
training—Research—Methodology.   5. Recreation—Research—
Methodology.   I. Latin, Richard Wayne, [date].   II. Title.
Q180.55.M4B417      1994
001.4'2—dc20        93–44092

Acquisitions editor:   *Ted Bolen*
Editorial/production supervision and
   interior design:   *Edie Riker*
Cover design:   *Design Solutions*
Production coordinator:   *Peter Havens*
Editorial assistant:   *Nicole Gray*

 © 1994 by Prentice-Hall, Inc.
A Paramount Communications Company
Englewood Cliffs, NJ 07632

Printed in the United States of America

10   9   8   7   6   5   4   3   2   1

ISBN 0-13-644014-2

Prentice-Hall International (UK) Limited, *London*
Prentice-Hall of Australia Pty. Limited, *Sydney*
Prentice-Hall Canada Inc., *Toronto*
Prentice-Hall Hispanoamericana, S.A., *Mexico*
Prentice-Hall of India Private Limited, *New Delhi*
Prentice-Hall of Japan, Inc., *Tokyo*
Simon & Schuster Asia Pte. Ltd., *Singapore*
Editora Prentice-Hall do Brasil, Ltda., *Rio de Janeiro*

# CONTENTS

## SECTION II   RESEARCH WRITING

## SECTION III   STATISTICS

# SECTION IV   MEASUREMENT AND RESEARCH DESIGN

## SECTION V   QUALITY CONTROL AND APPLICATION OF RESEARCH

## APPENDIX

# PREFACE

This book was written for students in health, physical education/exercise science, and recreation (HPER). Its primary objective is to provide instruction for HPER professionals on how to be producers and consumers of research. Numerous examples from each of these academic areas are cited throughout the text. Many students take a dim view of research classes and perceive researchers as overly cerebral "eggheads." To help alleviate this attitude, we have attempted to make this an easy-to-read, highly applied, and user-friendly textbook—and even, on occasion, humorous.

The book provides coverage in topics that are commonly discussed in a research methods class. This information should allow students to effectively write research proposals and theses to read and understand research published in their discipline, and conduct basic studies. Several topics are covered that are rarely dealt with in existing books, such as the role of research in universities, quality control, the need for and history of informed consent, and ethics in research. Note that this book was not intended to be voluminous, giving in-depth coverage of all aspects of research.

Students should focus on the book's instructional aids. At the beginning of each chapter is a brief list of key concepts discussed in the chapter. Following these are learning objectives/review questions. *Students should read these before and especially after reading each chapter.* If an objective is not met, *additional review of that topic is necessary.*

The section on statistics emphasizes interpretation. Many examples are integrated with various types of experimental and nonexperimental designs so that students can more easily understand the application of statistics to specific research problems. Statistics chapters provide example problems and their solutions that reflect research situations from the three disciplines. At the end of each of these chapters statistics exercises are given. The exercises may be solved by hand and/or by computer. The answers are in Appendix II.

The growth of our professions depends on its members being active producers and/or consumers of research. We trust that through the use of this book your knowledge of and appreciation for the research process will be enhanced.

# ACKNOWLEDGMENTS

One of the primary reasons I wanted to become involved in writing this book was due to the experiences I gained from teaching a course in research methods. Over the years it became more apparent that many students were apprehensive about taking the course. They tended to share the typical negative stereotypes about research and researchers. Therefore I would like to thank those anxious students who actually provided me with a tremendous challenge and source of motivation. Because of them, hopefully, future students will benefit.

Great appreciation is extended to all members of my family. They also provide me with a different, albeit important, form of encouragement. (I'm still not sure if they totally understand this "college professor" thing, however!)

I would also like to thank my co-author. He is a tireless worker, a source of inspiration, and a very nice person. Kris has been an excellent role model for me, especially in my early years as a faculty member. I know that my academic career would not have been as successful without him.

Finally, if I would have been asked at the beginning of my career if I would enjoy teaching, conducting, and writing research as much as I do now I would have replied, "No way!"—or words to that effect. It's funny how things can change.

*Rick Latin*

I wish to express appreciation to my wonderful wife, Carolyn, and my sons, Eric and Steve, for their support and understanding while writing this book. Without such a strong base, the task would never have been started. I also am very thankful for the love and support of my parents, Richard and Frederica, who always made me feel like a winner. Other key players in my life I wish to note are my sister, Diana, my brothers, Chuck, Steve, Bob, and Brian, and my parents-in-law, Nancy and Bill Heard. They contributed more than they could ever realize.

I also thank the many fine students in my classes at the University of Nebraska at Omaha. Their questions, joys, frustrations, enthusiasm, and patience with my numerous teaching "brainstorms" have allowed me to learn much about the art of teaching and realize that quality teaching demands a large amount of time, energy, and caring about people. Lastly, I thank my colleague, Rick Latin, who has been a joy to work with. For years we have shared much about our teaching and research, and I am the better for it.

*Kris Berg*

The authors also thank Andy Barela, graphic artist at the University of Nebraska at Omaha, for his excellent work in developing the figures and cartoons.

# CHAPTER 1

# INTRODUCTION TO RESEARCH

**KEY CONCEPTS**

Scientific method
Inductive and deductive
  reasoning
Fact, theory, and principle
Basic research
Applied research

Field research
Laboratory research
Internal validity
External validity
Independent and
  dependent variables

**AFTER READING THIS CHAPTER, YOU SHOULD BE ABLE TO**

- Explain the role of research training in graduate education.
- State the primary purpose of research.
- Describe common misconceptions about research.
- Explain the importance of staying current with developments in one's field.
- Define the scientific method and explain each step.
- Describe inductive and deductive reasoning.
- Explain how fact, theory, and principle are interrelated.
- Understand the limitations of making decisions based on tradition, trial and error, bias, and superstition.
- Differentiate between basic and applied research.
- State the pros and cons of field versus laboratory research.
- Define internal and external validity.
- Define and give an example of an independent and a dependent variable.
- Describe desirable characteristics of the researcher.

$W$hy is it that nearly all graduate degrees offered by universities and colleges in the United States require taking a course in research? There must be a good reason why such a requirement is so common. Tradition may be one, but a more persuasive rationale may be because research is so much a part of modern life that academics want students to understand the process, for the sake of general knowledge as well as for professional training. Newspapers, television, radio, and magazines regularly report research in some form. Research data are quoted to describe and justify expenditures. The local school board quotes figures about increasing enrollment and teachers' salaries to justify a bond levy. The city council cites traffic density data to justify widening the streets or to construct new entrance and exit ramps from an interstate. Advertisements proclaim that "9 out of 10 doctors recommend . . ." or that this beverage is "lighter than or less filling than. . . ."

We are bombarded during election years with surveys indicating the support and rank order of candidates. The media quote the latest study on cholesterol, fiber, fat. . . . While watching a ball game on television, we are inundated with batting averages, won-loss records against certain opponents, passing and running yardage, percentage of third downs converted. . . . Nearly everything we do is quantified by someone in order to make a decision. The decision may involve the products we purchase, how we eat and exercise, whether or not we smoke, and myriad other facets of our lives.

So, whether or not we realize it—or even like it—we live in a world of statistics and research. Consequently, it seems logical that an educated person today, particularly one with an advanced degree, should possess a basic knowledge of the research process.

## THE PRIMARY PURPOSES OF RESEARCH

Research, simply put, is a way to gather information and make a sound decision or judgment or develop new knowledge. A recreation therapist wishes to find a better way to work with patients who are physically limited. A coach wants to know how to build strength safely and effectively in junior high school athletes. A health teacher isn't sure how much time to spend lecturing as opposed to students' discussing, watching films, or listening to guest speakers. A playground supervisor would like to know what programs will be most popular during the summer. In order to find an answer and make a decision in each of these examples, an understanding of research could be very helpful.

## A COMMON MISCONCEPTION ABOUT RESEARCH

Many people, including a graduate students early in their programs, view research as dull, theoretical, and impractical. Researchers are seen as overly cerebral intellectuals with IQs surpassing 180 who wear white lab coats and work in highly sophisticated laboratories with extremely complex and expensive equipment. They are thought to deal only with esoteric topics—subatomic particles, the distance of the furthest galaxies, and other matters that the average person barely understands or can relate to.

Portraits of two researchers.

What people may not realize is that many professionals in all areas use research techniques in their daily work. They may do their research work in far less technical environments, such as schools, hospitals, parks, and businesses. They typically are not concerned with splitting atoms, but they are interested in and deal with everyday problems and questions. For example, health educators may use research to study the causes, prevention, and treatment of drug abuse, marital stress, and eating disorders. Physical educators investigate when it is safe and effective for children and adolescents to train with weights, how to develop the abdominal musculature without injuring the back, how to create students' interest in personal physical fitness, and what fitness tests to use. Recreation professionals investigate what activities to offer in a summer recreation program, the effects of recreational services on people, and the leisure-time practices and needs of people. All of these are very real problems that professionals in HPER can address, and sound research methods will typically provide the best way to find an answer.

Most of the research done by people in HPER is application oriented simply because these disciplines evolved from a host of other traditional, long-standing academic fields: Sport psychology is derived from psychology; exercise physiology from biology, chemistry, and physiology; and kinesiology from anatomy and physics. Health and recreation/leisure studies are even broader than the various subdisciplines in physical education. They incorporate knowledge across a wide array of academic disciplines. These fields draw their knowledge base from as many disciplines as can enhance knowledge of people as it relates to lifestyle and use of leisure time. Consequently, the disciplines and their related problems and questions are highly applied.

## RESEARCH IN OUR DAILY LIVES

### Staying Current and Being Professional

Staying reasonably up to date with today's rapidly developing knowledge is a demanding task even for the most dedicated professional. Toffler's *Future Shock* describes the rapidity of change in every facet of modern society and suggests that the rate of change is forever accelerating. In order to carry out our daily work as effective professionals, we must be consumers of a certain amount of research. Doing something well in this day and age implies doing it based on the best and most recent knowledge available.

Few of us would go to a dentist who didn't use a painkiller before removing a tooth. Similarly, people with whom we work should expect to receive accurate, current information. An expectation of reasonable quality should be held for any professional, and part of that quality can only be attained and maintained by reading research journals in your field. However, some understanding is needed to distinguish legitimate research from pseudo research. Madison Avenue cleverly overstates the benefits of one product and touts it as better than that of a competitor. Professionals with research training should be able to detect the limitations of such statements. Much of the public is unable to do so.

As an example, some of the lay literature exaggerates the benefits of the healthy lifestyle. Well before research data were available to document the cost-effectiveness of corporate fitness/health promotion programs, numerous articles claimed how fantastic the savings would be to corporations. Few if any data actually existed to support the claims. And so it is with vitamin and mineral supplements. Articles abound with claims of reduced illness, cures of disease, improved energy, and even reversal of the aging process. Research data simply don't support such dramatic effects. However, note how frequently pseudo health authorities appear in the media espousing their fantastic claims to the American public.

The point to be emphasized is that false and misleading advertising is rampant. Perhaps people would rather listen to a glamorous celebrity rather than be informed by an unknown professional in HPER. This makes our work more challenging, as we may have to correct some of the notions people have picked up from such sources. And hopefully we are able to differentiate sound from unsound sources of information and facts from fantasy and misconceptions. Well-informed professionals need to be able to distinguish fact from fiction. We need to know what characterizes sound research and the limitations in a study (and every study certainly has limitations). We then can provide people with facts rather than let them search for information from the wrong sources.

### Being a Consumer of Research

With a good understanding of the fundamentals of research, you are not only more likely to read research on your own but also are far more likely to comprehend it. Becoming a consumer of research should be a primary goal of any graduate research class. Being a user of research may well be a factor that separates the more successful professional from the average one. By reading research and thinking about ways to use some of the findings, your mind-set becomes one aimed at self-growth. This tends to improve your job performance. Consequently, a cycle of self-improvement is created that helps you be an achiever. So who says research isn't practical!

Adopting the mind-set and some procedures used in research can even be useful in your daily life. (Yes, this actually has occurred and is documented in the *Journal of Unbelievable Phenomena* [1962].) It may affect the way you plan your finances, organize a summer vacation, plan a career move, or even choose a graduate school. An educated person is often said not merely to know facts but also how to obtain and use those facts. Knowing how to use a library efficiently is a great boon to accessing information quickly and is a critical skill for living in the age of knowledge explosion. An experienced researcher can enter a library and in 20 to 30 minutes can walk out with a lengthy list of pertinent references. Compare this to the novice who meanders through three floors of the library looking for "some health journals." After a disappointing and frustrating 45 minutes of not finding anything of real use, the student exits the library in disgust.

The research process certainly isn't perfect, but for most of us it can't be beat in terms of maximizing the soundness of our decisions. The process, with regular use, becomes an invaluable skill that carries over into much of our professional life, including the planning of meetings, classes, budgets, and program objectives. In short, you may really become more productive professionally because of using an organized, scientific approach.

## THE SCIENTIFIC METHOD

The time-honored procedure used by scientists and most researchers to study what is of interest to them is known as the *scientific method*. It is a logical basis for answering questions and interpreting data. Because of its application to all academic disciplines and potentially any real-world problem, it is considered the foundation of the research process.

The scientific method involves several steps, as outlined in the following discussion. An example of a study dealing with two strategies to lower cholesterol is used for illustrative purposes.

*State the problem.*

- Does diet or exercise have a greater impact on cholesterol level?

*State a testable or measurable hypothesis.*

- Diet has a greater effect on cholesterol than exercise.

*Plan the methods to be used in carrying out the study.*

- Who will be the subjects? What will be their characteristics regarding age, sex, diet, physical activity, initial cholesterol levels, medical history, and so on?

- What measurements will be made? How and when will they be made?
- Define exactly what the two groups in this case will actually do? What will the diet consist of for each group? How will adherence to the diet be assessed? Exactly what will the exercise group do as regards the intensity, duration, frequency, and type of exercise? How will their adherence be determined?
- How will the data be treated statistically?

*Carry out the study:* The two groups follow the guidelines for exercise and diet set by the study.

*Analyze the data using appropriate statistics.*

*State the conclusion(s):* Diet and exercise are equally effective in reducing serum cholesterol.

*State a new research question.*

The scientific method allows making a decision, in this case, a comparison, based on data that are carefully gathered using sound measurement techniques. What the subjects actually did with their diets and exercise was carefully identified. The change in cholesterol was then judged to be noteworthy or statistically significant based on a predetermined criterion—that is, a significance level of .05, which means that there is a 5% probability that the decision made may be in error but a 95% probability that the decision made was correct. This is quite different than "eyeballing" the results and making a decision.

Most people looking for answers to a problem or trying to make a decision probably have some bias favoring one answer or outcome. For example, a dietitian may have hoped that diet exerted a greater effect on cholesterol, whereas a physical educator may have hoped for the reverse. Without using an objective statistical approach, it is all too easy for the dietitian or physical educator to pronounce small differences as being noteworthy. For example, if the cholesterol in the exercise group dropped from 190 mg/dl to 180 and that of the diet group from 195 to 183, is the difference in change between the two groups really meaningful? Is it valid for the physical educator to proclaim that exercise has a greater effect than diet?

Given the likely bias that many of us may have when making comparisons, there is a need for statistics to remove the subjectivity in the decision-making process. If the difference between the two groups is too small to be statistically significant, then one can be reasonably confident that the difference is not real and is most likely due to measurement error, chance, or the like. Consequently, use of the scientific method allows one to make a bias-free judgment. That does not mean it is always the best decision, but it will certainly tend to be better.

Research should not be viewed as a mere compilation of results from many independent studies. Rather, it should thought of as an ever-changing body of information that may yield different interpretations over time. New results engender new hypotheses that are then tested through the scientific method. Former "facts" may no longer be supported and are replaced by new results.

Consequently, the state of knowledge of a topic at any time must be thought of as temporary, with future modifications "baking away in the research oven."

## INDUCTIVE AND DEDUCTIVE REASONING

*Inductive reasoning* is making a conclusion or generalization based on a limited number of observations. Thus it proceeds from the specific to the general. All research that makes inferences or generalizations about the results of a study uses inductive reasoning. For example, if 40 vegetarians were studied and all were found to be introverts, one might conclude that all vegetarians are introverts. Obviously, the conclusion, though logical, certainly may not characterize all vegetarians. One can readily understand why researchers prefer having a reasonable number of subjects in a study—the conclusion is more likely to be true. The formation of theory from fact is also based on inductive reasoning because a generalization is made on a limited number of observations.

*Deductive reasoning* is the reverse of inductive reasoning: It proceeds from the general to a specific case. If a foreigner visited the United States and was taken to a location where tryouts were being held for a professional basketball team, it could easily be concluded that most men can dunk a basketball. The logic would go something like this: All American men can dunk a basketball. Joe is an American man. Therefore he can dunk a basketball.

The application of research is also based on deductive reasoning. We assume or deduce that what occurred in a sample of subjects in a study may also occur in other people similar to the subjects. If a study found estrogen replacement therapy to increase bone density of postmenopausal women, one might deduce that a similar change might occur in your 60-year-old aunt and you may encourage her to see her physician.

Inductive and deductive reasoning obviously do not always produce sound conclusions. The soundness of either method of reasoning is only as good as the premise used. For example, most American men cannot dunk a basketball as a movie title once suggested. Generalizing from a limited number of cases or to dissimilar people places severe limitations on deductive reasoning.

## FACT, THEORY, AND PRINCIPLE

The scientific method strives to obtain *facts*, that is, consistently observed events. For example, changes in cholesterol level associated with dietary changes or alteration in mood before and after recreational activity may be measured to see how consistently they are affected by selected variables. The consistency is determined with appropriate statistics that indicate whether or not the change more likely occurs because of the variable or chance. If the balance of studies detects similar change in a variable, then at some point a fact has been engendered.

*Theory* represents the integration of many facts into the explanation of a phenomenon. This complex process attempts to satisfy most facts associated with the phenomenon. For example, a theory of obesity must include knowledge about food intake, physical activity, metabolism, and the influence of genetics on these factors. As new information becomes available, theory must be modified accordingly. As stated previously, because new information is continually produced, fact and theory must be revised periodically. Consequently, it is important to understand that knowledge perpetually changes.

One of the most vital reasons for conducting research besides simply understanding ourselves and the world we live in is to guide behavior. Guides to behavior that are based on fact and theory are called *principles*. Many things we do professionally as well as personally are based on fact and theory. Weight training principles, dietary guidelines, and learning principles are examples. Professions obviously strive to develop guidelines for their practitioners as a means of improving the lives of people served. Consequently, research and the weaving together of fact, theory, and principle will always be vital components in the development of health, physical education/exercise science, and recreation as professions.

## OTHER, LESS SCIENTIFIC METHODS

Compare decision making with the use of the scientific method including statistics with that of making decisions based on *tradition*, *trial* and *error*, or *bias*. Many of our purchasing decisions are done on an emotional basis. Madison Avenue spends billions of dollars creating designs, colors, shapes, and sizes that they hope we will find attractive enough to buy. Think of the number and variety of cereal boxes in the supermarket. Consider the great number of shoes for runners, walkers, aerobic dancers, and tennis players. They are aimed largely at the visual and emotional regions of our brains. Incidentally, how do you think Madison Avenue actually selects the various colors, shapes, words, and pictures? Through research, naturally! When huge amounts of money are on the line, what else would you expect?

Although the scientific method is not perfect, it probably will yield the best information in most situations. The majority of people tend to make many of their decisions based on tradition, emotions, superstition, and overall poor logic. How many basketball players buy Air Jordans in the hope that these sneakers will improve their jumping ability? How many weight trainers follow the biceps routine of the current Mr. America? How many coaches switch to the offense or defense of the number one rated team after completion of the bowl games? How much oatmeal was sold in the last several years to people trying to lower their cholesterol when their cholesterol may have already been quite low? How much vitamin C is consumed by the average American? Why is a book about a new means of weight loss so likely to sell many copies? Is a Hollywood starlet qualified to write a book on physical fitness? Is a former professional athlete an authority on physical fitness for children?

Most of us realize how common these examples are, but we would be less likely to imagine how often we make decisions on the job in a similar manner. Think about the last time you made a fairly important change in something you do at the workplace or in your personal life. For example, have you changed what you teach or how you teach it? Have you dropped a unit while adding one? Have you altered your eating habits or exercise program? Have you installed a new offense with a team you coach? Have you added, deleted, or changed certain exercises done in your class? Have you used any facets of the scientific method in making a decision about any of these changes? If not, you are a particularly good candidate for improving the effectiveness of your decisions.

## BASIC AND APPLIED RESEARCH

*Basic* research is performed without a specific purpose in mind. Rather, it is done primarily for the sake of knowledge alone. In contrast, *applied* research is done with a specific question or application in mind. Consider a health educator who wishes to know if a six-week unit on drug education will change drug usage and attitudes in high school students. The researcher wishes to address a specific question. In comparison, a researcher in particle physics designs an experiment to accelerate subatomic particles to a velocity previously never reached. The purpose? Perhaps it is simply to see what happens. This somewhat vague approach demonstrates basic research. Although it is typically viewed that basic research is done with no specific purpose in mind, one might question whether or not this is actually so. The physicist may have some fairly specific hunches as to what may happen and why it may happen. By observing what does actually happen, more links between observations, theories, and hunches may be developed. So is it really nonpurposeful research? Perhaps it is not so important to answer the question as it is to realize that both types of research may exist on two ends of a continuum with neither one necessarily at the absolute end.

## FIELD VERSUS LABORATORY RESEARCH

*Field* research is done outside the tightly controlled environment of the laboratory: a school, classroom, gymnasium, park, hospital—any location that exists in the "real world." *Laboratory* research is conducted under more "sterile" conditions, which allows researchers to exert tighter control over an experiment. This control facilitates research being sound, but it can limit the application of the results. In real life, many factors may affect learning other than the experimental variable, and field research allows these other factors to operate. Some mistakenly feel that field research is inferior to laboratory research. This is certainly not true. Some settings make experimental research difficult if not impossible. This is certainly the case in many environments where HPER professionals work. It would be more accurate to state that experimental and field research each has its strengths as well as limitations. We discuss field and laboratory research in more depth in Chapter 14.

## INTERNAL AND EXTERNAL VALIDITY

*Internal validity* is the soundness or overall quality of research. Were measures carefully, accurately, and reliably made? Were appropriate statistical techniques used to analyze the data? Was the study conducted in a way that allows the possible effect of an experimental variable to be demonstrated adequately? Were the effects of other factors besides the experimental variable minimized? Good research deals with all factors that allow research questions to be soundly tested.

Laboratory research generally is characterized by higher internal validity than field research, because of the relatively tight controls that may be placed on a study. For example, the lifestyle of mice can be regulated strictly as regards diet, physical activity, temperature, and the like. The lifestyle of people living and working in a variety of environments makes regulation rather difficult. Demonstrating that a low-fat diet reduces cholesterol would thus be easier in the mice as compared to a group of people who may not fully adhere to the dietary regimen.

*External validity* deals with the potential application of the results of a study, or its generalizability. There is no statistic that provides a simple answer as to when and what can be applied. Rather, application is justified to the degree that the people and conditions involved in the potential application are similar to the subjects and conditions of the original experiment. For example, results of a study comparing two methods of teaching the tennis serve to 12-year-old novices may not be applicable to older, more experienced players. Similarly, the effects of a drug on subjects with high cholesterol may not be applicable to people having normal cholesterol levels.

Field research often allows greater potential for application than laboratory research because it is conducted in an environment more likely to be similar to conditions outside the lab.

## INDEPENDENT AND DEPENDENT VARIABLES

An *independent variable* is one that is manipulated or controlled by the researcher; the *dependent variable* is the behavior that is measured to determine if it is affected by the independent variable. For example, in a study examining the effect of consuming caffeine on anxiety level, caffeine is the independent variable and anxiety level is the dependent variable. It thus will be determined if the behavior (anxiety level) is dependent on caffeine (manipulated variable).

## CHARACTERISTICS OF THE RESEARCHER

Certain traits seem to characterize competent researchers, which suggests that they should be developed in people who are training to become researchers. Awareness of these characteristics may help you to train yourself accordingly, as well as to understand some of the requisites for success as a researcher.

***Open-Minded***   Researchers should be open to all possible options in deciding what questions to ask, strategies to use in studying a problem, and possible explanations for results. One shouldn't pigeonhole his or her thinking because it tends to narrow one's focus. Limiting the breadth of one's thinking reduces the likelihood of examining all possibilities. Many great scientific theories probably emerged due largely to the ability of someone to view a concept in an open, unobstructed manner.

***Knowledgeable in a Specific Subject***   The researcher must know a given field fairly well in order to ask appropriate questions. What problems or controversies exist? What constraints have limited the study of a given topic? For example, measurement of body fat even today is limited by the fact that calculation of body fat from underwater weighing is based on the dissection of a small number of cadavers performed decades ago. Equations were developed to predict body density based on the findings from these few cadavers, so use of the same equations for other people with widely varying ages and physical activity levels is not strongly justified.

*Intellectual Curiosity*   Few people would muster the time and energy to do research without having a reasonably good amount of intellectual curiosity. One couldn't develop much knowledge of a topic without considerable reading. Heightened curiosity leads to more reading and increased desire to learn. As knowledge is accumulated, intellectually curious people tend to want to know even more. Details become more important as the mind strives to connect and relate concepts and bits of information. This curiosity probably explains why many researchers do much of their work in one specific topic. As a few research questions are answered, more questions are raised and curiosity seems to lead to more research.

*Perseverance*   As stated, developing the knowledge and insights needed to do research takes time and effort. The research process itself involves numerous detailed steps often requiring several years for completion. Perseverance is obviously needed. Formulating the exact research question may take many hours of reading and discussion with other researchers. Writing the documents that are required by most universities to obtain approval to perform a study takes time. The study must be planned and explained in detail. The actual collection of data may take months. Then the data are analyzed statistically and the final portions of the research paper are written.

Typically, researchers will submit the study in an abstract form to be presented at a professional meeting. The manuscript is prepared and submitted to a research publication and is reviewed by several expert researchers on the topic who then suggest revisions to the author. The manuscript is revised accordingly and resubmitted in hopes of it then being accepted. It may or may not be accepted for publication, however. The *Research Quarterly for Exercise and Sport*, for example, typically rejects more than 80 percent of submitted manuscripts. If rejected, the author then will most likely resubmit the manuscript to a different publication. It is no wonder that the time from developing the research question to the date of publication in a journal typically is several years. This does require perseverance.

*Honesty*   In writing the results of a study for publication or presentation a researcher has ample opportunity to be dishonest. A person might plagiarize or, even more likely, alter data in order to support a given hypothesis or line of reasoning. Considerable pressure to publish and obtain funding for grants exists in many universities. Also, in order to gain a professional reputation, a person may decide to cut corners and do something unethical.

Another example of academic dishonesty is the placement of a faculty member's name before that of a graduate student under his or her supervision on a publication. Graduate students who write theses or dissertations should always be the first author of a study. This breach of ethics has occurred too often, and many professional groups and universities have written policy declaring that the student's name must be placed first.

Developing the state of knowledge in a discipline is seriously hindered by those who falsify data. If the item is published, it potentially misleads many other scholars and students. They may then do work based in part on the false findings presented, which may throw them off the track and cause considerable wasted time. Also, much of the information presented in textbooks is based on research findings. Falsification of findings can ultimately lead to students learning erroneous information. Consequently, a bit of misinformation may lead to considerable compounding of the act.

## SUMMARY

Training in research has been a hallmark of graduate education for many years. It is considered a key trait of a professional with advanced training because it makes one more logical and able to read and understand professional literature. These characteristics are essential to becoming and maintaining one's status as a quality professional. Although only a relatively small percentage of professionals actually conduct research, all of us should view ourselves as consumers of research.

The scientific method is an orderly and logical means of addressing problems and answering questions. Consequently, it is a very practical tool. Less scientific methods, such as tradition, superstition, trial and error, and mimicking the champions, are illogical and less useful.

Research, while sound and useful, isn't easy to do. It requires a high degree of open-mindedness, specific knowledge in a field, intellectual curiosity, perseverance, and honesty.

# CHAPTER 2

# ETHICS IN HUMAN SUBJECT RESEARCH

---

**KEY CONCEPTS**

Institutional review board
Informed consent
Confidentiality and
   anonymity
Invasion of privacy

Safe and competent
   treatment
Knowledge of results
The researcher's role

**AFTER READING THIS CHAPTER, YOU SHOULD BE ABLE TO**

- Explain the major concerns for ethical treatment of research subjects.
- Describe the process of informed consent and the components of an informed consent document.
- Discuss the issues of confidentiality, invasion of privacy, safe and competent treatment, and knowledge of results regarding research subjects.
- Explain the role of the researcher concerning the ethical treatment of subjects.

---

$R$esearch subjects have irrefutable rights that allow them to make informed decisions about participating in a study, and upon participation, to be treated in a safe, humane, and professional manner. The design of a study, the characteristics of the subjects, the methods used in an investigation, and the disposition of the researcher may all influence the ethical treatment of the participant. Therefore, before we delve into more detailed discussions on these and other research topics, it is important that we spend some time examining some of the basic considerations and rights of human research subjects.

## CODES AND GUIDELINES

In 1974, the U.S. Congress formed the National Commission for the Protection of Human Subjects of Biomedical and Behavioral Research to address ethical guidelines for human research subjects. The Belmont Report (1978), the published results of the commission's deliberations, is one of the keystone documents for research ethics in the United States. Federal agencies involved in human subject research, like the Food and Drug Administration and the Department of Health and Human Services, have regulations that reflect the recommendations of the Belmont Report. Many international codes, such as the Code of Nuremberg (1949) and the Declaration of Helsinki (1974), also address the protection of research subjects. Virtually every journal that publishes human subject (and animal) research has a policy statement on obtaining informed consent and ethical treatment of subjects that investigators must declare to have complied with. Many of these codes and guidelines have evolved from noted abuses of human subjects rights in the not so distant past. In short, ethics in human subject research is a serious matter that requires our attention.

## THE INSTITUTIONAL REVIEW BOARD

An institutional review board (IRB) is a panel of research experts who pass judgment on the quality and safety of studies before they can be conducted. Most institutions where human subject research is conducted have an IRB. It serves primarily as a means of protecting the rights of subjects and is an important research quality control measure. The IRB also protects researchers and the institution as well. Among the many other functions of the IRB is the evaluation and approval of proposed studies as well as the informed consent documents that will be used in an investigation. We discuss the IRB in much more detail in Chapter 17, but for now simply note that the IRB serves as a vital means of ensuring that sound and ethical research practices are utilized at an institution.

## INFORMED CONSENT

An investigator has an ethical commitment to ensure that a potential subject has sufficient information and comprehension so that a sound decision about participating in a study may be made. Informed consent is one of the subject's most important rights. Typically, the informed consent process involves the prospective subject reading a simple but thorough written document that provides the essential details of the study. After reading the document and discussing any questions with the investigator, the subject is usually in an informed position to determine whether or not to participate.

Informed consent statements vary in language, length, and detail. Studies that pose little or no risk may use very simple and brief consents, whereas investigations involving greater risk (even life-threatening in some medical research) need to employ much more elaborate consent forms and practices. It is important to emphasize that the language level of the consent form needs to written at the comprehension level of the subject, without using unnecessary "big words" or technical jargon. Needless to say a consent form geared for medical students would be considerably different than one aimed at fourth graders. This is probably the most significant problem and challenge that researchers have when preparing these documents. Remember, what seems like everyday language to the professional is usually quite foreign to the subject. The document needs to be written in a noncoercive and straight-forward manner that is respectful of the prospective subject. Finally, for subjects under the age of majority there are parental consents as well as youth and child assents that serve as consent documents. Examples of some consent forms are given in Appendix III.

## Components of an Informed Consent

As we have mentioned, consent forms may vary considerably in terms of content, language, and length. What follows are descriptions of some of the basic elements of an informed consent document. Check with your university for specific information regarding its consent form requirements.

*Background and Invitation to Participate*   This is a brief statement that provides some background about the study, the need to conduct it, and why the subject is being asked to participate. This is an important section because the researcher is trying to stimulate interest and inform the subject about why it is important to become involved.

*Explanation of Procedures*   The investigator must describe all of the procedures that the subject will be asked to perform and where the methods will be conducted. Sufficient details need to be provided for each aspect of the study—all pre- and postassessments, intervention of a treatment, and so on. Failure to provide critical components and characteristics (risky, unpleasant, costs, etc.) could be regarded as an act of unethical deception. Could you imagine a researcher approaching a subject during a study and saying: "Oh, we forgot to tell you that we'll need to perform a brain biopsy. Don't worry; it won't hurt a bit!"

*Potential Risks and Discomforts*   In this section the investigator must describe any apparent risk or discomfort that may occur during the study that may be considered important in the subject's decision to participate. Risks may be classified as physical (heart attack, pain, bruised skin, nausea), psychological (distress, anxiety, fear), legal (possible criminal action), economic (loss of job), or social (invasion of privacy). In addition, many universities and agencies require a statement of what type of medical treatment the subject may receive if injured during the research. The federal and international codes mentioned earlier also mandate the disclosure of foreseeable risks.

*Potential Benefits*  Two types of benefits may result from the research. One is the possible benefits to the *subject* and the other is to *society*. Therefore, in this section any benefits that are likely to be expected are described. These descriptions must be written in a way that does not guarantee or exaggerate the benefits, so that the subject is not misled. The possible benefits from the proposed research may or may not be of direct value to the subject. So if there are no direct benefits to the subject, it must be clearly stated. There always must be some benefit to society (advancement of knowledge, etc.) for a study to be ethically conducted. The societal benefit should be stated in this section as well.

*Rights of Inquiry and Withdrawal*  Subjects must be informed that they have the right to ask questions and have them answered by the investigator at any time. This is particularly true during the consent process, where clarification of uncertainties clearly affect a person's ability to make an informed decision. Subjects also have the right to withdraw from the study at any time they desire. Therefore, there needs to be a statement to that effect, and additionally they need to be informed that they are free to withdraw without fear of reprisal or future prejudice on the part of the researcher or the sponsoring institution. You may see where this may raise touchy questions about requiring students to participate in a research study as a class requirement or other such academic situations.

It is important to point out that when a subject provides consent it is considered unethical to ask him or her to waive any legal rights or privileges. Therefore, there cannot be any language in the consent form that requires the subject to relinquish any of these rights. This is also true for any language that absolves the researcher or the institution from any liability for negligent actions.

## Valid Informed Consent

We all have probably read and signed documents that we didn't really understand, such as a bank loan contract or an insurance policy. We sign on the good faith that the loan officer or agent is not trying to take advantage of us. All too often a subject hastily "reads" a consent document and agrees to participate with that same good faith. The point to be made here is that a signature from a subject doesn't necessarily imply that valid informed consent was obtained. Actually, the consent form serves only to "assist" the investigator in negotiating valid consent from the subject. To help verify that prospective subjects comprehend what they have just read and are in an enlightened position to provide a valid consent, it is suggested that the investigator ask them several questions about the document before signatures are obtained.

## CONFIDENTIALITY AND ANONYMITY

All observations that are made on research subjects should be treated in as confidential a manner as possible. This typically implies that only the investigator(s) or possibly those involved in gathering the research information have access to or knowledge of the identity of the subjects and their related measurements. When possible, codes or identification numbers should be assigned to subjects and their research records to protect their anonymity. Reporting of research results is usually done with group rather than individual data, which further masks the identity of singular observations. Individual results may only be disclosed or reported with the subject's permission.

## INVASION OF PRIVACY

It is certainly acceptable to make research observations of many public acts that would normally be viewed by others. However, it is considered unethical and an invasion of privacy to made clandestine observations of acts that would be considered personal or sensitive in nature. This is not to say that research of this type can't be ethically conducted, as, for instance, the many studies in human sexuality that have been done. When studying highly personal behaviors or utilizing covert observational techniques, it is essential to explain the rationale to the subjects and to obtain their permission and consent prior to any data collection.

## SAFE AND COMPETENT TREATMENT

A subject should expect the investigator to have a high degree of skill in making research assessments. The measurements should be made in a professional manner that respects the dignity of the subject and minimizes any potential risk or discomfort. Practicing new or unfamiliar skills during a study may predispose a subject to unnecessary risk, diminish the validity of the data that are collected, as well as reduce the credibility of the investigator in the eyes of the subject or others involved in the project.

## KNOWLEDGE OF RESULTS

A researcher's responsibility to research subjects doesn't end after the last measurement is made. An investigator has a professional obligation to provide subjects with feedback about their own outcome and the general results of the study and to acknowledge any promises that were made for consideration for participating in the study. Failure to provide knowledge of outcome conveys a negative, impersonal message about the researcher and is a breach of plain, common courtesy. Be assured that subjects prefer to work with nice researchers, so providing feedback in a friendly and timely manner not only enhances the investigator's reputation but may help in recruiting subjects for future studies.

## THE RESEARCHER'S ROLE

The investigator is the individual who is primarily responsible for the ethical treatment of research subjects. No IRB, federal agency, or international code can directly oversee the research process; therefore, it is incumbent on the researcher to employ safe, honest, and ethical practices. Unfortunately, a few researchers feel some guidelines and review boards are so restrictive that they limit their academic freedom. Those adopting this viewpoint sometimes attempt to justify some unethical practices to promote their own research agenda. Usually there is little merit to these claims, particularly when it is apparent that ego expansion and notoriety are placed ahead of scientific objectivity and professionalism. When we recall the characteristics of a competent researcher (see Chapter 1), it should be evident that these traits play an important role in ethical protection of subjects and the conduct of research.

## SUMMARY

Many boards, agencies, and codes exist for the protection of human research subjects. Among the ethical research rights are informed consent, confidentiality and anonymity, privacy, safe and competent treatment, and knowledge of results. Even though there are many external sources for the protection of subjects, the investigator is directly responsible for providing professional and ethical treatment of research participants. A summary of the research subject's rights is presented in Table 2-1.

**TABLE 2-1**   Summary of human subject research rights

| |
| --- |
| Informed consent |
| Confidentiality |
| Anonymity |
| No invasion of privacy |
| Safe and competent treatment |
| Knowledge of results |

# CHAPTER 3

# GETTING STARTED: INFORMATION RETRIEVAL

**KEY CONCEPTS**

Primary and secondary
references
Abstract
Bibliography
Index

Research review
Educational Resource
Information Center (ERIC)
Computerized information
retrieval

**AFTER READING THIS CHAPTER, YOU SHOULD BE ABLE TO**

- Identify several reasons for reviewing the literature before beginning to write a proposal.
- Describe why researchers should read primary rather than secondary references.
- List and define several sources of reference information and give examples of each.
- Describe how computerized information retrieval systems operate and their several advantages.
- Name several data based computer systems and the indexes which they search.

$\mathrm{B}$efore you begin to write a research proposal, some general as well as specific reading should be done. From this reading a general knowledge of the topic can be gained. This knowledge should include a familiarization with areas of controversy, designs, methods, and characteristics of subjects studied as well as those not yet studied, and recommendations made by others. If the literature is viewed with some of these aspects in mind, the results of your reading should be fruitful. Typically, graduate students tend to rush into reading the literature without much direction, which may require rereading the same information.

## PRIMARY AND SECONDARY REFERENCES

References are either primary or secondary. *Primary references* are the original article, report, or book; *secondary references* are those in which the original work is described or mentioned by someone other than the author of the original work. In the latter case, one is informed secondhand. Much of the information stated in textbooks is based on original work that is described, cited in the text, and referenced. The text is thus a secondary reference for that particular information. The difference should be understood because, when writing a research paper or proposal, it is assumed that references cited were read firsthand to provide the best possible understanding of the original work. Restriction to secondary references increases the probability that opinion and bias are transferred from author to reader. The effect is analogous to whispering a secret in someone's ear and having that person then whisper the secret to another person. With each person involved in the chain of communication, accuracy potentially drops.

To ensure the highest level of accuracy in reporting information, the original or primary reference should be read firsthand. As a result, the references cited by you in a paper indicate that you did read the original work rather than a translation or summary of the work by another author. Consequently, secondary references should be used only when the original work is not available. It is tempting but dishonest to do otherwise.

## BIBLIOGRAPHIES, ABSTRACTS, INDEXES, AND RESEARCH REVIEWS

Information from books, articles, and documents are contained in a *bibliography*. However, no summary or abstract is included, so the potential use to the reader is limited to the title. Examples of bibliographies related to HPER appear in Table 3-1.

*Abstracts* are compilations of information on a given topic and provide a bibliographical entry and a summary for each source. Typically, publications from dozens and even hundreds of journals are included in an abstract. The sole purpose in reading an abstract is to help make a decision as to whether or not the original work is relevant enough to justify reading all of it. Abstracts represent a source of information for previously published information as well as work yet to be published and so represents the most recent work being done on a topic. The process of writing, submitting a manuscript, revising it, and having it published typically takes a year or two. Therefore the "hottest" work usually appears in abstracts. Examples of abstracts pertinent to HPER are provided in Table 3-1.

**TABLE 3-1**   Examples of references in HPER

| *Type* | *Example* |
| --- | --- |
| Abstracts | Abstracts in Hygiene |
| | Annual Meeting Abstracts of the American College of Sports Medicine (published annually as a supplement to Medicine and Science in Sports and Exercise) |
| | Annual Meeting Abstracts of the Research Consortium of the American Alliance of Health, Physical Education, Recreation, and Dance (published annually as a supplement to the Research Quarterly for Exercise and Sport) |
| | Completed Research in HPER |
| | Current Index to Journals in Education |
| | Dissertation Abstracts |
| | Medical Abstracts |
| | Physiological Abstracts |
| | Sociological Abstracts |
| Bibliographies | Bibliography of Biomechanics |
| | Bibliography of Research Using Female Subjects |
| | Physical Fitness/Sports Medicine Quarterly |
| | Sociological Information Retrieval for Leisure Studies |
| Indexes | Education Index |
| | Index Medicus |
| | Index to Literature in Leisure, Recreation, Parks and Recreational Services |
| Research reviews | Annual Review of Public Health |
| | College Health Review |
| | Exercise and Sport Sciences Reviews |
| | Physiological Reviews |
| | Psychological Review |
| | Review of Educational Research |

The term "abstract" as used here refers to a compilation of sources of information. It should not be confused with the brief summary of an article which commonly appears on the first page below the title.

An *index* is identical to a bibliography except that it is limited to periodicals (e.g., journals and magazines). Usually no summary or abstract is provided. See Table 3-1 for examples.

*Research reviews* are thorough reviews written by an expert in a field and are useful when you want greater understanding about a specialized research topic. A large number of references are cited, which makes it useful, and commentary about the limitations to the research in general is given with recommendations to other researchers. Such reviews are very helpful to the student looking for a research topic. Examples appear in Table 3-1.

## JOURNALS

The disciplines of health, physical education, and recreation are fairly specific today, and consequently a wide variety of journals is available. A list of selected journals in HPER appears in Table 3-2.

**TABLE 3-2**   Selected HPER journals

| | |
|---|---|
| Health | American Journal of Clinical Nutrition |
| | Annual Review of Health Education |
| | College Health Review |
| | Death Education |
| | Educational Gerontology |
| | Health Education |
| | Journal of the American School Health Association |
| | Journal of Environmental Health |
| | Journal of Health Promotion |
| | Wellness Perspectives |
| Physical Education | Adapted Physical Activity Quarterly |
| | Dance Annual |
| | Dance Perspectives |
| | Dance Research Journal |
| | International Journal of Sport Sociology |
| | International Journal of Sports Biomechanics |
| | Journal of Biomechanics |
| | Journal of Educational Psychology |
| | Journal of Motor Behavior |
| | Journal of Physical Education, Recreation, and Dance |
| | Journal of Sport Psychology |
| | Journal of Sports Medicine and Physical Fitness |
| | Journal of Philosophy of Sport |
| | Journal of Teaching Physical Education |
| | Medicine and Science in Sports and Exercise |
| | Perceptual and Motor Skills |
| | Physical Educator |
| | Quest |
| | Research Quarterly for Exercise and Sport |
| Recreation | Adapted Physical Activity Quarterly |
| | American Corrective Therapy Journal |
| | Journal of Health, Physical Education, Recreation, and Dance |
| | Journal of Leisure Research |
| | Park Maintenance |
| | Parks and Recreation |
| | Recreation Management |
| | Therapeutic Recreation Journal |

## EDUCATIONAL RESOURCE INFORMATION CENTER (ERIC)

ERIC is a data bank established by the U.S. Office of Education in the 1960s that collects and stores information pertaining to education. ERIC's staff reviews articles, conference reports, government documents, and the like, and selects items to be indexed and abstracted in *Resources in Education* (*RIE*) or *Current Index to Journals in Education* (*CIJE*). *RIE* contains abstracts of conference reports, programs, and documents and is published monthly. *CIJE* abstracts periodicals only, also monthly. More than 700 journals are reviewed for possible inclusion in *CIJE*, with about 20,000 articles indexed annually.

Because ERIC is limited to coverage of education, areas such as biomechanics, exercise physiology, and therapeutic recreation are not specifically included. Consequently, some journals and conference reports in the disciplines of HPER are not in the ERIC data bank.

ERIC uses a thesaurus of descriptors that facilitates locating information for a specific topic within the system. Using the descriptors, a computer search can be used to develop a list of references. The abstracts for each reference can then be read to determine those references pertinent to your research.

## COMPUTERIZED INFORMATION RETRIEVAL

Widespread use of the computer to speed information retrieval began in the 1970s, and today computers are an integral part of most university libraries. A massive number of references are made available, which saves the researcher much time. Locating references manually in indexes, bibliographies, and so on, used to involve many hours in the library. Today key words or descriptors are typed on a computer terminal and the computer system searches for those terms in a data bank or data base. References containing the terms are then printed. The entire process may take only minutes. Furthermore, the data base is more current than paper sources because it is updated with new references that would not have yet appeared in the paper copies of indexes, or bibliographies. A good source of key words for a topic you are researching may be found in published journal articles. The words are typically listed after the abstract of the article on the first page.

Care must be taken in selecting descriptors to obtain useful references. One of the unique benefits of the computer approach is that several options that combine two or more terms, such as the *and, or,* and *not* options, are available that help to delimit the references. These options are important because they greatly influence the number of references listed. For example, a recreation therapist seeking information on recreational fitness activities for paraplegic children would want to narrow the topic so that only minimally related references would not be listed. Key words might include "fitness," "paraplegic children," and "recreation." However, "fitness" may be too broad, and instead more specific terms such as "strength" and "flexibility" may be used. Articles not having "strength" or "flexibility" in the title could be omitted. Thus one could limit the

printout of articles to only those having all the key words, three of the four key words, or so on. Typically, it is more difficult to delimit the search than it is to achieve a good number of references.

Reference librarians are most helpful in getting you started on a computer search and explaining special features. You may even work with a reference librarian who is a subject matter specialist in your discipline. He or she will also be able to assist you in a more effective selection of key words. Indexes currently available on computer data bases are listed in Table 3-3.

**TABLE 3-3**  Indexes currently available on computer data bases

| Printed Index | Data Base |
|---|---|
| Biological Abstracts | BIOSIS PREVIEWS |
| ERIC | ERIC |
| Index Medicus, including the subset Physical Fitness/Sports Medicine | MEDLINE |
| Psychological Abstracts | PSYCHINFO |
| Science Citation Index | SCISEARCH |
| Social Science Citation Index | SOCIAL SCISEARCH |
| Sociological Abstracts | SOCIOLOGICAL ABSTRACTS |
| Sociology of Leisure and Sports Abstracts | SIRLS |
| Sport and Recreation Index | SPORT |

## SUMMARY

Begin reading with at least a general direction as to what type of information is sought. A wide variety of resources, including abstracts, bibliographies, indexes, research reviews, ERIC, and computer searching, is available. Secondary references may be used to identify publications that you want to read, but primary references should be read to enhance understanding and accuracy.

# CHAPTER 4

# THE RESEARCH PROPOSAL

**KEY CONCEPTS**

Timetable for a thesis
Title
Abstract
Introduction

Problem
Review of literature
Methods

**AFTER READING THIS CHAPTER, YOU SHOULD BE ABLE TO**

- List and summarize the components of each chapter of a research proposal or thesis.
- State the components of a proposal that are not part of a published article.
- Explain why detail is required in the chapter on methods.
- Explain why all studies have limitations.
- Explain how the chapter on the review of literature should be written.

The typical research proposal and graduate degree thesis are explained in detail in the next several chapters. Examples are given throughout to facilitate understanding not only of the content that is to be included but also of how it may be written. The writing of the proposal or thesis is difficult for most students and consequently it is where they are more heavily penalized in the evaluation of their work by professors and journal reviewers.

It should be noted from the outset that there is no one universal standard regarding the number of chapters or even the exact components of each chapter. There is, however, a definite pattern as to what is recommended or required at most institutions. One finds considerable variation across departments on a single campus, which indicates that the faculty making up the membership of a thesis committee determines the specific content of each chapter. Furthermore, the components explained here hold true for most types of research performed in the disciplines of health, physical education/exercise science, and recreation/leisure studies.

With these institutional, departmental, and academic idiosyncracies understood, we now proceed to discuss the comprehensive thesis. The research paper or journal manuscript is briefer and does not include all aspects of the thesis. The thesis format is explained chapter by chapter, and where appropriate, omissions or variations in the journal article are noted. Similarly, the research proposal ends with the methods chapter. Very often students enrolled in a research methods class write a proposal but never carry out the remainder of the study. This is not all bad because it assures that all graduate students have at least participated in the planning of a study, which provides considerable insight into the world of research that is inherent in much of graduate work. The chapters that follow the methods chapter are explained in Chapter 5 in the same detail as are the chapters that make up a research proposal because some students writing a thesis need this information explained in detail and also because it adds to every student's general understanding of the purposes and features of the results, discussion, and so on. This information should be helpful in reading these sections in a journal article.

For students considering writing a thesis, we urge you to plan well ahead. It takes about one year to accomplish the numerous steps, including discussing a topic with a professor, writing and defending the proposal, obtaining approval of the institutional review board, and so on. See Table 4-1 for a list of the steps and the estimated time to complete each. Note how many steps depend on your own motivation. Some students can work effectively on their own, but others have difficulty. Student self-discipline, motivation, and need to graduate at some predetermined date vary considerably in our experience.

## COMPONENTS OF THE THESIS

The chapters of a thesis are similar to the plans and specifications for building a house. Numerous details must be considered and written down to ensure that all facets of the project are considered. The sequence and content of the chapters are similar to the steps followed in the scientific method. As a matter of fact, the thesis is nothing more than an elaboration of the scientific method. Following

**TABLE 4-1**   Timetable for a thesis

| Step | Estimated Time |
| --- | --- |
| 1. Obtain committee chair and committee. | As early as possible |
| 2. Write proposal. | Self-motivation |
| 3. Distribute copies to committee. | One week ahead |
| 4. Defend proposal. | 1–2 hours |
| 5. Revise proposal. | Self-motivation |
| 6. Submit to IRB. | Self-motivation |
| 7. Wait for IRB review and approval. | 1–4 weeks |
| 8. Conduct study. | Self-motivation |
| 9. Write final chapters. | Self-motivation |
| 10. Defend thesis (see steps 3 and 4) | 1–2 hours |
| 11. Revise. | Self-motivation |
| 12. Submit for final approval. | Five minutes! |

the recommendations given here, writing a thesis or research proposal should be a logical, step-by-step, cookbook affair. Dividing the various chapters into components allows you to work on various sections of each chapter in small blocks of time rather than being forced to work for long, tiresome periods. Flexibility is gained, and it may even enhance work efficiency.

The components of the thesis and research paper are listed in Table 4-2. Note that the introduction and problem chapters are often combined into a single chapter, as are the results and discussion chapters.

Research writing is usually done in the second or third person—that is, he, she, or they. Much of the proposal is written in the future tense because it is yet to be accomplished. In the proposal the review of literature chapter is written in the past tense because it deals with work already accomplished.

**TABLE 4-2**   Components of the thesis

Title
Abstract
Chapter 1: Introduction
Chapter 2: The Problem
Chapter 3: Review of Related Literature
Chapter 4: Procedures or Methods
Chapter 5: Results
Chapter 6: Discussion
Chapter 7: Summary and Conclusions
References
Appendix

# TITLE

A title should describe what a paper is about so that potential readers can decide whether it is of interest to them. Computer searches for identifying related published information are based on identification of key words in titles. Consequently, it is important to use meaningful words to describe a work. Typically titles are about 10 to 15 words long, with nouns as key words. Jargon is avoided to ensure reader understanding. If the title of an article is vague or too broad, it may not be read by many people. An overly brief title makes it difficult for readers to decide if the study is related to their needs and interests. Below are several titles with a comment regarding their suitability.

### Health Risks in Children

This title is too short. It does not describe any specific traits of the children, such as age, sex, or socioeconomic level. It also fails to indicate any specific aim of the study: Was it comparative? Were risks measured before and after some experimental variable was administered? In the following version, determine if it meets the criteria of being both precise and concise.

### Health Risks in 12- to 15-Year-Old Latchkey vs. Nonlatchkey Students

### Hematological Changes Occurring as a Result of Exposure to Various High Altitude Environments

This title is adequately descriptive in informing the reader of the purpose of the study, but some of the words are not needed.

### Hematological Changes from Exposure to High Altitude

This version conveys as much information as the first one but does it in far fewer words. A good rule of thumb for effective research writing is to strive for brevity. If something can be communicated clearly in 100 words, then the same information stated in 150 words contains some "fat." Most readers prefer getting the facts as quickly as possible. Newspaper articles are written with this in mind, as are journal articles, in order to minimize the length and cost of printing each issue. Everyone is busy these days, so learn to get right to the point.

# ABSTRACT

An abstract is a summary of the thesis or article. It very briefly describes the purpose of the study, subjects, methods, results, and conclusions. In journal articles the abstract is usually printed in italics or boldface immediately below the title and is limited to about 100 to 150 words.

# CHAPTER 1:  INTRODUCTION

The introduction is treated as a single chapter here, although it is often combined with the problem chapter of the thesis. The main purpose of an introduction is to justify the need for the study. In order to do this, key studies from the literature should be cited that document the need. For example, if there is a conflict on some topic, then studies citing the conflict as well as those that support each side should be referenced. Conflicts in the research literature abound because researchers naturally gravitate to topics of disagreement and controversy; and the existence of conflict by itself nearly justifies research that attempts to resolve the problem. Textbooks and articles often point out areas of unsettled knowledge, as do professors in their classrooms. Articles that review the state of knowledge on a specific topic frequently appear in research journals. Specific recommendations for future research are typically provided, and serve to highlight the direction of that research as well as suggestions for improving the methods used to study a topic. Also, a wealth of references are immediately available in review articles.

Many studies published in the fields of health, physical education, and recreation in the 1950–70s were performed using college-age male subjects. Although these studies reported on the responses or characteristics of certain-age males, the responses of older and younger males as well as females were relatively unknown. Since that time these other populations have been more commonly used as subjects. Consequently, 10 to 20 years ago the study of these other groups were often the main rationale for a number of investigations.

Improved research techniques open the door to replicate old ideas to verify the results. Use of modern strength assessment equipment has caused researchers to reevaluate techniques to improve muscular fitness. Computer software is widely available to perform complex statistical analyses that were infrequently done because of lack of computer hardware and software. These limitations can now be overcome and consequently allow researchers to reexamine problems and questions that even today may not be resolved.

In summary, the introduction chapter is critical to understanding the overall meaning and value of a study. It should emphasize the importance of asking good research questions and documenting the need for their answers. If your professor does not buy the reason for doing the study, the remainder of your proposal obviously becomes less meaningful. When researchers submit their work for publication, they, too, must clearly substantiate its value. Failure to accomplish this task normally results in rejection.

It may be helpful at this point to refer to a recent copy of a research publication in your field. Read the first several paragraphs of the article. The term "introduction" may not appear as a central or side heading, but it actually is the introduction. Note that references are cited to make the reader aware of the state of knowledge on a particular topic. The length of the section is often quite short, typically just several paragraphs, but do not confuse brevity with less importance. The last paragraph is commonly phrased something like: "The purpose of this study is to. . . ." Scan several articles and see how similar they are in length, content, and even the semantics used in the last sentence. A definite pattern emerges.

Some professors prefer the introduction as a separate chapter because it is so vital in the planning of research. Having one purpose for an entire chapter and considering how brief it typically is in a journal article should emphasize its importance.

Most of the introduction chapter is written in the past tense because it cites and describes the results of previous studies. Only the last sentence, "The purpose of this study," is written in the future tense for a proposal. If a study is actually conducted and completed, then the same sentence is stated in the past or present tense.

## CHAPTER 2: THE PROBLEM

The problem chapter provides an overview of the study: statement of the purpose or problem to be addressed, hypothesis, delimitations (scope), limitations (variables that could not be controlled), and significance of the study. In a proposal, the future tense is typically used in most sections because at that time the study is merely a plan that is to be critiqued by a professor or committee. If the proposal is written for a graduate thesis rather than a class project, a thesis committee will examine the plan and most likely suggest revisions that will then be used when actually conducting the study. At the completion of the study, the verbs must be changed to past tense to reflect the fact that the work was done.

The information given in the problem chapter does not appear in a separate chapter in journal articles, as most of it is implicit in the context of the study or it appears in other sections of the manuscript (such as the methods or discussion). It exists as a separate chapter in the thesis proposal to draw attention to components of the study that might otherwise be neglected or not fully appreciated by the student who is learning research skills. Hence, it is included to make sure the student author typically carrying out that first piece of research pays adequate attention to several important facets of the study.

### Purpose of the Study

This is a brief statement that identifies the specific intent of the study. It should identify an exact problem to be studied. Commonly this is a difficult statement to write, as most students tend to be concerned with solving a major problem that has many different variables. A research problem is usually very specific and addresses only one or two key factors involved in a given phenomenon. For example, a physical educator with an interest in weight training states the problem to be the determination of the best means of increasing muscular strength and bulk. Although this is an interesting topic, it is extremely broad. Numerous variables affect the acquisition of strength and muscle mass: frequency and intensity of training, quantity of work per training session, work/rest ratio, type of apparatus used, and diet. To carry out such a training study would require a large number of groups and subjects, making the study unrealistic.

Here the novice researcher would be advised to select perhaps one variable for investigation. For example, comparing the effects of one, three, and five sets would be far more manageable. Now three experimental groups plus a control group (a group not receiving the independent variable) would probably suffice in addressing the problem: Is there a significant difference in strength development when one, three, and five sets of selected weight training exercises are compared? This graduate student will address a meaningful problem and be able to provide closer supervision of the training sessions as well as measure strength more accurately and reliably with fewer subjects. Also, the student may be able to carry out the study *and* graduate in a reasonable time!

In sum, focus the purpose of the study: Do not attempt to answer all the questions in the world about the topic. Save something for other researchers! The following example of stating the purpose of a study may be helpful. The statement suggests doing one thing well rather than many things poorly: "The purpose of this study will be to determine if recreational activity and socioeconomic status are significantly related."

## Hypotheses

A hypothesis is a statement of the likely outcome of a study. It is often posed as a question. It can also be thought of as a prediction of findings based on the relevant literature.

### Statistical Hypotheses: Null and Directional

*Statistical hypotheses* are stated in either a null form or a directional form. In the former no significant effect or relationship is anticipated. For example, using the example of body fatness and TV watching, the null hypothesis might be stated as "Body fatness and time spent watching TV will not be significantly related." The directional hypothesis is stated such that a significant difference or relationship is predicted to occur. In this case, TV watching would be projected to *be* significantly related to body fatness. Another example would be stating that red balls will enhance catching and throwing skills more than yellow and blue balls.

Does it make a difference which way the hypothesis is stated? Typically most people new to research find it is easier to conceptualize the outcome of statistical analysis by using the null form. If statistical significance is found, the researcher can readily identify which experimental effect is superior or whether or not a real relationship exists. However, achieving statistical significance is more likely to occur when using the directional statement. This concept is more fully discussed in Chapter 9. For now, it is probably easier to state hypotheses in the null or no difference format.

### Research Hypotheses

*Research hypotheses* are stated according to the results the researcher actually expects. They might appear as follows: Students will catch more playground balls when using yellow balls rather than red balls. Research hypotheses are used in this section of the research paper. Statistical hypotheses are used to test the research hypothesis. Hypotheses are not usually stated in journal articles because they are implied by the purpose of the study. Using the ball color experiment as an example, the purpose of the study would be to compare the effect of ball color on catching ability. Logically the research hypothesis then states what the expected outcome will be.

## Delimitations

Delimitations are the "what, who, where" of a study and serve to summarize what is included in the study: the nature of the subjects, the location of the study, its duration, and variables studied. An example might be: "Eighty 7- and 8-year-old children enrolled at Rockbrook Elementary School in Omaha, Nebraska, will be subjects in a 12-week study in which throwing and catching skills with 9-inch rubber playground balls of three different colors will be compared." In journal articles this information is covered in the methods section of the paper.

## Limitations

Limitations are uncontrollable events that may interfere with the results of a study. In our example study on ball skills, obviously other factors may affect learning as well as performance while testing subjects. The amount of ball handling that occurs outside the experimental procedure may affect skill level. Some youngsters may be playing on teams or informally with parents and siblings and other children may have little or no outside activity using balls. Performance during pre- and posttesting may be affected by children's emotions (performing in front of a strange adult), attitudes ("I hate ball games because I'm no good"), physical injury, and the like. Though some of these factors may be unknown to the researcher, the researcher is obligated to define any factors that are anticipated to affect the outcome.

One common limitation is the duration of the study. Short-term studies may be limited simply because some phenomena do not dramatically change in 10 or 12 weeks. Studies examining bone density change through exercise or diet should last many months because bone responds slowly to these stimuli. A 12-week study may conclude falsely that these variables have no effect on bone simply because of the overly short duration of the study.

Stating limitations in a distinct section of the proposal ensures that the student recognizes the possible influence of other variables. No study can perfectly control all factors in the environment, and therefore even the best designed and best planned studies have one or more limitations. In published articles, limitations are often mentioned in the discussion section or are implied.

## Definition of Terms

Certain terms, because they have multiple meanings, should be defined in the context of a particular study. For example, the word "health" is defined differently in the dictionary as compared to its meaning in the professional field of health education. If health is assessed in a study, it should be defined operationally or functionally so that all readers understand the context to which it applies. The term "physical fitness" would need to be defined because of its different meanings—health-oriented fitness or athletic fitness, for example.

Definitions should adhere to what is commonly accepted and used in the professional literature.

Some terms are defined in graduate theses simply to assist committee members outside the discipline to understand the study. Many universities require that at least one thesis committee member be from outside the department. A Ph.D. in the psychology department may have difficulty understanding the specific meanings our disciplines attach to some words. Comprehension is facilitated by defining the words as used in the discipline and proposal. Abbreviations and acronyms should be defined as well.

### Significance of the Study

The significance of a study refers to its application and meaning to the real world. For example, if red playground balls were found to enhance ball skills more than blue and yellow balls, this information might be applied to other groups of 7- and 8-year-old children with similar characteristics. If TV watching were found to be related to body fatness, it may justify a study in which TV watching was experimentally limited in a group of people to see if it reduced body fatness.

The phrase "significance of the study" should not be confused with the term "statistical significance." The latter deals with a statement of mathematical probability (see Chapter 9 for a discussion).

## CHAPTER 3:  REVIEW OF LITERATURE

In the research proposal the chapter on the review of literature is written in the past tense because it deals with already published work. It usually has three sections: introduction, body, and summary. The introduction is brief and need only indicate titles for sections of the body and that a summary is included. In essence, it informs the reader how the literature analysis is organized. A review of literature is not a separate section in journal articles but, instead, is embedded within the introduction and discussion sections.

The body comprises the vast majority of the review chapter. It is usually divided into several subsections. The most common misunderstanding that students have about this chapter is that it is a series of paragraphs in which one study is summarized per paragraph. Such an approach fails to collate the main themes about literature on the topic. It certainly is easier to compose, for it requires no collation and comparison of findings across studies. However, this is exactly what the chapter is supposed to do, and quite honestly it requires a bit of work. The task is to *analyze* the literature rather than merely list results of studies.

The task is somewhat difficult for students because they do not usually have an in-depth knowledge of the topic. Faculty who publish on a regular basis, on the other hand, do possess in-depth training in statistics, experimental design, and the subject matter in their field. Furthermore, they read research literature regularly and have a good feel for its content. Obviously, one cannot expect a graduate student to have this level of expertise, but the only way to learn how to analyze literature is by "jumping in and getting wet!" Most professors adjust their level of expectation to coincide with the level of training of their students.

An understanding of literature analysis can be greatly enhanced by reading a review of the literature on any topic in a research publication. If you are able to obtain a review of the topic you are working with, so much the better. Notice that the review is organized around concepts or themes, rather than the one study per paragraph approach. A review of literature on aerobic training, for example, may be organized into headings on exercise intensity, duration, frequency, and mode of exercise. Several paragraphs under each topic will depict the overall findings and cite individual studies to document the observations. For example, a sentence in one paragraph may be stated as follows: "Numerous studies have reported that the minimal exercise intensity that elicits an improvement in maximal oxygen uptake is 50 percent of maximum (several key studies are cited in parentheses to document the statement)." Several of these cited studies can then be summarized regarding the characteristics of the subjects, their initial fitness level, age, and so on. A second paragraph might describe studies that report other levels of exercise intensity threshold.

These studies should then be analyzed to determine what they may have in common that helps explain the different findings. Perhaps some of the studies observed a lower intensity to be effective in older and less fit subjects. Differences in training programs need to be analyzed as well as limitations to studies, such as sample size, design, and methods. Note again that the literature is being analyzed rather than just summarized study by study. The term "review" perhaps connotes the wrong impression to students. Perhaps "critique" or "analysis" better suggests the correct way to write this chapter.

The purpose in reviewing the literature is to develop an understanding of the state of knowledge about a topic. It includes not only the findings of many studies but also the methods used to study the problem. Consequently, much can be learned by carefully noting the instruments and procedures used to measure variables. There are often several means of assessing a variable, and the advantages and disadvantages of each should be examined.

A summary is the last component of the chapter. In lengthy review chapters, summaries are sometimes written for each subsection as well.

## CHAPTER 4: PROCEDURES OR METHODS

The procedures or methods is a "cookbook" chapter that provides precise details regarding how the study was conducted. It describes the subjects, the means of collecting data, the treatment used if the study is experimental, and the statistical analysis. The purpose in describing the methods in such detail is to allow replication of the study by others, an essential step in research, and so that others can judge how the methods may have affected the outcome of a study. For example different means of measuring a variable may affect the scores, as might the procedures for administering a test or the means of statistically analyzing the data. Informed readers wish to know these details so they can intelligibly interpret the findings.

The methods chapter is written in the future tense for the proposal be-cause it is only a plan at that point and will be subject to review and revision. The first two components of this chapter may be thought of as preliminary pro-cedures because they are steps to be accomplished before data are collected. Similarly, the last two parts of the chapter deal with data collection and analysis and hence are done while actually carrying out the study. They may be viewed as operational procedures.

## Subjects

The source of subjects, criteria for being a subject, their general characteristics, and the sampling technique used to obtain them are described. The source may be a particular school, recreation setting, or the like. Criteria might include sex, age, medical or fitness status, or some special trait such as being a female gradu-ate student in recreation/leisure studies. The sampling procedure refers to the means of selecting people with the defined criteria at the given location(s). Random sampling means everyone with the needed criteria at a defined location is a possible subject. For example, every child at a school might be assigned a number, and 100 numbers are drawn out of a hat or from a table of random numbers. A number of sampling procedures exist, and the procedure used should be stated to inform the reader because it affects the scores obtained (e.g., the mean rate of school absenteeism from 100 randomly selected students would quite likely be different than the mean from children with a chronic illness or an unstable family). More details about sampling are covered in Chapter 7. Last, a statement should be made that approval from an institutional review board was received and that all subjects signed an informed consent document.

## Treatment or Experimental Design

The treatment or design refers to how the study will be conducted: how subjects will be placed into groups (if appropriate) and the activity performed by the subjects. It is important to describe the experimental procedures in detail for two reasons. First, the results of the study will depend on the treatment applied to the subjects, and second, other researchers may wish to replicate the study to de-termine if similar results occur in other groups. They need detailed information in order to accomplish either of these functions. For example, if a recreator wished to measure the effects of high-risk outdoor activities on self-confidence, then details regarding the exact activities used, their risk, involvement with other people, physical surrounding, number of activities used, duration of the program, and so on, must be known. Similarly, if one is studying the effects of a health unit on nutrition and its effects on eating habits at home, great detail would need to be given describing the unit: media used, its duration, activities used in class, the number of different teachers used, special training of teachers for the unit, the collection of data describing food consumption, and so on. As a test to determine if these details were adequately given, students can ask them-selves if they could almost perfectly repeat the protocols with only the informa-tion given.

### Data Collection

As with the treatment or design section, considerable detail must be provided for possible replication and for full understanding of data collection. Details may include equipment or instruments used, validation of procedures, site of data collection, time of day, physiological status (e.g., fasting), omission of previous exercise the day of data collection, warm-up or practice trials, sequence of tests, and motivational strategies. For example, in an exercise physiology experiment, it would be necessary to explain the treadmill protocol used (e.g., speed and duration of each stage and criteria for determining if maximal oxygen uptake was achieved). The name and model number of the treadmill, gas analysis equipment or metabolic cart, and EKG unit are often given as well. If a practice trial was given to subjects running on the treadmill, this, too, should be noted.

In motor learning experiments involving use of novel tasks such as juggling or balancing tasks, the amount of practice should be controlled. If a number of different tests are administered, the sequence of tests should be explained because fatigue, emotional changes, and learning from performing one task may affect performance on ensuing tests.

### Data or Statistical Analysis

Each statistical procedure used to analyze data is stated and the level of significance used. This section is usually quite brief. Here is an example: "Mean and standard deviation were calculated for each variable. A one-way analysis of variance (ANOVA) was used to compare the change in catching skill across the three groups. The .05 level of significance was used." Commonly used statistical procedures are not usually cited, but unusual ones are in order to verify their use.

## SUMMARY

The research proposal is a plan for research. It is divided into chapters that coincide with the steps composing the scientific method. The introduction provides a justification for the study. The problem chapter is a summary of the purpose, hypotheses, delimitations, limitations, definitions, and significance of the study. The review of literature is an analysis or critique of the pertinent published work, and the methods chapter details how the study will be conducted.

# CHAPTER 5

# RESULTS, DISCUSSION, CONCLUSION, AND REFERENCES

$T$he research proposal, being a plan for research, ends with the methods chapter. Once data have been collected and analyzed, the remainder of the research paper is written. This includes the results, discussion, conclusion, references, and appendix.

## CHAPTER 5: RESULTS

The results chapter is a brief statement of meaningful findings without an explanation. A logical place to begin is to state whether or not the hypothesis being tested was accepted or rejected. This is based on the results of an appropriate statistical procedure. Tables and figures (graphs) often supplement the narrative in this chapter. Numerical details are best depicted in tables and figures because they greatly simplify the comprehension of large amounts of data. Attempting to read a mass of numbers in paragraph form is exceedingly difficult. Therefore, the text is best limited to identifying statistically significant findings and stating associated statistical information such as significance level. (These details on statistics will make more sense after having covered the section in this text on statistics; see Chapters 7–12).

This section or chapter should be brief if the methods chapter provided adequate details on procedures and the data are explained in the discussion. Occasionally writers restate or even add new information such as the statistics used to analyze the data. We view this as needless repetition of information that should have been presented in the methods chapter. Similarly, data are sometimes partly interpreted in the results. We believe the results are best presented by stating only the outcome with as little verbiage as possible. Let the facts or data stand on their own. Interpretation should be made in the discussion.

### Tables

Tables are an effective way to present the results of a study because it is far easier to extract key information from a table than from text. An example of data presented in tabular form appears in Table 5-1. The guidelines of the American Psychological Association (APA) will assist you in producing attractive and effective tables.

1. Place the title above the table.
2. Number tables consecutively.
3. Place a table in the text on the page immediately following where it is first mentioned.
4. Use parallel lines to separate column headings from the body of the table, and place one at the bottom of the table.
5. Indicate units of measure for each variable.
6. Do not use vertical lines.
7. Report the sample size in the title if describing only one group.
8. Place each table on a separate page.

**TABLE 5-1**  Sample table: Physical characteristics of subjects ($N = 25$)

| Variable | Mean | SD | Range |
|---|---|---|---|
| Age, yr | 19.8 | 2.6 | 18.3–24.7 |
| Height, cm | 164.5 | 7.8 | 156.5–174.0 |
| Weight, kg | 62.2 | 5.1 | 54.0–66.7 |

# CHAPTER 6: DISCUSSION

The discussion chapter is an explanation and interpretation of the results. It usually comprises the following topics (without formal headings): comparison with the results of other studies, how the results relate to theory, limitations of the study, implications, and recommendations.

The results are compared with those of other studies, and relevant findings that may both agree and disagree are cited. Then an analysis of the studies is done to determine why the results conflict or agree. For example, some years ago several studies reported that elementary school–age children were unable to improve their maximum oxygen uptake with training. In writing the discussion for a paper with such a finding, the author would cite other studies with similar results and try to identify common factors in these studies such as intensity, frequency, and duration of training. Similarly, those studies that observed significant gains in maximum oxygen uptake are analyzed. Were their subjects possibly more mature? Was maturity assessed in any of these studies? Was there a greater volume or intensity of training than used in the studies not showing significant change? An analysis of differences in studies requires attention to detail and the ability to generalize. One should approach such analysis much like Sherlock Holmes searching for clues.

In some cases, differences in results across studies may have little to do with the experimental treatment used in the study but, instead, may reflect differences in methods of measurement. For example, researchers who study the effects of various levels of physical activity on incidence of disease, body fatness, or cholesterol level commonly use a method that requires subjects to record daily the type and amount of physical activity. This method is limited by the memory and cooperation of the subject to record data accurately and regularly. A second technique employs wearing a motion sensing device that counts vertical or horizontal movements during the day. The latter probably is a more valid and accurate way to quantify physical activity. Researchers using the recall method may tend to find less impressive associations with cholesterol, cardiovascular disease, or fatness than those using a motion sensing device. Consequently, it is important to analyze studies reporting different results thoroughly because an explanation should be offered as to why the differences occurred.

A second component of the discussion chapter is relating the results to theory and accepted principles dealing with the topic. For example, if a study assessed personality traits of recreation administrators, these traits might logically be related to what is known in the psychological and sociological literature about personality development. Theory X might suggest that people who prefer working with others in an open, relatively unstructured rather than a more structured environment have a common set of psychological traits. The researcher can compare the traits identified with those proposed by the theory to see how well the theory fits the subjects. As another example, a researcher finds that abdominal girth is significantly related to mortality rate. The task is to identify some logical cause of the relationship. Perhaps it blends well with a theory that excess body fat in this region results in more fat being carried in the blood to the liver, which then increases cholesterol production from this added source of energy.

In both examples the researcher can only use sound logic in attempting to relate the results to theory. No means of proving the conjecture are available, as the results of the study only offer indirect support. The attempt to relate results with theory is called *speculation*. It demands a good knowledge of one's general discipline. It is an excellent brainteaser for most students because it is a more complex, intellectual task than writing the more structured components of the research paper. It is important in reading articles to be able to distinguish between speculation and explanations directly supported by the results. Writers often use such terms as "may," "possibly," "could," and "suggest" to indicate when they are speculating. The danger in failing to recognize a statement as speculation is that a reader may assume that it is actually a fact or finding in a study. Readers of research need to be able to make a clear distinction between fact and speculation.

A third component in the discussion is the limitations of the study. These extraneous or contaminating variables are ones that may not have been adequately controlled for and may have had some effect on the outcome of a study. In the research proposal, these are covered in the problem chapter as well as in the discussion. The reader is referred to that chapter for clarification if necessary. Common limitations are small number of subjects, use of a measuring instrument or method that is less than ideal, and short duration of a study. Sometimes limitations are not addressed directly and the reader must inspect the study for possible flaws.

A fourth component in the discussion is implications. Implications refer to possible applications of the results. If a recreator finds in a study that injury rate of children on certain playground apparatus is significantly higher than on others, then an implied application may be to alert school and recreation professionals about the finding so that they may modify use of the apparatus, warn children, or even remove it from playgrounds.

Indeed, the application of research to the real world is the reason most research is conducted, but great caution is needed to prevent the application to unjustified situations. Typically, researchers must resist the tendency to apply the results of a single study to many other cases because the situations may be markedly different. What happened in one environment with one group of people may not hold true for many other situations. In the playground study example, perhaps the apparatus was dangerous only because of the age of the children studied. Swinging ropes may be more dangerous for very young children, whose upper body strength is limited, or for heavy children with low strength related to body weight, or in playgrounds with inadequate sand below the equipment. Many factors may make the application somewhat specific, and if these factors do not exist, the generalization outside the study may be unjustified.

The issue of application of results of a study is known as external validity (see Chapter 14). It is an important point, though, so before we leave it, here is another example to consider. If a study found that visualization significantly aided the play of professional tennis players, is it justified to have novices use the technique? The results of a study are only justified to the subjects of the one study. Thus the only logical application is to others outside the study with as many similarities as possible to the subjects and conditions inherent in the original experiment, that is, other professional tennis players.

Last, recommendations are made in the discussion. This may be helpful to others who read the paper and may plan to carry out a study on the topic. Making recommendations also acknowledges that some insights have been developed about the research process in general as well as the state of knowledge on the topic. Therefore, it is worthwhile to be included in the graduate thesis. Typical recommendations include studying subjects with other traits (e.g., age, sex, fitness level, maturity level), considering alternative methods of measurement or experimental design, citing the need for longterm or longitudinal study, etc. In short, anything which may be helpful to other researchers is appropriate.

## CHAPTER 7: SUMMARY AND CONCLUSIONS

In journal articles the summary and conclusions are given at the end of the discussion section. In a thesis it is a short, single chapter. The summary is an overview of the need for the study, the statement of the problem, methods, and results. The conclusions are statements that are justified from the results. That is, they are not speculative comments. Researchers often use the word "justified" or "warranted" in their statement of the conclusions to make it obvious that the conclusions are data-based and statistically tested, and not speculations. One conclusion is usually written for each hypothesis tested. Here is a typical way to state a conclusion: "The following conclusion is warranted from the results of this study: The use of visualization before competition enhances playing performance in professional tennis players."

## REFERENCES

References are those sources actually cited or used in the preparation of a research paper. A bibliography lists literature for additional reading and should not be confused with references. References cited in the text should also appear in the reference section. Errors are common, so it is wise to double-check.

**Reference Styles**

A great variety of reference styles are seen in research publications. Every journal seems to have its own unique format. However, three basic styles exist. The *name and year* style (e.g., Johnson and Kumquat, 1988) is the easiest to use because no numbering is required. If references are added or deleted as the paper is being prepared, the changes are easy to make. The disadvantage is that reading is made more laborious because a series of names that may be of little interest to many readers must be passed over. When several references are cited consecutively, as is common in the introduction and discussion, the list of names can become lengthy and slows the reader. To combat this problem, the phrase "et al." meaning "and others" may be used in the text after the initial citation in which the authors' names are listed. For example, "Johnson, Smith, and Kumquat (1989)" is listed the first time the citation is made, but thereafter "Johnson et al." is used.

The *alphabet-number* system numbers and lists all references alphabetically. Only the number is given in the text, which aids reading and reduces printing costs (e.g., "The relationship of health knowledge and behavior is significant but explains only a small part of the variance in health behavior (11)."). However, the reader, unless he or she refers to the list of references, is not informed of the date of the work, which sometimes is relevant.

In the *order of citation* system, each citation is listed in the references according to the sequence cited in the paper. Consequently, authors' names are not listed alphabetically. This system has the same advantages and disadvantages as the alphabet-number system, but many people like the names of authors to appear alphabetically.

**Components in the List of References**

In addition to selecting the reference style to use, one must also consider the format when listing the names of the authors, title of article, journal title, volume, and so on. Of the many styles or formats employed, we describe the APA style (1983) here because of its wide use and preference.

*Periodicals*   McCall, L. T., & Washington, S. D. (1990). Differences in recreational patterns of the elderly living in retirement centers and privately. Leisure Sciences, 9, 167–171.

> *Names.* The authors' names are given with last name first followed by the initials. All authors are listed. Use an ampersand (&) before the name of the last author when there are multiple authors.
> *Date.* Give the date of publication in parentheses following the last authors' name and close with a period.
> *Title of Article.* State the title of the article, capitalizing only the first letter of the first word except for proper nouns and the first letter following a colon. Do not use quotation marks or underline the title of the article. Close with a period.

*Title of Journal.* State the full title of the journal and underline it. Capitalize the first letter of key words. Underline only the volume number but do not include "Vol." Give inclusive page numbers and end with a period. Use commas before and after the volume number.

**Books**   Day, R. A. (1983). How to write and publish a scientific paper. Philadelphia: ISI Press.

*Author.* Use the same guidelines for periodicals. If the book is edited, place "Ed." or "Eds." in parentheses after the name of the last editor.
*Date.* Use the same guidelines for periodicals.
*Title of Book.* Capitalize only the first letter of the first word except for proper nouns. Underline the title. Close with a period.
Place of Publication. State the city and the state if the former is not well known.
Publisher. State the full name of the publisher but omit details such as "Inc.," "Co.," and "Company." Close with a period.

The reader is referred to the *APA Manual* for more details on references.

## Locating the Citation in the Text

Place the citation at the point in the text where it relates. This may be at the end of a sentence if only one point is made, but often the citation needs to be placed within a sentence. For example: "Smaller values were reported in several investigations (Carson & Newman, 1989; Wellman & Denzi, 1991), but these values may reflect a lower baseline level (Beckman & Irish, 1992)." Here the first two citations substantiate an observation, and the third refers to an explanation of the observation. Had all three citations been lumped together at the end of the sentence, as some writers like to do, one wouldn't know which references support each point. To avoid confusion, keep the citation "close to the action." Also, when citing several studies within parentheses, list them alphabetically.

## Accuracy

The accuracy of references has recently been highlighted by several publications. Among the studies was an analysis of 973 references in the 1988 and 1989 volumes of the *Research Quarterly for Exercise and Sport*. Forty-seven percent, or 457, of the references contained at least one error. A total of 171 errors was found in the references. About 16 percent of all errors were in titles and 13 percent were initials of authors (Stull, Christina, & Quinn, 1991). Similar analyses of other publications indicate error rates of 28 percent for the *American Journal of Epidemiology* and the *American Journal of Public Health* (Eichorn & Yankauer, 1987) and 50 percent for the *Journal of the American Medical Association* (Goodrich & Roland, 1977), all prestigious publications.

The problem is obviously widespread, which should not condone the occurrence of errors. Rather, all researchers, student and professor alike, should take greater care in seeing that reference information is accurate. As suggested by one journal editor, researchers must check references against the original source rather than secondary sources and check for typographical errors (Yankauer, 1991). As explained in Chapter 3, primary rather than secondary references should be used to minimize transferring information biased by opinion and possible misinterpretation, and now we can add a third reason: to ensure accuracy of references. Although checking the accuracy of references is hardly a fun task, it is a responsibility of all researchers. Failure to be accurate here may well suggest lack of accuracy in other facets of a manuscript or article.

## APPENDIX

An appendix is a supplementary item sometimes included in a proposal or paper to present information that may be helpful to some readers but not necessary to its understanding. Items may include informed consent forms, correspondence, data collection forms, additional tables or figures, questionnaires or surveys used, and details of a measuring system. If one or more of these is included, each is listed as a separate appendix preceded by a cover page with its own title (e.g., Appendix A, Informed Consent Form; Appendix B, Letter of Invitation to Parents).

## SUMMARY

The results, discussion, and conclusion are not written until the research proposal has been approved and data collected and analyzed. The results chapter presents the basic findings and is typically accompanied by tables and possibly figures. The discussion is a comparison of the results with those of other findings and an integration of this new information with established theory and practice. The conclusion briefly states the major finding(s) of the study.

References may be cited within the text and listed at the end of the paper in several ways. An advantage of the author-date style is the ease in adding or deleting references. Far too commonly errors appear in the references, demonstrating that care must be given in accurately citing information from the primary reference.

# CHAPTER 6

# THE ART OF RESEARCH WRITING

**KEY CONCEPTS**

Getting started
Collating reference material and writing
Common faults in writing

**AFTER READING THIS CHAPTER, YOU SHOULD BE ABLE TO**

- Explain why several drafts and proofs of a paper should be made before submission.
- Define plagiarism and explain how to make decisions when some possibility for plagiarism exists.
- Explain why research writing should be brief and exact, and why clichés, jargon, and redundancy should be minimized.
- Properly use symbols, abbreviations, and numbers.
- Effectively use an accepted style guide.

$P$robably the most difficult part of writing for most people is simply getting started. Writer's block occurs even in veteran writers, so perhaps more than experience is needed. Let us share some of our observations based on our collective experience with students, as well as our own writing, in the hope that we can facilitate not only your getting started but also getting the job done with quality and efficiency.

## GETTING STARTED

### Select a Topic

Select a topic that is of great interest to you. You will be spending a good bit of time in preparing it, so you may as well enjoy it as much as possible. Pick a topic that relates to your field of study. It could be something dealing with teaching, such as curriculum, methods, or media; it could relate to some issue of health care, such as fitness in the elderly, osteoporosis, cardiovascular disease, or diabetes; or it could deal with rising health care costs or the types of recreational activities people pursue.

### Read about the Topic in a General Way

Do some general reading on the topic; you will have ample time later for highly specific reading. A good place to start may be a recently published text from a course that you really enjoyed. What particular chapters are of interest to you? Skim through to find one or two chapters and then within each specifically search for topics with controversy. These topics obviously need to be further researched, and it is possible that your proposal could be designed accordingly. Review articles are written by experts with knowledge and experience with research on a topic, so what better place to search for recommendations for future research. Avail yourself of the writer's expertise, as it is free, quality advice. Also, remember that any journal article typically contains the justification for the study in the introduction, whereas recommendations to other researchers are made in the discussion section. Both places might contain rationales for a proposal.

Studies often need replication to determine if similar results are observed in subjects with other traits. This implies that a study in a journal could be modified by using different subjects or the same type of subjects but eliminating a limitation to the study. For example, a study might not have found significant results because the duration of the treatment may have been too short. Your proposal could repeat the experiment but for a longer period. This is a legitimate rationale for doing a study.

### Consider the Availability of Equipment and Subjects

If your intention is to write a proposal for a class but not actually to conduct the study and write a thesis, realize that you do not have to be concerned with actually having access to sophisticated laboratory equipment or being able to obtain subjects with specific traits. One may assume that the necessary equipment and subjects are available to you. On the other hand, students planning on doing a thesis must be careful to plan a study that can reasonably be done given the limitations of time and the environment they are in. Does your institution have the laboratory equipment needed? How accessible will the lab be to you? Will you need the assistance of trained personnel to collect data? If so, will you have to pay them out of your own pocket? Can the study be conducted in a reasonable time to coincide with your graduation plans? All of these questions, as well as others, need to be addressed before you launch into a study. The professor teaching your research methods class will likely be invaluable in answering some of the questions, and you may need to consult other faculty as well.

## Simplify the Study

Limit the complexity of the study. As discussed in Chapter 4, students typically wish to take on far more than is reasonable for a novice researcher at the graduate level. It is far better to delimit the study to one or two variables and to have a well-conducted study than to attempt to do too much and reduce both the quality of the work and your level of satisfaction.

## Discuss Your Plans

A useful way to help get started is to discuss your initial plans with the professor teaching your research methods class or some other professor with expertise in the topic of interest. Ask the professor for his or her reactions to the plans. Perhaps the professor may even help you fine-tune the topic or develop it so that it is based on the very latest research findings. Another possibility may be that this professor has conducted research on the topic and may have several useful suggestions concerning how your proposal might blend in with some of his or her current or previous work. Faculty in our department are somewhat accustomed to students in our research methods class knocking on their door to discuss plans for a proposal.

## Put It on Paper

Get something down on paper, at all costs, as soon as possible after having the research proposal explained in your research methods class! The longer you wait, the more difficult starting becomes because more material is covered in class, an exam is soon staring you in the face, and so on. In our research methods class, we require students to write a proposal. Over many years we have learned that it is extremely helpful for students to submit the first several chapters early in the semester. We critique the draft, and placing little weight on it as far as a grade is concerned. By being forced to start early, students find the rest of the semester's work more relevant because many aspects of it are related to their own proposal. Also, receiving feedback early allows them to determine what they need to revise in order for the final version to be acceptable. This submit-revise-resubmit cycle is exactly how research journals operate. So, the student experiences the same procedures as do faculty who publish.

## COLLATING REFERENCE MATERIAL AND WRITING

Writing ability is critical in the research process simply because the end product of most research is the written form. Unless research can be communicated orally at research meetings or in print, little is accomplished. Similarly, for the student, the grade for writing a proposal is the end product. One's ideas may be organized, logical, and meaningful, but unless the ability to express the information is demonstrated, the best ideas, plans, and logic may prevent the award of a reasonable grade.

The remainder of this chapter is aimed at helping you to write effectively. Effective writing tends to give your work a positive "halo effect." It cannot replace good logic, organization, and content, but it certainly does not hurt.

## TIPS FOR GOOD WRITING

### Code and Organize Your References

Students typically reproduce a number of articles to use in writing a paper. Once sitting at the word processor or, heavens forbid, in front of a yellow pad, the problem of actually knowing what to say confronts the writer. Two steps may be helpful in getting by this block. On the cover of each copied article, indicate what chapter(s) information in this article pertains to. For example, perhaps it relates to the introduction, methods, or discussion. Note this on each article so that it can easily be identified. Stack the articles according to the section or chapter of the paper they pertain to.

### Develop an Outline

Much of this has already been done within the framework of each chapter of the proposal, but an outline will be needed within certain sections or chapters, such as the introduction, review of literature, and discussion. To do this, begin reading the sections of the articles that apply. For example, if developing an outline for the introduction, read and highlight these articles and develop the outline as you go along. Or you might try an initial outline something like this:

1. What is known?
2. What is not known?
3. What is controversial?
4. What are the limitations and recommendations of other studies?

These two steps alone may greatly help get you started. However, a special tip may be useful for the introduction, review of literature, and discussion. The difficulty here is trying to collate and compare a number of studies. A useful technique is to make a table that includes the key elements needed (see Table 6-1).

**TABLE 6-1**   Example of table method of summarizing literature

| Authors | Year | Subjects | Design | Results | Limitations |
|---------|------|----------|--------|---------|-------------|
| Smith and Howard | 1988 | 110 children, K–grade 3 | PE curriculum: fitness vs. traditional (games, skill and some fitness) | Fitness significantly greater than traditional on 3 of 5 fitness tests but no differences on social variables | Three different teachers. Study only 6 weeks long. |

The table method allows you to see the key elements of a number of studies simultaneously. It facilitates analysis of studies because they can be grouped according to findings—for example, those reporting significant effects, those not reporting significant effects, characteristics of subjects, or limitations. Tables are sometimes used in review articles for the same reason that they are used to help write a section of a paper: to facilitate interpretation.

An older technique widely used in the writing process is to summarize a study on a 3 × 5 or 5 × 7 card. The basic reference information is recorded at the top, and key points noted on the card. When writing a particular section, the relevant cards are used to glean information. This technique may be left by the wayside because it is more time consuming than reading and underlining or highlighting a copy of an article. Also, if more information is needed than was recorded on the card, the original article still has to be read.

### Keep a Dictionary Close By

There is no excuse for misspelled words. An advantage of word processors is the spelling check available in most software.

### Keep a Thesaurus Beneath the Dictionary

A thesaurus provides a list of synonyms. Most of us, if we were to examine the number of times we use some words, would be utterly astounded at the frequency of use. Writing the introduction, review of literature, and discussion is particularly likely to cause the overuse of certain words—"studied," "investigated," "found," and "concluded" are examples. The software for many word processors contains a thesaurus, so when you are looking for a "new" word, a listing is made available on the screen.

A thesaurus is helpful in selecting alternative words, but it should not be used to search for overly long, infrequently used, and not commonly understood words. Such words do not add to the quality or comprehensibility of a paper; rather, it does just the opposite and should be avoided.

### Use a Word Processor

The time saved through the efficiency of the word processor is enormous. Revision is facilitated because entire pages do not have to be retyped. Entire paragraphs or sections can be moved at the stroke of several keys. And, as previ ously mentioned, it can verify the spelling of words and provide a quick source of synonyms. If you do not already own a word processor, seriously consider purchasing one. Most universities make word processors available to students through microcomputers or mainframes. Furthermore, free classes are usually offered to help get you started.

## Review the Paper Several Times

Many students review or proof their papers only once before submitting them. One review is insufficient simply because there is too much to attend to. If striving for an A grade and high-quality work, separate reviews, each with a singular purpose, will be superior. First review the paper for content, as this is the most important aspect of any paper. After making revisions, review just for grammar and repetitiveness of words. Then review purely to make sure all necessary components have been included. Can you imagine the look of shock on a student's face when a paper is returned and the grade suffered because a major section was omitted? Have we seen it? Oh, yes we have, and we will again because there are enough components in a research paper to allow it to happen to a slightly disorganized student rapidly trying to assemble a paper in the last two days before a due date.

## Understand and Avoid Plagiarism at All Costs

Plagiarism is defined by Random House (1967) as "the appropriation or imitation of the language, ideas, and thoughts of another author and presentation of them as one's ideas." Note that the ideas and thoughts of others are included in the definition, so it is not merely limited to just their words. If the exact words are used, it is necessary to cite the reference and place the words in quotations or to indent and single space the words that are quoted. Both techniques visually highlight the fact that the words are not your own.

A valid question about plagiarism arises when one considers whether or not nearly all information in a research paper is based on the thoughts and ideas of others, and therefore should be footnoted. An effective rule of thumb here is that if the idea or thought is known to you from past knowledge or experience or it is considered general knowledge, then it does not need to be footnoted. This leaves much to the writer's sense of ethics, which usually suffices if the reason for plagiarism is understood. However, realize that if others, such as the professor grading the paper or a journal reviewer, disagree with your not having referenced something, you will be held accountable. In some cases, the penalty may be as severe as receiving a failing grade for a paper or even being dismissed from an institution. Obviously, academics take plagiarism extremely seriously. We have seen several students expelled from the university or receive automatic failing grades for plagiarism. A student writing a paper has two options when confronted with the issue of referencing information: Discuss it with your professor if time permits or simply reference the source. The worst that can happen is that you have more references than necessary. However, this is not usually a concern unless it becomes excessive.

*So, when in doubt, cite the reference!*

## COMMON FAULTS IN WRITING

Writing is an art form with a thousand and one rules, most of which we know intuitively from the daily reading we do and from our formal education. Although it is beyond the scope of this book to review the many rules of grammar and composition, we would like to share with you the most common writing mistakes made by graduate students. If you are able to avoid many of these, your papers will be much the better.

*Verbose and Pedantic Style*   Verbosity refers to being overly wordy—in other words, beating around the bush. Many of us remember writing themes and papers to meet a length requirement. Such a requirement is commonly made to ensure that all students do some minimum of work, which is believed to be conducive to achieving a learning objective. Although it is undoubtedly of some value when working with groups of students, it may not be optimal in trying to produce the best quality of work because it encourages padding and quantity, often at the expense of quality. Writing in research, however, emphasizes brevity and clarity. This saves time for readers, and by saving space, allows for publication of more studies in a given journal over a year. Some research publications limit the length of submitted manuscripts to about 25 pages, which includes references, tables, and figures. In addition, the number of references is even limited in some publications. Therefore, researchers tend to write succinctly. With practice, your ability to be brief and to the point will improve. See Table 6-2 for some examples of wordiness.

Pedantic writing occurs when writers strive to show off their intellect by using uncommon words. One could say: "Deport oneself to an environment conducive to academic endeavor," which more simply could be stated as "Go study in a quiet place." Similarly, one could say, "Assume the supine position in a comforting manner for a period following neuromuscular activity" or "Take a rest after exercise." The object of writing in research is to aid communication. The examples here are more a puzzle rather than an aid.

Do not confuse the use of scientific terminology with being pedantic. Terminology exists to give exact meaning to words, and this enhances communi-

**TABLE 6-2**   Examples of wordiness

| Wordy | Alternative |
| --- | --- |
| Long period of time | Long time or long period |
| Month of June | June |
| At a rapid rate of speed | Fast |
| Decreased number of | Fewer |
| In close proximity to | Near |

cation. Although the phrase "The respiratory exchange ratio exceeded 1.05 for all subjects" may seem pedantic to some readers, to those trained in physiology of exercise the terms are well known, easily understood, and the meaning exact. Attempting to say it much differently would likely require more words that may not be as well understood. All disciplines have their "lingo"—and for a good reason.

*Clichés* Clichés are figures of speech that are best deleted. They do not enhance meaning but do add length to one's writing. Some common clichés are listed in Table 6-3.

*Subject–Verb Agreement* A sentence structure in which a subject is followed by a phrase in which the object is plural often tends to cause subject–verb disagreement. For example:

Proper intake of all essential nutrients (is, are) vital to good health.
**Answer:** *is*, which agrees with the subject, *intake*.

Control of all variables in a study (is, are) important.
**Answer:** *is*, which agrees with the subject, *control*.

Each participant recorded (his, their) intake of all food and drink consumed for two weekdays and one day of a weekend.
**Answer:** *his*, which agrees with the subject, *participant*.

*Parallelism* Phrases in a sentence should use the same grammatical form. Here are some examples:

The following were obtained from the subjects: medical history, height and weight, and then we measured their blood pressure.
**Correct:** The following were obtained from the subjects: medical history, height and weight, and blood pressure.

When teaching young children, wear a smile on your face, be organized, have supplies ready, and if an emergency occurs you should have previously developed a plan.
**Correct:** When teaching young children, wear a smile on your face, be organized, and have supplies as well as an emergency plan ready.

**TABLE 6-3** Common clichés

| Cliché | Preferred |
| --- | --- |
| First of all | First |
| A considerable amount of | Much |
| Last but not least | Last |
| At this particular time | Now |
| Accounted for by the fact | Because |
| It is suggested that | Possibly |

*Misused Commas*   Commas should clarify meaning, but if improperly used they can change the meaning of a sentence. Examine these illustrations:

> The student, thinks the teacher, is a fool.
> > The student is thought to be the fool by the teacher.
>
> The student thinks the teacher is a fool.
> > Here the teacher is thought to be the fool.

*Vogue words*   Vogue words enjoy short-term popularity. If they remain in common usage, they become clichés. Ease communication by using simpler words. Some examples follow: *exacerbate, ameliorate, interface, expertise, via, vis-à-vis.*

*Redundancy*   Repetitiveness adds length without meaning because both words mean the same. Here are some common examples: *basic essentials, refer back, viable alternative, authentic replica.*

*Jargon*   Jargon is technical terminology often mixed with obscure, long words. A few examples are borrowed from Day (1983). See if you can understand what is meant by each.

> It has been posited that a high degree of curiosity proved lethal to a feline.
> **Answer:** Curiosity killed the cat.
>
> From time immemorial, it has been known that the ingestion of an "apple" (i.e., the pome fruit of any tree of the genus *Malus,* said fruit being usually round in shape and red, yellow, or greenish in color) on a diurnal basis will with absolute certainty keep a primary member of the health care establishment absent from one's local environment.
> **Answer:** An apple a day keeps the doctor away.
>
> A sedimentary conglomerate in motion down a proclivity gains no addition of mossy material.
> **Answer:** A rolling stone gathers no moss.

*Symbols*   Symbols are used in research to denote certain statistics and mathematical functions. Their main value is that they save space on the printed page. Some of the rules for using symbols, which are not widely known, are described here.

1. Do not capitalize the letters unless the unit is derived from a person's name or in the case of L, for liter, which is done to avoid confusing the lowercase letter l with the number 1.
2. Do not use a period after the letter and do not add an *s* to make it plural. (There are exceptions to the *s* rule, however.)
3. Leave one space between the symbol and number.
4. Examples: cholesterol = 200 mg/dl, body weight = 82 kg

*Misuse of Words*   Day (1983) cites several words commonly misused by writers. Note how the meaning is altered in each example.

ONLY.   The word *only* can be positioned in several places in the following sentence. However, note the change in meaning depending on the location.

> I hit him in the eye only yesterday.

> I hit him in the only eye yesterday.

> I only hit him in the eye yesterday.

IT.   If the antecedent is not clear, the meaning can be changed. "Free information about venereal disease. To get it, call 654-7000." Problems with confusing antecedents commonly occur when a sentence refers to something in a previous sentence but two or more words could be the item being referred to. To avoid the problem, restate the word for which *it* refers.

VARYING.   The word means "changing." It is often used instead of "various," which means "different." For example: "Varying responses were obtained, depending on the quality of the feedback provided."

*Abbreviations*   Abbreviations, as are symbols, are used to save space in writing, which in turn often facilitates reading. Writing the name of our national professional organization, the American Alliance of Health, Physical Education, Recreation, and Dance, becomes tedious for the writer as well as reader. However, overuse of abbreviations, particularly if they are not commonly used, can be aggravating. Sometimes experimental groups in studies are abbreviated. For example, imagine a study in which four groups based on their preference of recreational activities are compared. One group might be abbreviated the VO for those selecting vigorous outdoor activities; a second group is termed MO for moderate outdoor acitvity; a third group is termed the SI group because of their preference for social interaction while they recreate; and a fourth group is labeled SA for sedentary activities done alone. The abbreviations are logical when first defined, but they are not standard and require the reader to deal with four new abbreviations as they read the article. It frustrates most readers to have to refer several times to the spot where the abbreviations are initially defined. Consequently, minimize the use of uncommon abbreviations.

Define the abbreviation the first time used and put the abbreviation in parentheses. This also includes the abstract, as the information here should be self-explanatory. Do not use an abbreviation in a title because it may create problems for indexing and abstracting services, as well as information retrieval systems. Use only standard abbreviations, such as those listed in the *Council of Biology Editors Style Manual* (1978) or those in Systeme Internationale (SI) units.

*Tense*   Tense is a tricky issue that is usually not addressed in textbooks on research methods. The current thought is to use the present tense for previously published work because, by virtue of it being published, it is accepted as established knowledge. For example, "The literature clearly shows a trend. . . ." However, the writing that you do in the preparation of a proposal or manuscript is not yet published or accepted by the academic community as accepted knowledge and therefore, to distinguish it, the past tense is used (Day, 1983, pp. 142–143). For example, "The literature reviewed clearly showed a trend. . . ."

This means that in writing a proposal, the future tense will be mixed with the present tense. In writing the results chapter of a thesis, the past tense should be used; the discussion will include past (your own work) and present (published work).

*Active versus Passive Voice*   Researchers generally have used the passive voice (third person) rather than the active voice (first person), perhaps trying to be modest. Consequently, we typically read: "It was found" or "Smith and Johnson reported" rather than "I" or "we." It is not wrong to use the active voice, and some experts recommend it because it is more direct, precise, and less verbose (Day, 1983). Some journals even encourage authors to use the active voice. However, because the issue is somewhat new and controversial, it would be wise to check with your professor.

*Nonemotional Language*   Write in a somewhat detached, nonemotional manner. You may not win a Pulitzer Prize using this style but it helps to obtain objectivity. Superlatives and qualifiers such as "extremely," "unusually," "very," "considerably," and "marked" are best deleted because they are inexact. Use less emotional words and let the numerical values and significance levels influence readers.

*Numbers*   The guideline used by the American Psychological Association is to use words to express numbers below 10 and figures for numbers 10 or greater (e.g., five subjects, 15 subjects). Figures are also used for numbers below 10 if included in a list of numbers some of which are greater than 10 (e.g., 3, 56, 78, 13). Use numbers whenever they immediately precede a unit of measure (e.g., 3 in., 5 kg) or are used in a statistical or mathematical sense, such as fractions and ratios (e.g., $F$ ratio = 3.17, 2.5 times larger, 3:2 ratio). Use numbers when referring to time, age, dates, points on a scale, and amounts of money (e.g., 3 months, 5 years old, 5 on a scale of 1–7, $5.00).

## EXAMPLES OF WEAK WRITING

We would like to share some of our favorite examples about how not to write. A list of words and expressions to avoid in writing taken from Robert Day's book "How to Write and Publish a Scientific Paper" is presented in Table 6-3. Day's "Ten Commandments of Good Writing" (1983) (see Table 6-4) provides an effective summary of common writing errors. See how well you can identify the errors.

**TABLE 6-4**   Ten Commandments of Good Writing

1. Each pronoun should agree with their antecedent.
2. Just between you and I, case is important.
3. A preposition is a poor word to end a sentence with. (Incidentally, did you hear about the streetwalker who violated a grammatical rule? She unwittingly approached a plainclothesman, and her proposition ended with a sentence.)
4. Verbs has to agree with their subject.
5. Don't use no double negatives.
6. Remember to never split an infinitive.
7. When dangling, don't use participles.
8. Join clauses good, like a conjunction should.
9. Don't write a run-on sentence it is difficult when you got to punctuate it so it makes sense when the reader reads what you wrote.
10. About sentence fragments.

Source: Day, Robert A. How to Write and Publish a Scientific Paper (2nd ed.), Philadelphia, ISI Press, p. 139, 1983.

## USER-FRIENDLY REFERENCES ON WRITING

Several excellent books on effective writing are surprisingly brief. They are filled with many useful tips that either we never learned before or simply forgot. Day's book is masterfully done because it is simply written, fairly short (188 pages), and covers each segment of the research paper as well as information on manuscript submission, the review and publishing process, preparation of conference reports, and much more. Another valuable reference on writing is Strunk and White's *The Elements of Style* (1979). This 92-page classic covers elementary rules of usage, principles of composition, misused words and terms, and style. It is loaded with many useful examples of errors we all commonly make and see. A third reference that every graduate student should know is the *American Psychological Association's Publication Manual* (1983). It covers every aspect of writing papers that one might wish to know, and it is beautifully organized. It goes beyond the items listed in the two previous books to include great detail on headings, margins, numbers, tables, figures, references, and typing instructions. It is difficult to imagine anything on writing not covered in the *APA Manual*.

## SUMMARY

Good research writing is an art. To be a good artist or writer, one must practice. Write so that your work can be quickly and easily understood. No one enjoys being confused and lost halfway through a sentence or paragraph. A helpful tip to remember when writing is the KISS principle: Keep It Simple, Stupid! Or our version: Keep It So Simple! Keep the format short and simple, the paragraphs short and simple, and the sentences short and simple. It makes for a smaller target when your paper is being graded!

# CHAPTER 7

# BEGINNING STATISTICAL CONCEPTS

---

**KEY CONCEPTS**

Measurement scales:
  nominal, ordinal,
  interval, and ratio
Parametric and
  nonparametric statistics
Descriptive and inferential
  statistics

Populations and samples
Random sampling
  procedures
Tips and notations on
  computation

**AFTER READING THIS CHAPTER, YOU SHOULD BE ABLE TO**

- Identify data by their level of measurement.
- Differentiate between parametric and nonparametric statistics.
- Distinguish between descriptive and inferential statistics.
- Describe what populations and samples are.
- Describe several commonly used random sampling procedures.
- Perform simple statistical operations by identifying standard computational notation.

*Statistics*, the study of the summary, analysis, and evaluation of data, is perhaps the most vital tool for research. The primary function of statistics is to reduce a large amount of data to a useful numerical value that represents a particular trait about the data. As we have mentioned time and time again, research is no place for making unsubstantiated guesses, hunches, or speculations. Most research decisions are based on hard facts that are generated through the use of appropriate statistical techniques. Effective professionals in HPER or any field must have at least an elementary knowledge of statistics so that they may make decisions about the correct use and interpretations of statistical procedures. This is an essential skill, whether for producing or consuming research.

It has been our experience that once the word "statistics" is mentioned some students lapse into tremors and shock. After they are revived, they confess to having terminal cases of "math anxiety." It's time to dispel some myths and purge those negative feelings. In the process of performing this exorcism, we would also like to present our philosophy, which we think is a pragmatic one, about the presentation of statistics in this text.

From a math standpoint, the statistical procedures that will be presented involve nothing more complicated than arithmetic. If you can add, subtract, multiply, divide, and find a square and square root with a calculator, you're in business. Performing calculations from an equation is much like following directions on a road map. If one knows what the signs and symbols are, that person will have no problem getting to the destination. With equations it's just a matter of performing calculations in order to get to the end result. Nevertheless, as straightforward as this is, it would be very unlikely that a modern researcher would perform statistical computations by hand. There are numerous statistical software packages (Minitab, SPSS, SAS, etc.) for mainframes and personal computers that tremendously expedite and simplify the data reduction and analysis processes. It can be argued that once someone understands the basic tenets of a statistic, particularly those related to its function and meaning, hand calculations are of little value. However, some initial number manipulation may be warranted to reach that level of comprehension.

Being a competent user of statistics doesn't mean that one needs to become a professional statistician. Most researchers are users of statistics, not mathematicians. They know what tool to select for the job, how to apply it, and how to interpret the results of its use. In everyday life, one can be an effective user of many tools without truly comprehending their underlying mechanics. How many pilots understand the elaborate engineering and mechanical operations of their aircraft? How many physicians understand the microelectronics of an EKG machine? We effectively operate and maintain sophisticated automobiles, but do we really know how they work? A chef can bake a delicious cake without understanding the essential chemical reactions as it cooks. The list goes on and on. Statistical purists may resent this statement but, we think it's true: One can effectively *use* statistics without understanding all of the intricate "engineering" details.

Having said these things our philosophy should be apparent. We will present the basic theory and appropriate selection, application, and interpretation of statistical procedures commonly used in HPER research. By reducing hand calculations and providing many relevant examples of their use and interpretation, we hope you will find this a *user-friendly approach*.

## LEVELS OF MEASUREMENT

Consider what the number 23 means. "Are you kidding? It means 23 of something, last time I checked," you say. Sure it does, but 23 of what? For instance, the number 23 could be Michael Jordan's uniform number, or 23 could represent the rank of a student in a class of 500. The number 23 could depict the temperature in degrees Celsius or the weight of an object in pounds. All of these representations of the number 23 typify a type of measurement that varies in terms of complexity. Levels of measurement allow us to know something about the intricacy of the numbers or data that we are generating from our research. It is important to know the level of measurement because it directly affects our choice of the correct statistical procedure.

### Nominal Level

*Nominal* (meaning "name") level data are the most rudimentary because they only provide information about a difference. Uniform number 15 is not the same as number 10 or interstate highway number 80 is different than number 29 are examples of nominal values. Nominal levels are also associated with counted categorical data. Categories need to be defined in such a way that they are mutually exclusive; an observation can belong in only one classification and not another. For instance, you could categorize athletic shoes as Nike, Adidas, Reebok, or the like. The categories are mutually exclusive, because a shoe can't be classified as both a Nike and an Adidas or a Reebok. A frequency count of observations in each category is made and used in a statistical analysis. If you walked through a fitness center and counted the varieties of shoes on people's feet you might come up with something like Nike = 10, Adidas = 6, and Reebok = 4. These frequency counts may now be used in a statistical analysis. Even though this level of measurement is very basic, it is important to identify because many observations in HPER only meet this level of precision.

### Ordinal Scale

*Ordinal* (meaning "order") level data demonstrate ranks, so they have the ability to show difference and direction of difference. Thus they provide more information than nominal data. Someone who finishes second in a road race did better than someone who was third, and of course, third place was better than fourth. What we don't know from rank data is the amount of difference between each because there is no equality of units. For instance, the difference between second and third place may have been 0.5 second and the difference between third and fourth may have been 30.0 seconds.

### Interval Level

*Interval* (meaning "equal intervals") level data have all of the properties of ordinal data plus equality of units. Therefore, on a Celsius temperature scale we know that 25° is warmer than 20° by 5° or 5° is 15° less than 20°. Therefore, interval level data inform us about difference, direction of difference, and amount of difference in equal units.

### Ratio Level

*Ratio* (meaning numbers may be presented as "ratios") level data are the most complex because they have all of the elements of interval level, plus they have an absolute zero point. What is an absolute zero? No, not –273°C, or at least not exactly. An absolute zero point represents the absence of the trait being measured. Variables such as weight, distance, and time have meaningful absolute zero points. Interval level zeros are not absolute. For example, if it is 0°C is there no temperature? Sure there is, and it is quite cold. If someone can't do at least one pull-up, does that mean she has no upper body strength? Of course not. Absolute zero points also allow us to make comparisons like 5 inches is half the distance of 10 inches or 60 seconds is three times as long as 20 seconds. Without an absolute zero point such comparisons are not valid. Does something that is 40°C have twice as much heat energy as something that is 20°C? The object is 20° warmer but, not twice (100%) as warm. The reason is that the zero point on the Celsius scale is not an absolute zero. Because the true absolute zero point for temperature (i.e., absence of heat energy) is –273°C, then 40° = (273 + 40 = 313) and 20° = (273 + 20 = 293). Therefore, 313/293 = 1.068—or 40° is only 6.8% warmer than 20°!

## PARAMETRIC AND NONPARAMETRIC STATISTICS

Statistical analyses can be classified as parametric or nonparametric types. *Parametric* statistics are used when data are interval or ratio level and when the populations from which the observations were made are thought to be normally distributed. Interval and ratio level data are considered *measured or continuous*. That implies that they may be measured with increasingly greater precision. For example, distances could be measured to the closest 1, 1/2, 1/4, 1/16, 1/32, 1/64, . . . inch. The level of precision is limited only by the sophistication of the instrument being used.

    *Nonparametric* statistics are used when data are nominal or ordinal level or when the populations from which the observations were made are thought to be nonnormally distributed. Sometimes these statistics are referred to as distribution-free analyses. We have mentioned that nominal and ordinal level data are considered counted and ranked data, respectively. They are also referred to as *discrete* data because the observations are treated as whole values. For instance, when obtaining frequency counts for a divorced/not divorced classification, one cannot have a count of 57.5 divorces because there is no such thing as half of a divorce.

Parametric statistics are more powerful than their nonparametric counterparts because they are more likely to reject a false null hypothesis (see Chapter 9). However, when the criteria for the use of a parametric analysis cannot be met, a nonparametric alternative must be used. Examples of statistics from both of these divisions are given in upcoming chapters.

## DESCRIPTIVE AND INFERENTIAL STATISTICS

Statistics may also be classified as descriptive or inferential, depending on their use. *Descriptive* statistics are employed to measure a trait or characteristic of a group without generalizing that statistic beyond that group. The average 40-yard dash speed of a football team, the mean number of miles you drove your car per month this year, your grade point average, and the range of your class test scores on the last research exam are all examples of descriptive statistics.

*Inferential* statistics are used to make generalizations or inferences from a smaller group to a larger group. What exactly does it mean to infer or generalize? An *inference or a generalization* is a type of prediction that is made by measuring a trait from a smaller representative group and estimating what it would be in the larger group. The ability to infer is not so much based in the computation of the statistic but the purpose for using it—that is, the researcher *wants* to make inferences. In order to make valid inferences, it is critical that the subjects in the smaller group are good representatives of the larger group. Here is an illustration.

A health educator is interested in determining the cholesterol levels of the 10,000 students on a university campus so that they can be compared to national norms. Does the researcher need to test all of the students to answer this question? No, thank goodness. This is because of the power to infer with statistics. The researcher obtains a group of 100 subjects who are a good model of the entire student body. (How this is done is discussed in the next section, on sampling.) He now tests the subjects and determines their cholesterol levels. Because the 100 subjects are representative of the entire student body, an inference may be made to estimate (usually with good accuracy) what the typical cholesterol levels of all 10,000 students would be. From this example it should be needless to say that inferential statistics are one of the most valued tools of a researcher.

## SAMPLING PROCEDURES

### Populations and Samples

In our discussion, we have referred to large and small groups of subjects. These groups are more correctly called a population and a sample, respectively. A *population* is an all-inclusive group that is operationally defined by the researcher. Definitions may range from broad to specific descriptions. Based on the definition, membership in the population is mutually exclusive. That is, a subject is either in the population or is not. Although we referred to the population as a "large" group, it may not be big at all. For instance, all university professors in HPER in the United States would define a fairly large population but, all university professors in HPER in the United States with annual incomes above $150,000 would probably be very small (maybe none!). In short, a population's size is dictated by the researcher's definition of it. Also, it's easy to see by the definition if one is included in the population or not. A trait or characteristic of a population is known as a *parameter*. For instance, the Greek letter μ (mu) is the symbol representing a population parameter mean.

A *sample* is a representative subset of the population that contains the essential elements of that population. A trait or characteristic of a population is known as a *statistic*. Anytime a researcher is interested in making inferences he/she needs to have a sample that is a good representation of the population. How does one obtain a good model sample? Let's look at several ways this can be done.

## Random Sampling

One of the fundamental principles of inferential statistics is that subjects are drawn from a population using a *random sampling* technique. By definition, when random sampling is used every constituent in the population has an equal probability of being selected for the sample. Random sampling is an impartial process and will result in what is called an *unbiased* sample of a population. An unbiased sample is one that is more likely to be representative of the population, whereas a *biased* sample contains some type of systematic error and is not as good a representation.

Random sampling can be accomplished many ways. One method is to use *random numbers*, which can be generated by computer or from statistical tables. If our health educator wanted to form a random sample of 100 from the university population of 10,000, he first would need to get a list of all 10,000 students (easy; go to the registrar's office) and assign each a number from 1 to 10,000. Then he could use a computer to select randomly any 100 numbers from 1 to 10,000. The students matching the random numbers are now in the sample. If the population is large and the process of assigning numbers to the entire population is performed by hand, this sampling procedure can be quite time consuming.

Another method that can be used especially when a population is large is called *systematic counting*. With this procedure the researcher uses some type of list or inventory of subjects in a population: A phone book, a list of licensed drivers, or an index of registered voters are examples. Suppose that we would like a random sample of 200 subjects and we have an alphabetical list of 30,000 drivers at our disposal. We could simply go down the list counting off every 150th person to be part of the sample. Of course any time a "list" is used, the sample is biased to the character of what the list is composed of. For instance, if a telephone book is used, the sample is biased to people who have phones. Nonetheless, this is a commonly used sampling technique for broad-based public opinion surveys.

The last procedure that we will describe is known as *stratified random sampling*. This method is used when the investigator has reason to believe that a population has distinct subgroups or strata and wants to have the appropriate representation from each. In our population of 10,000 university students, a conspicuous subgrouping could be freshmen, sophomore, junior, and senior students. Of course these students are both of the male and female variety. After consulting with the registrar, it is found that the percentage of the population of each class and the breakdown of men and women. Table 7-1 illustrates the composition of a stratified random sample of 100 students for this university. A random sampling procedure would be used to assign the requisite number of subjects into each stratum.

How different would the sample be if we used the random numbers approach instead of stratification? That is difficult to say. Normally, a very large random sample will contain representatives of all of the strata. The smaller the sample size, the more likely biased representation becomes even if random sampling is used. To that end, stratified random sampling offsets some of the potential of forming a biased sample and should be used when forming smaller samples.

Having said all of this about random sampling, we must confess that it is difficult to obtain a true random sample. It isn't very often that a researcher could have access to or the freedom to manipulate all of the subjects in a population. For instance, what if someone were interested in studying the physical fitness levels of high school football players in the United States. That would be a massive population from which to draw a random sample, and probably large portions of it would be inaccessible to the researcher. Or if someone wanted to do school-based research, it would be difficult to randomly select students and place them into classes where different teaching methods were being studied. So in those types of cases investigators use the best sampling technique that they can and describe that to the consumer of research. The consumer then decides if legitimate inferences or generalization can be made.

Oftentimes researchers will draw up specific delimitations for subjects and will include any volunteer subject who meets that description. This certainly

**TABLE 7-1**   Example of a stratified random sample

| University Population $N = 10,000$ | | | |
|---|---|---|---|
| Percent men = 45    Percent women = 55 | | | |
| | | *Sample (n = 100)* | |
| *Subset* | *Percent* | *Men* | *Women* |
| Freshmen | 29 | 13 | 16 |
| Sophomores | 26 | 12 | 14 |
| Juniors | 24 | 11 | 13 |
| Seniors | 21 | 9 | 12 |
| | *Total:* | 45 | 55 |

isn't a random sampling technique, and the ability to make generalizations may be quite limited. However, when random sampling from a population is not practical or possible, this is how samples may be obtained. Many studies in HPER are based on this approach.

How many subjects do we need in a sample to make accurate inferences? Generally speaking, a larger random sample will be a better model of the population than a smaller one. There are equations that may be used to estimate the size of a sample based on an acceptable level of error that is defined by the researcher. An equation for sample size and a discussion on this topic are presented in Chapter 18.

### Randomization into Groups

Once potential study subjects have been identified, the researcher may need to make decisions about group placement. The investigator should not allow the subjects to select what group they would like to be in as this represents a form of selection bias that weakens the experiment. It is critical in some types of research that groups are equivalent at the onset of a study, and the best way to ensure this is to randomize the subjects into groups. Random numbers, blind draws of coded cards, and other such unbiased methods may be used. More is said about randomization of subjects in Chapter 14.

## SOME COMPUTATIONAL NOTATIONS AND TIPS

In our discussion of selected statistics, equations and sample problems will be provided. These problems may be solved through the use of a computer, by hand, or as a form of checking your work, by both approaches. The emphasis placed on any of the approaches is at the discretion of your professor. To help you understand statistical problem solving, we give some tips on computation.

As we said before, solving math problems is no different than reading a road map. If you know what the signs and symbols mean, you'll have no problem getting to your destination. With equations, it's just a matter of performing calculations in order to get to the end result. To help you remember the order of computations we present a phrase that you probably learned in grade school. (We learned it in grade school, too, so it is a very old phrase!) *Please Excuse My Dear Aunt Sally* is the order of operations for *P*arentheses, *E*xponents, *M*ultiplication, *D*ivision, *A*ddition, and *S*ubtraction. Simply do the operations in parentheses first (start with the pair the furthest in, then work outward), followed by exponent operations (e.g., square or square root), then multiplication or division, and addition or subtraction. Remember this and you can't go wrong.

Statistical equations are composed of some math symbols that you should be very familiar with, as well as a few that you might not be. The symbol $X$ refers to the value of any variable in a distribution or column of scores. When a subscript appears with $X$, such as $X_1$, it refers to the position of the score in the distribution. Thus, $X_3 = 57$ means the third score or variable in the distribution has the value 57. The symbol $N$ or $n$ refers to the total number of scores in a distribution. Technically, $N$ denotes the size of a population, whereas $n$ refers to the size of a sample. However, frequently $N$ is simply used to denote the number of observations in a group regardless if it is a sample or a population. If $N = 20$, that means there are 20 scores in that distribution. If subscripts appear with $N$, it represents the number of scores in a certain group. For instance, $N_3 = 18$ means that there are 18 scores in group number 3. The symbols $X$ and $N$ frequently appear with the exponent for squaring—for example, if $X = 12$, $X^2 = 144$ or if $N = 9$, $N^2 = 81$. What does $N_1^2 = 49$ mean? It means that the number of observations in group 1 squared, or $N_1^2 = 7^2 = 49$.

The symbol $\Sigma$ is the Greek letter sigma, which expresses the operation of addition. In some statistical texts sigma may have notations like sub- and superscripts associated with it. They are used to indicate starting and stopping points of summing operations. We will not use these notations, however, so any time you see $\Sigma X$ in an equation assume that it means sum all of the variables in that column. Therefore, the sign $\Sigma X$ says to sum all of the variables in a distribution. So, given the variables 1, 2, 3, 4, 5, $\Sigma X = 15$.

Now for some quick application. Given the variables 1, 2, 3, 4, 5, then $\Sigma X = 15$. What is $\Sigma X^2$? The order of operations says to do exponents first, then addition (remember, $\Sigma$ is the sign for summation or addition), so this expression says to square all of the $X$ variables first, then sum them. So $\Sigma X^2$ is $1 + 4 + 9 + 16 + 25 = 55$. What does $(\Sigma X)^2$ equal? That expression indicates that we sum all of the $X$ variables first, because it is in parentheses, then square that sum. Therefore, $(\Sigma X)^2 = 15^2 = 225$.

All of this seems straightforward enough, and it is if you know the signs and the order of operations. By the way, there is a great deal of squaring and summing of variables in the computation of statistics, and you will see the operations $\Sigma X^2$ and $(\Sigma X)^2$ many times. These two operations are often mistaken for one another. In our examples, $\Sigma X^2 = 55$ and $(\Sigma X)^2 = 225$, and as you are well aware, 55 does not equal 225. Confusing these operations (or any other for that matter) will lead to calculating the wrong statistical value and will start a domino effect ending with a terrific headache! So, for those of you who are uncertain about these two operations, review this last section before you go on.

## SUMMARY

Statistics are probably the researcher's most important tool. Statistics may be classified as parametric or nonparametric and may be used for descriptive or inferential purposes. In order to make accurate inferences, a researcher needs to have a representative sample of a population, and the best way to establish a model sample is through a random sampling technique. Effective professionals in HPER or any field must have at least an elementary knowledge of statistics so that they may make prudent decisions about the correct use and interpretations of statistical procedures. This is an essential skill for both producers and consumers of research.

## STATISTICS EXERCISES

1. Indicate the level of measurement for the following:
   a. Driving on U.S. Highway 6
   b. A runner's time of 18 min 30 sec in a road race
   c. A student 27th in a class of 157 students
   d. 44 women in a recreational golf league
   e. The average daily temperature of 35°F last March
   f. Locker number 16
   g. A systolic blood pressure reading of 124 mm Hg
   h. A score of 20 correct out of 25 test items
   i. A football lineman who weighs 275 lb
   j. A swimmer who finished third in a race

2. For the following data sets, calculate $\Sigma X$, $\Sigma X^2$, and $(\Sigma X)^2$:

| Group A | Group B | Group C |
|---------|---------|---------|
| 1 | 3 | 7 |
| 3 | 4 | 2 |
| 6 | 9 | 1 |
| 8 | 3 | 5 |
| 4 | 6 | 2 |
| 7 | 2 | 4 |

# CHAPTER 8

# CENTRAL TENDENCY, VARIABILITY, AND THE NORMAL CURVE

**KEY CONCEPTS**

Central tendency      Range
Mean      Standard deviation
Median      Normal curve
Mode      z score
Variability      Nonnormal distributions

**AFTER READING THIS CHAPTER, YOU SHOULD BE ABLE TO**

- Explain the concepts of central tendency and variability.
- Describe the characteristics of the normal curve and explain how it may be applied to sets of data.
- Calculate measures of central tendency and interpret the results.
- Calculate measures of variability and interpret the results.
- Calculate z scores and interpret the results.
- Describe what nonnormal distributions are.

$M$easures of central tendency and variability are some of the most commonly used and important descriptive statistics. These statistics perhaps represent the most basic form of statistical analysis and are utilized in most every form of research. The concept of the normal curve is the cornerstone of many other statistical techniques. We explore these ideas in this chapter.

## CENTRAL TENDENCY

The general purpose of statistics is to reduce a large amount of data to one meaningful numerical value. In the case of measures of central tendency, that value is the one that best typifies or is the most representative of all of the scores in a distribution. There are three measures of central tendency: the *mean, median,* and *mode.* Let's look at each.

### The Mean

We are exposed to means, or average values, on a daily basis, and you have probably calculated a mean value numerous times in your life. The *mean* is simply the arithmetic average of a distribution of scores and is the most commonly used measure of central tendency. The customary symbols for the mean are $M$ and $\overline{X}$. The equation for the mean is

$$M = \frac{\Sigma X}{N}$$

and given the variables 1, 2, 3, 4, 5, $M = 15/5 = 3.0$. The mean is used when the data are interval or ratio level. The mean is usually regarded as the most reliable and meaningful measure of central tendency.

### The Median

The *median* is the point in a distribution where 50% of the scores lie above and below. The symbol for the median is MED (in some cases the entire word is used). To determine the median of a distribution, all of the scores need to be ranked from highest to lowest in order. If there is an odd number of scores, the median is the score that is the exact midpoint; for an even number of variables, the two middle scores are averaged.

Median for odd $N$:   MED = 6, 7, 8, 9, 10 = 8.0

Median for even $N$:   MED = 6, 7, 8, 9 = (7 + 8)/2 = 7.5

This approach is used only when there are not many tied scores. (If there are several tied scores, another data analysis must be done, which will not be presented here, but is used in any commercial statistical software.)

The median is the measure of choice when data are ordinal level (medians can be computed for data that are ordinal level or higher) or when a distribution has a small $N$ size and some atypical or outlying scores in it. Let's say that a physical education instructor has her seventh grade class perform a push-up test for muscular endurance. In the class she has a junior Olympic gymnast who does unusually well. Compare the effect that this atypical score has on the mean and the median.

$$\text{Data: } 17, 19, 20, 22, 25, 27, 100$$

$$M = 230/7 = 32.9$$

$$\text{MED} = 22.0$$

You can see that the atypical score of 100 push-ups inflated the mean value. Thus, in this case, the median is a better representation of the group's performance.

### The Mode

The *mode*, the crudest measure of central tendency, is not used very often. The mode simply is the most frequent score in a distribution and can be obtained by quick inspection of a distribution that is ranked in numerical order. It may be possible that two scores occur the most frequently. If this occurs the distribution has two modes, or is *bimodal*.

$$\text{Data: } 10, 9, 9, 8, 7, 7, 7, 5, 3, 2$$

$$\text{Mode} = 7$$

### Application of Mean and Median

The primary use of the mean and the median is as an index of the most typical score in a distribution. These statistics also allow for comparison of individual scores within a distribution (85 is 10 points higher than the mean of 75) and to compare to like values between other distributions (Group A MED = 40 vs. Group B MED = 35). We will be using these statistics frequently because the mean is used extensively as a component in other parametric statistics, and the median appears in some nonparametric equations.

## MEASURES OF VARIABILITY

Measures of variability indicate something about the dispersion of scores in a distribution. These statistics provide information about how spread out scores are and if the scores are similar to one another or not. The most common measures of variability are range and standard deviation. Each of these statistics requires that data be interval or ratio level.

## Range

The *range* measures just what its name implies: the distance between the end-points in a distribution. The range is determined by taking the difference between the high and low scores in a distribution, with some statisticians advocating adding 1 to that difference. Here is an example of a range calculation:

$$Range = High\ score - Low\ score\ or$$

$$Range = (High\ score - Low\ score) + 1$$

$$Data: 3, 4, 5, 6, 7, 8, 9$$

$$Range = 9 - 3 = 6\ or\ (9 - 3) + 1 = 7$$

The range is a weak measure of variability because it is based on the extreme scores in a distribution and is determined by only two scores. Therefore, it doesn't give any information about the spread of all the scores in the group. Sometimes the range is reported in a table by reporting the high and low scores. For example, reporting a range of 25 for a group of test scores tells nothing about the extreme scores. However, if the high and low scores are reported instead, like 90 to 65, more descriptive information is given, plus one can easily calculate the range, if desired.

## Standard Deviation

The *standard deviation* is the most frequently used measure of variability and is much stronger than the range. The standard deviation provides information on the average algebraic distance each score in a distribution is away from the mean. The basis for computing a standard deviation is called a *deviation score*, which is the difference each score in the distribution is from the mean $(X - M)$. When these differences are squared, summed, averaged, and unsquared, the standard deviation is the result. The most common symbols for the standard deviation are $S$ and $SD$.

One equation for $SD$ is based on computing a distribution mean:

$$SD = \sqrt{\frac{\Sigma X^2}{N} - M^2}$$

Another equation doesn't require a calculation of a mean:

$$SD = \frac{1}{N}\sqrt{N(\Sigma X^2) - (\Sigma X)^2}$$

Table 8-1 contains examples of each.

**TABLE 8-1**  Example calculations of standard deviation

| X | $X^2$ |
|---|---|
| 1 | 1 |
| 2 | 4 |
| 4 | 16 |
| 6 | 36 |
| 8 | 64 |
| 9 | 81 |

$$\Sigma X = 30, \Sigma X^2 = 202, (\Sigma X)^2 = 900, M = 5, N = 6$$

$$SD = \sqrt{\frac{202}{6} - 5^2} = \sqrt{33.67 - 25} = \sqrt{8.67} = 2.94$$

$$SD = \frac{1}{6}\sqrt{6(202) - 900} = .167\sqrt{1212 - 900} = 2.94$$

As you can see from these examples, either equation will give you exactly the same value, so the choice of which to use doesn't matter.

By the way, it is impossible to have a negative *SD*, as you can see from the squaring and square root processes. So if you have hand-calculated a negative *SD*, check your work.

### Interpreting *SD*

How is *SD* interpreted? From our examples we can say that the scores in the distribution differ from the mean on the average 2.94 units. A larger *SD* means there is more variability in scores or they are spread out more, whereas a smaller *SD* means that the scores are closer together or more similar. The *SD* from different distributions with scores reflecting the same variable may be compared as well. If Group A has a *SD* = 10.5 and Group B has a *SD* = 5.3, which distribution has more variability in scores? Group A, of course, does. The *SD* has many more applications in other statistics and concepts, which we will discuss in Chapters 10, 11, and 18.

### Variance

The square of *SD* ($SD^2$) is a statistic called *variance*. Variance is another measure of the variability of scores and is used extensively in the calculation of many other statistics. However, variance is rarely used in place of the *SD* as a descriptor of a distribution's variability. This is because variance is expressed in squared units as opposed to the original units of the data. We'll be discussing variance in more detail later on.

## THE NORMAL CURVE

The normal curve is a statistical model that is used to visualize data, interpret distributions of scores, and most importantly make predictions and probability statements. The normal curve has several notable characteristics. The mean, median, and mode on the curve are identical and make up the vertical midpoint. The curve is perfectly symmetrical, that is, the halves are mirror images of one another. The right side of the curve is composed of positive values or values above the mean, and the left side contains negative values that are below the mean.

Many of the things observed in our work and in life approximate the model of the normal curve. For example, if one were to measure a variable such as body weight on many subjects and make a frequency graph of the scores, the resulting figure would be bell-shaped. This bell shape is representative of the normal curve. Measurements of things like height, IQ, income, or strength would result in a curve of the same shape. (Figure 8-1 shows what a bell-shaped curve looks like.) So, if one can assume that the variable that is being measured approximates the normal curve, then it can be presumed that the variable will conform to the characteristics of the model curve. Again, because many of the observations we make will approach the normal curve, we may use the model to make numerous statistical decisions.

Many so-called normal curves are used to make statistical judgments. The model that we will be discussing is called the *unit normal curve*. The total area under the curve is equal to 1 (one square unit, thus the name "unit" normal curve) or 100%. The unit normal curve has a mean that equals 0 and is divided into *SD* units that have a size equaling 1. As can be seen in Figure 8-2, approximately 68% of the area under the curve would be between ± 1 *SD*, about 95% of the area would be between ± 2 *SD*s (actually, 1.96 *SD*s), and close to 99% of the area would be between ± 3 *SD*s (actually, 2.58 *SD*s). Also notice in Figure 8-2 that the tails of the curve don't touch the baseline and would extend into infinity. This means, technically, that there are an infinite number of *SD*s on the curve. For instance, Michael Jordan has an annual income that is probably 10 *SD*s above the mean. But, because about 99% of the area can be accounted for within ± 3 *SD*s, we don't get too concerned about the remaining 1%.

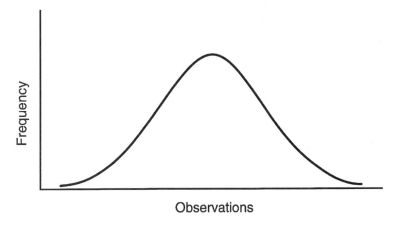

Figure 8-1   A normal curve.

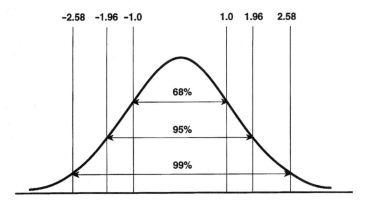

Figure 8-2   Some areas of the normal curve.

Of what value is knowing the characteristics of the normal curve? Lots! First of all, it is important to understand that when references are made to a defined area under the curve one is actually accounting for the percent of the total scores in a distribution that are represented by that area. By applying the model on data from an actual distribution of scores, we can make many statements about how the data are dispersed. The *M* and *SD* from a distribution may be substituted in the following equations to determine the 68%, 95%, and 99% values for that group of scores:

$$68\% = M \pm 1\ (SD)$$
$$95\% = M \pm 1.96\ (SD)$$
$$99\% = M \pm 2.58\ (SD)$$

In these equations *M* and *SD* are the mean and standard deviation of the distribution, and 1, 1.96, and 2.58 are the actual number of *SD* units above and below the mean that correspond with 68%, 95%, and 99% of the area under the curve, respectively. These intervals are also known as *confidence intervals*, of which more will be said later.

### Application of the Normal Curve

Let's say that a researcher has measured the percent body fat of 1000 women. The resulting distribution has a *M* = 25.0% fat and a *SD* of 5.0. Therefore, the scores would be distributed in the following manner:

$$68\% = 25.0 \pm 1\ (5.0) = 20.0\ \text{to}\ 30.0\%\ \text{body fat}$$
$$95\% = 25.0 \pm 1.96\ (5.0) = 15.2\ \text{to}\ 34.8\%\ \text{body fat}$$
$$99\% = 25.0 \pm 2.58\ (5.0) = 12.1\ \text{to}\ 37.9\%\ \text{body fat}$$

Now many statistical statements can be made about this distribution. Here are some examples. Also, examine the figure below each example. The shaded area depicts the percent of the scores referred.

1. Sixty-eight percent of the scores are between 20.0 and 30.0% body fat. How many actual scores does this represent? Because there are 1000 scores and 68% of them are between these values, then 1000 (.68) = 680.

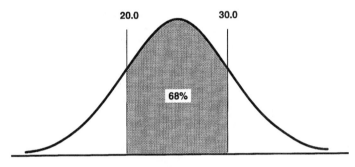

Figure 8-3

2. Thirty-two percent of the scores are either lower than 20.0 or higher than 30.0% fat. How many scores are there? There are 320 scores, as 1000 (.32) = 320.

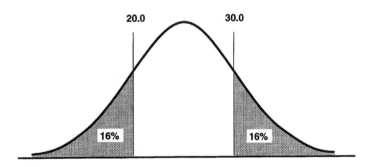

Figure 8-4

3. What percent of the women had body fat percentages above 30.0? Think for a moment about this. Each half of the curve represents 50% and 1 *SD* above the mean represents about 34% of the area—34% + 34% = 68% for ± 1 *SD*, right? Therefore, we are interested only in the percent of the area above 1 *SD*, so 50% − 34% = 16%. Now we can say that 160 women have body fat levels above 30.0% (1000(.16) = 160).

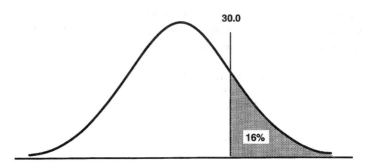

Figure 8-5

4. What percent and number of women have percent body fats below 20.0? The answer is identical to problem 3, 16% and 160, for the same reason. The only thing different is that now we are only interested in the area under the curve that is below 1 *SD*.

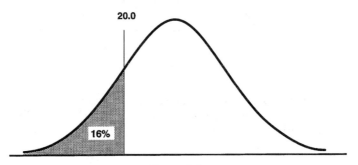

Figure 8-6

If you understand the logic that was used in examples 1 through 4, then the rest will be easy. All we are basically doing is solving for a portion of the area under the curve, and that can be done by simple deduction.

5. What percent and number of women have body fat percents above 34.8 and below 15.2? We are referring to 5% of the distribution because 2.5% of the scores are above and 2.5% below these values. This represents 50 scores, as 1000 (.05) = 50.

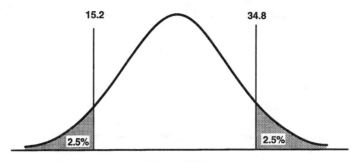

Figure 8-7

6. What percent and number of the women have body fat percents below 12.1 and above 37.9? In this case we are interested in 1% of the scores because 0.5% of the scores are above and 0.5% below these values. So there are only 10 scores at these levels, as 1000 (.01) = 10.

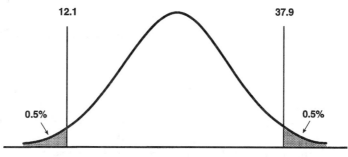

Figure 8-8

7. Put on your thinking cap for this one! What percent and number of the women have body fat percents below 30.0? The answers are 84% and 840 women. The area in this case is all of the area below +1 *SD*, and because the area from the mean to +1 *SD* equals about 34% and the entire area to the left of the mean is 50%, it follows that 50% + 34% = 84%.

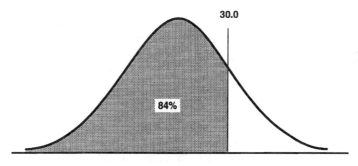

Figure 8-9

8. What percent and number of the women have body fat percents below 12.1? Because we are referring to scores that are –2.58 *SDs* from the mean, which refers to 1/2 of 1% of the scores, there are only 5 scores in this category because 1000 (.005) = 5.

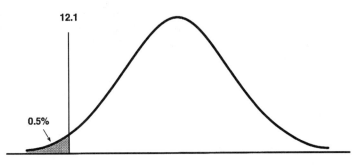

Figure 8-10

Why have we bothered with all of these examples? Because a fundamental understanding of the normal curve and its applications is vital to the study and use of statistics. You will see the 68%, 95%, and 99% intervals and the corresponding *SD* units of 1, 1.96, and 2.58 used again and again, so it may be worth your while to commit them to memory now. (These will be the only numbers that we'll ask you to memorize!)

## THE *z* SCORE

The *z* score is a statistic that is used to convert a raw score from a distribution into units of the normal curve called standard deviation units. (The unit normal curve is sometimes referred to as the *z* distribution.) A *z* score provides information about how far a raw score is away from the mean, in *SD* units. The equation for the *z* score is

$$z = \frac{X - M}{SD}$$

where *X* is the raw score, *M* is the mean, and *SD* is the standard deviation of the distribution. Using the *M* = 25.0 and *SD* = 5.0 from the women's body fat example, what would be the *z* scores for 18 and 35% body fat?

$$z = \frac{18 - 25}{5} = -1.40 \quad z = \frac{35 - 25}{5} = 2.0$$

A positive *z* score tells us how many *SD* units a score is *above* the mean, whereas a negative score is interpreted as the number of units *below* the mean. Recall that the mean of the unit normal curve or *z* distribution is 0 and a *SD* equaling 1. Therefore, a *z* score of −1.40 means that a score of 18% body fat is 1.40 *SD* units below the mean of 25 and a *z* score of 2.0 means that a body fat of 35% is 2.0 *SD* units above the mean. Thus the *z* score informs us about the exact position of the raw score in a distribution. What would be the typical range of *z* scores? Because about 99% of all scores in a distribution are between ± 3 *SD*s, then 99% of all *z* scores will range between −3.0 and +3.0. Look at the *z* distribution in Table F to confirm this fact.

The z score may also be used to compare raw scores from different distributions. Say that someone has a score of 45 kg on a grip strength test and a score of 25 cm on a low back flexibility test. Without any other statistical information, however, we wouldn't know how good these performances are relative to the group or each other. Furthermore, comparing grip strength and flexibility scores in their original units would be like comparing apples and oranges. Given the following information, however, we may convert the scores into the same unit of measure (that is, *SD* units) by computing a z score for each and then make comparisons: Grip strength *M* = 40.0 kg, *SD* = 3.0 and flexibility *M* = 30.0 cm, *SD* = 4.0.

$$\text{Grip strength } z = \frac{(45-40)}{3} = 1.67 \quad \text{Flexibility } z = \frac{(25-30)}{4} = -1.25$$

With the z score information, it can be concluded that a grip strength of 45 kg was 1.67 *SD* units above the mean and was a better score than a flexibility of 25 cm, which was −1.25 *SD* units below the mean.

## A FINAL WORD ON MEANS AND STANDARD DEVIATIONS

As you may now realize, the *M* and *SD* provide much integral descriptive information about a distribution's scores. It would be rare that you would read a research article and not find means and standard deviations reported. Therefore, a table that contains the *M* (or in some cases the median), *SD*, and range of key experimental variables is essential and should be part of any published or presented research.

## NONNORMAL DISTRIBUTIONS AND CURVES

There are times when a distribution of scores will not fit the model of the normal curve. These atypical distributions are called *skewed* and result in curves that are *nonnormal*, particularly in shape and appearance. A skewed curve has a tail that represents few scores and is classified by the direction that the tail is pointing. A *positively skewed* curve has the majority of its scores depicted in the left or lower value side of the distribution with the tail pointing in the positive direction (see Figure 8-11). An exam that was too difficult for the level of a class (e.g., a test for an advanced statistics course given to an introductory class) would probably result in a positively skewed distribution and curve.

A *negatively skewed* curve is just the opposite, where most of the scores are on the right or higher value side with the tail pointing in the more negative direction (see Figure 8-12). A distribution of grades in graduate courses would usually result in a negatively skewed distribution, because graduate students typically perform at a higher academic level and few Ds or Fs (and even Cs sometimes, but we won't discuss grade inflation!) are given. Annual incomes of residents living in Beverly Hills would result in a negative skew as well.

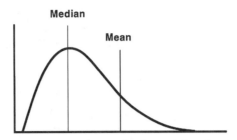

Figure 8-11   A positively skewed distribution.

Therefore, knowing something about the skewness of a distribution may inform the researcher about the tendency of high or low performance of the group. How is skewness determined? The amount and presence of skewness may be judged by "eyeballing" the shape of a curve of a distribution or by examining its measures of central tendency. As we mentioned previously, the mean of a distribution is more affected by extreme scores than is the median. Therefore, in a positively skewed distribution, where there are fewer but higher scores, the mean will be higher than the median. This notion is depicted in Figure 8-11. The opposite is true in the negatively skewed distribution, because the fewer but lower scores are on the lower end of the distribution, which will reduce the size of the mean. So the mean is less than the median. This concept is illustrated in Figure 8-12.

An easy way to remember these concepts is to recall that the mean is "pulled" toward the tail in the skewed distribution. There are equations that may be used to determine the amount of skewness in a distribution; they are beyond the scope of this discussion. Also, when a distribution is markedly skewed, it won't accurately conform to the properties of the normal curve. Any application of the normal curve in this case may be suspect. In these cases nonparametric analyses should be used.

## SUMMARY

Measures of central tendency provide information about the most representative score in a distribution, with the mean and median being the most commonly used. Variability statistics show the dispersion of scores in a distribution. The

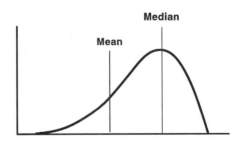

Figure 8-12   A negatively skewed distribution.

range and standard deviation are the most routinely used statistics for this purpose, with the standard deviation being the better of the two. The normal curve is an important statistical model that is used to visualize data, interpret distributions of scores, and to make predictions and probability statements. A fundamental understanding of the normal curve and its applications is vital to the study and use of statistics. Positively and negatively skewed curves reflect distributions that do not conform to the normal curve model.

## STATISTICS EXERCISES

| Percent Body Fat | Percent Income for Recreation | Stress Index |
|:---:|:---:|:---:|
| 13 | 10 | 7 |
| 8 | 15 | 8 |
| 5 | 12 | 12 |
| 11 | 9 | 15 |
| 6 | 10 | 6 |
| 7 | 20 | 9 |
| 9 | 11 | 5 |
| | 13 | 14 |
| | | 11 |

1. For the data sets above compute the following:
   a. Mean and median
   b. Range and standard deviation
   c. Confidence intervals of 68%, 95%, and 99%

2. Using Table F, determine the area under the normal curve for the following $z$ scores:
   a. Above $z = 1.50$
   b. Below $z = -.25$
   c. Between $z = -.50$ and $z = .75$
   d. Above $z = 2.25$ and below $z = -1.45$
   e. Between $z = 1.00$ and $2.50$

3. Given the following test results, compute $z$ scores to determine the better test scores:

   | Health Test | Recreation Test |
   |:---:|:---:|
   | $M = 75.0, SD = 7.0$ | $M = 50.0, SD = 4.0$ |

   a. Health score = 78 or recreation score = 55
   b. Health score = 85 or recreation score = 59
   c. Health score = 80 or recreation score = 48
   d. Health score = 65 or recreation score = 45
   e. Health score = 72 or recreation score = 52

CHAPTER 9

# PROBABILITY AND HYPOTHESIS TESTING

KEY CONCEPTS

Theoretical probability
Probability and the normal
  curve
Hypothesis testing
Two-tailed vs. one-tailed
  tests

Sampling error
Level of significance
Type I and Type II errors
Sampling distributions

AFTER READING THIS CHAPTER, YOU SHOULD BE ABLE TO

- Define and provide examples of theoretical probability.
- Explain how probability statements are related to the normal curve.
- Describe all of the components related to and be able to conduct a general hypothesis test.
- Differentiate between Type I and Type II errors.
- Explain the concept of statistical significance.

Hypothesis tests are perhaps the most important statistical procedures used by the researcher. These tests allow an investigator to make objective decisions about the outcome of a study. As important and useful as these procedures are, one must realize that they are not exact proofs. All research decisions are made within a certain probability of being right or wrong. In this chapter we discuss some of the basic elements of probability and general hypothesis testing.

## PROBABILITY

We are exposed to a variety of probability statements on a regular basis: "There is a 40 percent chance that it will rain today." "The odds are 75 to 1 of the Chicago Cubs winning the World Series." "The potential of winning the lottery is 1 in 10,000,000." "A male between the ages of 55 and 65 has 1 in 100 chances of dying from heart disease." All of these are probability statements that imply the likelihood or chance of a certain event occurring. Probability plays an informational role in many aspects of our lives.

Statistical decisions are not exact but are made with a certain probability or chance of being right or wrong. Therefore, a fundamental knowledge of probability is requisite for understanding many statistical tests. Because entire courses and texts are dedicated to the topic, our presentation of this material will be quite basic.

### Theoretical Probability

Classical or *theoretical probability* is a traditional way of expressing the statistical likelihood of an event occurring and is the kind we are the most familiar with. Probability statements are commonly symbolized by using the small letter $p$ and are expressed in proportions of 1.0. A probability of 1.0 is 100% certainty of an event occurring; conversely a probability of 0 means there is 0% chance of an event occurring. Therefore, probability statements range from 0 to 1.0. Theoretical probability may be defined as.

$$p = \frac{\text{The number of ways an event can occur}}{\text{The number of possible events}}$$

A number of examples from the world of gambling illustrate some probability statements. If we were to flip a coin, what is the probability that it will come up tails? Because there is only one tail on a coin, the number of ways it can happen is one but, there are a head and a tail on a coin, so there are two possible events. The probability of a tail appearing after a toss is $p = 1/2 = .50$, or 50%. What about the probability of rolling a single die and it coming up 3? There is only one 3 and six possible events, so the probability would be $p = 1/6 = .167$, or 16.7%. How about a roll that would produce either a 2 or a 5? There would be two ways the event could occur with six possible events, so $p = 2/6 = .333$, or 33.3%. What would be the probability of pulling a jack from a deck of cards with a blind draw? There are 4 jacks in a deck, and there are 52 cards in a deck, so there are 52 possible events. The probability would be $p = 4/52 = .077$, or 7.7%. How about pulling a red ace under the same conditions? That would be $p = 2/52 = .038$, or 3.8%. We could go on and on. The point of this is to appreciate exactly what theoretical probability is because we will be using it a lot.

## Probability and the Normal Curve

Recall that the applications of the normal curve include the abilities to make predictions and probability statements. Making these determinations is very straightforward if it is remembered that when we are referring to a specified area under the curve, that area relates to a percent of a representative distribution. In the simplest sense, think of the number of observations in the given area or percent of the distribution in question as the number of ways the event can occur and all of the observations in the distribution as the number of possible events. Let's apply this to an example.

A health educator is interested in determining the incidence of systolic hypertension of men between the ages of 40 to 50 years in her community. The prevalence of hypertension is of interest to her for the programming and staffing of risk reduction programs and to compare the values to national averages. She obtains a random sample of 300 men in her town and measures their systolic blood pressure and finds the $M = 125.0$ mm Hg (millimeters of mercury) with a $SD = 15.0$. This distribution would be divided accordingly:

$$68\% = 125.0 \pm 1\ (15.0) = 110 \text{ to } 140 \text{ mm Hg}$$
$$95\% = 125.0 \pm 1.96\ (15.0) = 95.6 \text{ to } 154.4 \text{ mm Hg}$$
$$99\% = 125.0 \pm 2.58\ (15.0) = 86.3 \text{ to } 163.7 \text{ mm Hg}$$

Imagine if we were to assign all 300 subjects a number and put the numbers in a hat. This is just another way of referring to all of the observations or the number of possible events. What is the event that we are talking about? It is the 40- to 50-year-old men's systolic blood pressure measurements, of course. Now we will specify certain blood pressure readings and make some probability statements.

What would be the probability that if any one subject were selected at random (drawn out of the hat), he would have a blood pressure reading between 110 and 140 mm Hg? Because 68% of the distribution has a blood pressure measure between those values, then 68% of 300 subjects = 300 (.68) = 204. So the number of ways the event can occur is 204 and the number of possible events is 300 (all of the possible blood pressures). Therefore, the probability is $p = 204/300 = .68$. The logic for the remaining probabilities will follow the same pattern.

What would be the probability that if any one subject were selected at random, he would have a blood pressure reading above 140 mm Hg? Because 16% of the distribution is above 1 $SD$ from the mean that represents 48 subjects (300 (.16) = 48), therefore, the probability is $p = 48/300$, or .16. What would be the probability that if any one subject were selected at random, he would have a blood pressure reading below 96 mm Hg? Because only 2.5% of the distribution is below this level, then $p = 7.5/300 = .025$.

We could go on making numerous determinations in this fashion. However, prediction statements that are based on probability and inference may also be made about the population that the subjects are representing. Because these 300 men were randomly selected, they probably are a good model of 5000 such men in the community. Because of this we may make fairly accurate generalizations from the sample. For instance, if 16% of the sample of 300 has blood pressures lower than 110 mm Hg, then probably 16% of the population of 5000 does as well. If this is true, then how many men in the population would we expect or predict (we are using these terms interchangeably) there to be? We would predict that there would be 800 men because $p = 800/5000 = .16$ and 16% of 5000 = 800. If blood pressure readings between 110 and 140 mm Hg are considered normal for this age group, how many men in the population would we expect to have normal readings? We would expect 3400 men to have normal blood pressure because $p = 3400/5000 = .68$ and 68% of 5000 = 3400. What if readings above about 155 mm Hg are considered very high, how many men would we predict to fall into this category? The predicted number would be 2.5% of the population, 125 men with very high blood pressure, because $p = 125/5000$ and 2.5% of 5000 = 125.

The previous examples were based on a calculation of probability and were presented that way to illustrate the concept. Actually these problems could be solved easily by computing z scores, referring to the z distribution table, and reading a probability directly from it. For instance, from our same sample of 300 men, the z score for a blood pressure of 110 mm Hg would be $z = (110 - 125)/ \ 15 = -1.0$, whereas a z score for 140 mm Hg would be $z = (140 - 125)/15 = 1.0$. By inspecting the z distribution table, we determine that about 34% of the area under the curve is from the mean of 0 to a z score of 1.0. This is also true for $z = -1.0$. Therefore, 68% of the area under the curve is between z scores ± 1.0. Identifying the area under the curve is the same as the probability of a z score occurring. Thus the probability of any z score being between z scores of ± 1.0 is .68. So the probability of any of the 300 men having a blood pressure between 110 and 140 mm Hg is $p = .68$. All of the other problems may be solved using this same approach.

You can now see how the normal curve can be used with both a sample distribution and a population. Furthermore, the z distribution can be used to make probability statements by relating probabilities to areas under the curve. Also, it's apparent that probability and the ability to predict are related to one another. In subsequent chapters we'll be discussing prediction as well as determining the accuracy of predictions in much more detail. As you might guess, normal curve concepts play an important role in these techniques.

## HYPOTHESIS TESTING

Recollect that we defined *research hypothesis* as a scientific hunch that an investigator has about the expected outcome of a study. Decisions to accept or reject the research hypothesis must be based on an objective and logical statistical process generally called *hypothesis testing*. The hypothesis test is a strict statistical operation that is built on making probability statements for two possible states of reality. Simply said, the researcher uses statistical tools to determine if her guess about the anticipated results was correct or not. An appropriate statistic is selected and used to reflect a certain characteristic, or event, in the research. It is this objective "piece of evidence" that is used to represent the event in question (e.g., a difference or a correlation between two groups) and is the prime ingredient in the hypothesis test.

The importance of understanding the nature, use, and interpretation of a hypothesis test in research cannot be underestimated. Each of the statistics that we will be discussing from this point on will have a hypothesis test associated with it. All hypothesis tests are based on the same logic, so an understanding of the basic steps and components, regardless of a specific statistic, is essential. The following discussion addresses the parts of a general hypothesis test.

### The Null and Alternative Hypotheses

The two states of reality that the hypothesis test is predicated on are the null and alternative hypotheses. Sometimes these are referred to as *statistical hypotheses* because statistical procedures are used to estimate whether they are true or not. It is important to emphasize at the start that the null and alternative hypotheses are merely statistical statements that are used in the hypothesis test and they may or may not bear any resemblance to the research hypothesis. The researcher uses the results of the hypothesis test to draw conclusions about the validity of the research hypothesis. As we will soon see, these hypotheses are stated in such a way that one or the other *must* be true, but not both.

The *null hypothesis* ($H_0$) is traditionally defined as a statement of no difference or no relationship. This hypothesis may be written numerous ways, depending on the research condition and the statistical test. For instance, the null hypothesis for comparing two population means ($\mu$) would be written as $H_0$: $\mu_1 - \mu_2 = 0$ or its equivalent $H_0$: $\mu_1 = \mu_2$. Both of these statements say the same thing; there *is no difference* between the two population means. As we indicated, a null hypothesis may be stated in many ways, and we will provide illustrations of these as subsequent statistics are presented.

The *alternative hypothesis* ($H_A$) is the logical state of reality that must exist if the null hypothesis is not true. In our example of comparing two different population means, the null hypothesis stated that there was no difference between them. If this is not true, then what has to be true? Right! *There is a difference between them.* The alternative hypothesis in this case is written as $H_A$: $\mu_1 - \mu_2 \neq 0$ or $H_A$: $\mu_1 \neq \mu_2$, both of which say that there is a difference between population means. Note that the alternative hypothesis doesn't provide any information about the amount of difference—and it doesn't need to because it is just the logical option to the null.

### Sampling Error or Something "Real"

At the heart of the hypothesis test is the issue of whether what is observed (a difference or a relationship) is due to sampling error or something "real." *Sampling error* occurs when chance or random effects cause an event to occur in a manner different from what is expected. Sampling error is always present, as there is always some probability or chance (even if it is a very remote chance) for any event to occur. Let's use coin tossing to illustrate some concepts.

If a friend were to toss a coin 10 times, what would be the expected number of head and tail counts? That's easy: Probability says that you would expect five head and five tail tosses. What if your friend came up with four heads and six tails, would you be alarmed and think that he was using a coin that was rigged? Of course not, because it would not be at all unusual to come up with a four to six count. What made the tosses come up four and six instead of five and five? Chance or sampling error is responsible.

If your friend continued with another set of 10 tosses and came up with a three tail and seven head count, you say, "No big deal, it's sampling error," and you're right. What about a one head and nine tail split? One would not expect this type of count to happen very frequently, but it can, and it's probably due to sampling error and not a rigged coin. What about 100 coin flips that came up 1 head and 99 tails. Could sampling error have produced this? The answer is yes, but it would be a rare event because the odds against this type of occurrence would be 1 to 99. Even though there is a remote chance that sampling error could cause this to occur, a more likely explanation would be something crooked is going on!

There is an important point to all of this. Ultimately, the researcher has to make a decision about whether or not sampling error is responsible for an event occurring. We will discuss how this is done in a moment, but right now we need to relate the concept of sampling error to the null hypothesis.

The null hypothesis is essentially a statement that implies that sampling error or chance could cause the event in question to occur frequently or often. Remember that a statistic is a measure of the event in question. The alternative hypothesis, conversely, is a statement that implies that the event in question could be caused by sampling error, but it would be a rare occurrence. If it is concluded that sampling error would rarely cause the event to occur, then it is probably due to something else. We are calling that *something "real"* (i.e., a "real" difference or a "real" relationship). For example, what if we observed a 1% difference between two population means, which in practical terms is deemed very small. Could we dismiss the 1% difference to sampling error, or does it represent a small but real difference between the two means? This is exactly the kind of decision that is made with a hypothesis test. The key to making this type of determination is deciding on a statistical reference point that defines the probability of an event in question occurring often versus rarely due to sampling error.

## Level of Significance

The *level of significance* is the statistical reference point that is selected either to accept or reject the null hypothesis. This level is set by the researcher and simply defines the probability of an event in question occurring often versus rarely due to sampling error or chance. Figure 9-1 is a modification of one presented by Fox (1969). Examine it to see what this means. The probability that sampling error had caused the event in question to occur could range from $p = 0$ to $p = 1.0$ or

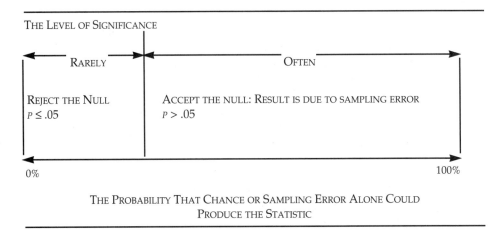

THE PROBABILITY THAT CHANCE OR SAMPLING ERROR ALONE COULD
PRODUCE THE STATISTIC

Figure 9-1    An illustration of the .05 level of significance.

from 0 to 100%. The researcher must decide on a point somewhere between the range of 0 to 100% that will functionally define whether an event may occur often or rarely due to chance. What level would you feel comfortable with? If sampling error could produce an event up to 50% of the time, would you consider that often? Probably. What about 20% of the time? That's not very often. How about 5% of the time? Most would agree that 5% isn't very often and 1% of the time is surely a rare event. Remember, this is entirely up to the researcher to define. However, we will soon see that researchers in HPER typically use the 5% and 1% values for making statistical decisions.

So what does it mean if a researcher chooses a significance level at 5% or $p = .05$ at which to test the null hypothesis? Essentially, the investigator is proposing that any event, as reflected by a statistic, that can occur due to chance more often than 5% of the time is probably due to sampling error. If this occurs the researcher accepts the null hypothesis. Conversely, if the statistic can occur due to chance less than or equal to 5% of the time, it is rare and is probably not due to sampling error but to something real. In this case, the null hypothesis is rejected in favor of the alternative.

The researcher needs to define an acceptable and reasonable level of significance to assist in making a sound statistical decision. How does the researcher decide what an acceptable level of significance is? The primary factor to consider is the willingness of the researcher to be wrong if incorrectly rejecting the null hypothesis. A *Type I error* is made when the null hypothesis is rejected when it is actually true. In other words, the researcher has falsely concluded that a statistic was reflecting a real effect when in reality it was one of those rare instances of sampling error. The probability of making a Type I error is called the *alpha level*, or $\alpha$, which is in fact the level of significance that we have been discussing all along. An alpha level of .01 means that there is a 1 chance in 100 of rejecting the null hypothesis when it is true. So if a researcher wants to reduce the

**TABLE 9–1**  Decisions for rejecting or not rejecting the null hypothesis

|  | $H_0$ Is True | $H_0$ Is False |
|---|---|---|
| Reject | No: Type I error | Yes |
| Accept | Yes | No: Type II error |

likelihood of making a Type I error, he just simply lowers the alpha level, perhaps from $p = .05$ to $p = .01$ or even $p = .001$.

In much of the research that is done in HPER and in many other disciplines, alpha levels of .05 and .01 are commonly used. The reason for the use of these levels is probably bound in tradition and convenience, because most statistical tables are based on these levels. However, a researcher could justifiably use alpha levels of .075, .15, .025, and so on, if so desired. Is there really much difference between the .05 and .06 levels of significance? This has been a much discussed topic recently, and we'll have more to say on it later.

Lowering the alpha level to a more rigorous quantity reduces the chance for making a Type I error but, simultaneously increases the probability of making a Type II error. A *Type II error* is made when the null hypothesis is accepted when it is false. The probability of making a Type II error is called the *beta level*, or β. Now the researcher has falsely concluded that a statistic was due to sampling error and accepted the null hypothesis, when in reality it was something real and the null should have been rejected in favor of the alternative. The nature and calculation of beta are beyond the scope of this discussion. However, it is true that when a researcher decreases the chance of making a Type I error, there is an increase in the probability of making a Type II error, and vice versa. Table 9-1 summarizes the correct and incorrect decisions related to rejecting or not rejecting the null hypothesis. Table 9-2 illustrates the effect that raising and lowering the alpha above and below .05 has on Type I and II errors.

So if it is not possible to have an equally low probability of making both errors, which one is more important *not* to make? The answer to this quandary is based on the type of research problem the investigator is dealing with. For instance, if a medical scientist had developed a new treatment that may revolutionize the management of an illness and replace a standard therapy, the scientist would want to be very certain that the new approach was superior to the old one. Because of the potential impact on the field and the negative consequences

**TABLE 9-2**  Effect of alpha level and probability of errors

| ALPHA | TYPE I | TYPE II |
|---|---|---|
| .01 | Decreased | Increased |
| .05 | — | — |
| .10 | Increased | Decreased |

The .05 level is a compromise between the pitfalls associated with .01 and .10.

of making a wrong decision, it is very important that a conservative approach is taken before claiming a difference. (We should keep in mind that the outcome of only one study should never be a reason for dramatic change. Good science demands replication!) In this case, reducing the chance of making a Type I error is more important, and making a Type II error would be more acceptable, because this would suggest no change in medical treatment. This can be accomplished by the use of a more stringent alpha level, such as .01 or .001.

For less critical research decisions, decreasing the chance for a Type II error would be more appropriate. This could be accomplished by using a more liberal alpha level, like .10, where it is easier to reject the null hypothesis. For example, let's say that a researcher wants to compare two different hand soaps that are both known to work, to see which one cleaned better. Would it really matter if it was concluded that one was better than the other, if in fact there was no difference between them? Probably not, so in this case making a Type I error is more acceptable. In summary, it is the responsibility of the researcher to decide which error is the less important and to set the alpha level accordingly.

## Other Points to Consider

In a hypothesis test the researcher calculates an appropriate statistic and compares it to a value from a statistical table. There are many such tables, and they are referred to as *sampling distributions*. Basically, sampling distributions are probability tables that provide values for the chance occurrence of a particular statistic. We noted that the normal curve is actually a probability distribution called the $z$ distribution with the $z$ score as its statistic. We have already made several probability statements about this distribution, but here are a few more. The chance occurrence of a $z$ statistic with a value greater than $\pm 1.96$ is $p = .05$, and greater than $\pm 2.58$ is $p = .01$. Does this look familiar? The values $z = 1.96$ and $z = 2.58$ are actually significance levels (alpha) for the chance occurrence of $z$ at the .05 and .01 levels, respectively. Sampling distributions for other statistics will also have probability values that represent significance levels of .05, .01, and so on.

The investigator compares the statistic that is calculated to one that is obtained from a sampling distribution at the desired alpha level. The statistic obtained from the sampling distribution is called a *critical statistic or value*. In order to determine the critical statistic, a value known as the *degrees of freedom* must be determined. (We provide details on how the degrees of freedom are determined for the respective statistics in subsequent chapters.)

For example, if a significance level was set at .05 and a calculated statistic was greater than or equal to the critical value, that means that the probability that sampling error could cause that statistic to occur would be less than or equal to .05, or $p \leq .05$. because a statistic this size may rarely happen due to chance (in this case less than or equal to 5% of the time). We conclude that something other than sampling error caused it to occur, that is, something real. Of course, there is a small chance ($p \leq .05$) that we are wrong. On the other hand, if the calculated statistic is less than the critical one, that means that the probability that sampling error could cause that statistic to occur would be greater than .05, or $p > .05$.

Because a statistic this size may happen often due to chance, in this case more often than 5% of the time, we conclude that sampling error caused it to occur.

How does the investigator use this information then? If the calculated statistic is less than the critical statistic, the researcher accepts the null hypothesis. However, if it is greater than or equal to the critical statistic, the null hypothesis is rejected. At this point the hypothesis test is completed, but the researcher is left to the task of interpreting the results and determining what it means in relation to the originally stated research hypothesis. This is probably the most challenging task in the research process. We'll have more to say about this in a moment.

### Steps in the Hypothesis Test

Now that we have discussed the nuts and bolts of a general hypothesis test, it's time to put it all together. If you follow all of the steps outlined in Table 9-3, you can't go wrong. Let us illustrate the entire process with a hypothetical research situation.

**TABLE 9-3**   Steps in a hypothesis test

1. State the null and alternative hypotheses.

    $H_0: \mu_1 = \mu_2$
    $H_A: \mu_1 \neq \mu_2$

2. Set the significance (alpha) level.

    .05, .01, .001, etc.

3. Determine the appropriate statistic.

    Independent or correlated $t$, $r$, ANOVA, etc.

4. Determine the critical statistic value.

5. Place the critical values on a curve and determine the areas of "do not reject" and "reject."

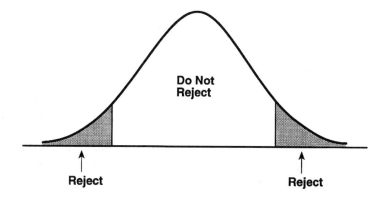

6. Calculate the statistic and place it on the curve.
7. Do not reject or reject the null hypothesis.
8. Draw a research conclusion.

A physical educator is interested in knowing if there is a significant difference in the vertical jump height of college women's basketball (BB) and volleyball (VB) players. The investigator's research hypothesis is that there will be no difference between the jump height of the athletes from these two sports. The researcher obtains a random sample of 100 athletes from each sport and finds that the basketball players had a mean vertical jump of 27.0 in., whereas the volleyball players had a mean of 25.0 in. In order to determine if the 2-in. difference in jump height was due to sampling error or represented a real difference, she performs a hypothesis test.

She starts off by stating the null and alternative hypotheses: $H_0$: $\mu_{BB} = \mu_{VB}$ and $H_A$: $\mu_{BB} \neq \mu_{VB}$. Remember, stating the null and alternative hypotheses has nothing to do with the original research hypothesis; they're simply tools used to test it. She feels that the .05 level of significance is satisfactory for this research problem and will use that as the alpha level. The appropriate statistic in this case is called an independent $t$, and the $t$ sampling distribution will be used to test it. (We haven't discussed the $t$ statistic yet, but we will soon.) Looking at the $t$ sampling distribution, she finds that the critical values of $t$ at the .05 level are $t = \pm$ 1.96, then places those values on a model distribution, and labels areas of "do not reject" and "reject." Those labels work like red and green lights and will tell you what decision to make. Next she calculates the $t$ statistic and determines that $t = 2.50$ and places it on the model distribution. Because the calculated $t = 2.50$ is greater than the critical value of $t = 1.96$, and falls in the reject zone, the null hypothesis is rejected in favor of the alternative.

She concludes that the 2-in. difference in vertical jump height is not due to sampling error but represents a real difference. Of course, there is a 5% or less chance she is wrong. So her research hypothesis that there would be no difference in the vertical jump height is now rejected. A summary of the steps in this hypothesis test appears in Table 9-4.

### Two-Tailed versus One-Tailed Hypothesis Tests

In the previous example note that critical values were ± 1.96 and were placed on each end of the curve. In this case that means that the area under the curve from the mean of zero to 1.96 is about 47.5%, with the remaining 2.5% outside that value. This is also true for -1.96. Therefore, 95% of the sampling distribution values are between ± 1.96 and 5% of the values are outside those values, with 2.5% on each tail of the curve. Why is the probability divided up that way? When a researcher cannot hypothesize about the direction of the outcome of a study, a *two-tailed hypothesis test* must be used. In the jump height example, a two-tailed test was used because the researcher had no notion about which group was going to be better than the other.

If an investigator has a strong sense about the direction of outcome in a study, then a *one-tailed hypothesis test* may be used. Simply said, it is easier to reject the null hypothesis with a one-tailed test because all of the probability is shifted to one tail of the distribution. Doing this allows for a smaller critical value, which means that the calculated statistic does not have to be as large to be

**TABLE 9-4**  Summary of a hypothesis test comparing jump height

1. State the null and alternative hypotheses.

   $H_0: \mu_{BB} = \mu_{VB}$

   $H_A: \mu_{BB} \neq \mu_{VB}$

2. Set the significance (alpha) level.

   .05

3. Determine the appropriate statistic.

   Independent $t$

4. Determine the critical statistic value.

   $t = \pm 1.96$

5. Place the critical values on a curve and determine the areas of "do not reject" and "reject."

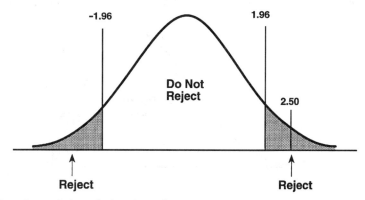

6. Calculate the statistic and place it on the curve.

   $t = 2.50$

7. Do not reject or reject the null hypothesis.

   Reject the null.

8. Draw a research conclusion.

   The 2-in. difference in vertical jump height is statistically significant ($p \leq .05$).

able to reject the null hypothesis. When a one-tailed test is used, the alternative hypothesis is actually the research hypothesis, because this is what the researcher thinks is going to happen. Perhaps an example will help.

A health educator wants to determine if a smoking cessation program is effective. It would be unlikely that a smoking cessation program would cause subjects to *increase* their rate of smoking, and if the program was ineffective smoking rates would probably stay the same. The most likely outcome if the program is effective is that the smoking rates should *decrease*. This situation justifies the use of a one-tailed test. The investigator conducts the study and determines that there was a 20% reduction in smoking rates. He is now ready for the hypothesis test. This test is summarized in Table 9-5.

The null and alternative hypotheses are now stated directionally with the null appearing as $H_0: \mu_{Pre} \leq \mu_{Post}$ and the alternative as $H_A: \mu_{Pre} > \mu_{Post}$. Note

**TABLE 9-5**   Summary of a one-tailed hypothesis test

1. State the null and alternative hypotheses.

$H_0$: $\mu_{Pre} \le \mu_{Post}$
$H_A$: $\mu_{Pre} > \mu_{Post}$

2. Set the significance (alpha) level.

.05

3. Determine the appropriate statistic.

Correlated $t$

4. Determine the critical statistic value.

$t = 1.67$

5. Place the critical values on a curve and determine the areas of "do not reject" and "reject."

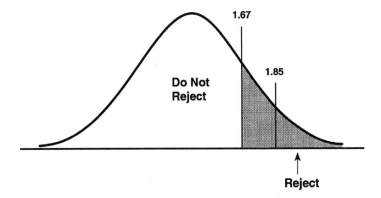

6. Calculate the statistic and place it on the curve.

$t = 1.85$

7. Do not reject or reject the null hypothesis.

Reject the null.

8. Draw a research conclusion.

The 20% reduction in smoking rate is statistically significant ($p \le .05$).

what these hypotheses are saying. The null indicates that there will be no difference between the pre- and posttest means, suggesting that the program was not effective. The null also states that there will be an increase in smoking rates, making the posttest mean larger that the pretest mean and thus insinuating that this was a really bad program. The alternative states that the pretest values will be greater than the posttest, meaning that smoking rates decreased. This is exactly what the researcher anticipates.

The correct statistic is the correlated $t$, and by using the $t$ distribution, it is found that the critical value for a one-tailed test is $t = 1.67$ at the .05 level. The calculated statistic is $t = 1.85$. These values are placed on the model distribution with areas of reject and do not reject on it. It can be seen that the calculated $t = 1.85$ falls in the reject zone; therefore the null hypothesis is rejected. Because the

$t = 1.85$ may occur due to chance or sampling error less than or equal to 5% of the time, it is concluded that the 20% reduction in smoking rates was real.

   If the researcher had used a two-tailed test instead, the critical values would have been higher. In this example, the two-tailed critical values would have been $t = \pm 1.96$. Because the calculated $t = 1.85$ does not exceed or is equal to $t = \pm 1.96$, the null hypothesis would not have been rejected and a different research conclusion would have been made. Therefore when the investigator has a strong idea about the direction of outcome, a one-tailed test should be used. Examples of one-tailed tests are presented in subsequent chapters.

## Interpretations after the Hypothesis Test

You may have read results of statistical analyses reported in a research journal that said something like "there was a significant difference between the two groups, $p \leq .01$" or "there was no significant difference between the two methods, $p > .05$." There are two important points to make about these statistical statements. One deals with how the probability statements are made. When stating that a finding is "statistically significant," the direction of the probability arrow points in the "less than" direction. This statement means that the probability that sampling error could cause that statistic to occur would be *less than or equal to* the stated alpha level. Because a statistic this size may rarely happen due to chance, it is concluded that something other than sampling error caused it to occur, that is, something real. However, when stating that a finding is "not statistically significant," the direction of the probability arrow points in the "greater than" direction. The interpretation of that statement is that the probability that sampling error could cause that statistic to occur would be *greater than* the stated alpha level. Therefore, because a statistic this size may happen often due to chance, we conclude that sampling error caused it to occur.

   The other important point is that when making statements of statistical significance, the significance level must be reported. The consumer of research can't assume that all of the tests were done at the usual .05 level. For example, an investigator may have set an alpha level of .20 for the hypothesis test, which would take on quite a different interpretation than the .01 level. So we have to remember that statistical significance is defined by the researcher's selection of whatever the probability level for alpha is.

## Practical versus Statistical Significance

The level of significance may have nothing to do with the magnitude or meaning of an observed effect. For instance, how meaningful would it be if a health educator showed a 2% change in cholesterol levels after a six-month modification program, even if that change was statistically significant at $p \leq .001$? All that result means is that there is less than or equal to a 1 in 1000 chance that the 2% change in cholesterol was due to sampling error. In the real world, a 2% change in cholesterol has little practical significance. The size of difference, statistical significance, and size of treatment effects are discussed in more detail in subsequent chapters.

The hypothesis test is used to make a statistical decision, and once that is made it is up to the researcher to draw the appropriate conclusions and speculations from the results. In the hypothesis test comparing jump height, it was concluded that basketball players had a 2-in. greater vertical jump height than volleyball players. What does that mean? Was a cause and effect relationship demonstrated? Does a 2-in. height differential have much practical meaning? What is this difference attributed to? How do these results compare with others that have been reported? All of these are questions that the researcher must answer.

We must be mindful that hypothesis tests are based on reasonable levels of probability of making good research decisions, but they don't provide unequivocal proof. It is tempting to overinterpret the results of analyses like these simply because they are a form of objective evidence. (Statistics don't lie, do they?) Hypothesis tests are highly valued tools of research, but they are only as effective as the person who uses them. It is incumbent on the researcher to use hypothesis tests correctly and to interpret the results from them in a cautious and scholarly manner.

## SUMMARY

Probability plays an important role in making research decisions. The normal curve and many sampling distributions are based on probability statements and are used extensively in hypothesis testing. The hypothesis test is a vital tool for making research decisions. When performing a hypothesis test, the researcher needs to do the following: state the null and alternative hypotheses, set a level of significance in regard to Type I or II errors, select an appropriate statistic and sampling distribution, compare a calculated statistic to a critical statistical value, decide whether to accept or reject the null hypothesis, and draw a research conclusion. Because the hypothesis test doesn't provide absolute proof, the researcher ultimately has the responsibility of arriving at the appropriate conclusions.

## STATISTICS EXERCISES

For the following research conditions, perform a hypothesis test (show all major steps) and provide the appropriate research conclusion.

1. A health researcher compares a program of dieting (D) to a program of dieting and exercise (DE) on blood cholesterol levels. The DE group had a mean reduction in cholesterol 20% greater than the D group. This resulted in a calculated statistic of $t = 4.50$ with critical $t \pm 2.30$ at $p = .05$. What do you conclude?

2. A recreation researcher wanted to compare the average percentage of income spent on leisure activities from families in Utah and Nebraska. The results showed that Utah families averaged 18.0% spent, whereas the Nebraska families averaged 12%. The calculated $t = 3.25$ with critical $t \pm 2.65$ at $p = .05$. What do you conclude?

3. An exercise science researcher is interested in comparing running four days per week to six days per week on improving aerobic capacity. The conclusion of the study indicated a 3% mean difference between the two groups favoring six days per week. This resulted in a calculated $t = 1.25$ with critical $t \pm 2.45$ at $p = .05$. What do you conclude?

4. A health researcher wanted to compare biofeedback to a relaxation technique in reducing stress levels. At the conclusion of the study the biofeedback group reduced stress levels 10%, whereas the relaxation group reduced 12%. This resulted in a calculated $t = 1.85$ with critical $t \pm 2.25$ at $p = .05$. What do you conclude?

5. A physical education researcher wanted to compare the results of percent body fat measures obtained by underwater weighing (UWW) and skinfolds (SK). The results showed a mean 3.1% fat overestimation by the SK. This resulted in a calculated $t = 7.95$ with critical $t \pm 3.75$ at $p = .01$. What do you conclude?

CHAPTER 10

# RELATIONSHIPS AND PREDICTION

## PURPOSE OF CORRELATION

Researchers and practitioners are often interested in studying the relationship between two or more variables. A swimming coach may want to know the relationship between swimming performance and strength. A health researcher may wish to know how well related eating habits and knowledge of nutrition are. Correlations are the statistics that provide a quantitative means of expressing a relationship, and it is used widely in research.

Correlation is also used in prediction. For example, skinfold thickness can be used to predict the density of the body, which in turn is used to estimate body fatness. Universities use achievement tests and grade point average to predict success in graduate school. Buying and selling stocks is based on the prediction of what future stock prices will be. Prediction is commonly used in everyday life as well as in research.

## CONCEPTS IN CORRELATION

A *positive* correlation means that as one variable becomes larger, the other variable also *tends* to increase. Examples are age and height in children (as children increase in age, they tend to become taller), education level and income, height and weight, and fat intake and incidence of cardiovascular disease. The word "tend" is important because, as for the example with strength and age, not every child 8 years old would be expected to be stronger than any 7-year-old child, and so on. This would be true only if the correlation was perfect and positive. Figure 10-1 is a *scattergram* depicting the relationship between these two variables. When the plotted data run diagonally uphill from left to right, the correlation is positive. Note the exception in the overall trend with the third data point. This subject is older than the first two subjects but has less strength. Thus we know that the relationship is less than perfect. If all the data could be connected with a straight line, then the correlation would be perfect—very unlikely because of human variability.

A *negative* correlation means that as one variable increases, the other variable *tends* to decrease. Examples of negative correlations are age of adults and strength (as adults grow older, they usually lose strength), education level

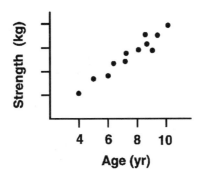

Figure 10-1   Relationship between strength and age in children.

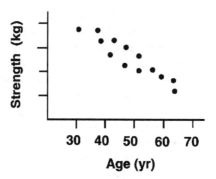

Figure 10-2    Relationship between strength and age in adults.

and smoking, and speed (mph) to sprint 40 yards and percent body fat. Again the term "tend" is appropriate unless the correlation was perfect. For example, a few adults may be older but stronger than some of their colleagues, which makes the relationship less than perfect. These exceptions can be seen in Figure 10-2, which illustrates the relationship between the age of adults and strength. In negative correlations, the data run downhill from left to right. With a perfect negative correlation, the data form a straight line going downhill.

The size of correlations can also be estimated by the degree that the data in a scattergram are clustered around a line running through them, called the *line of best fit* or *regression line*. Figures 10-1 and 10-2 show data very closely clustered to the line of best fit. As stated, if the data formed a straight line, the correlation would be perfect. The data in the figures very nearly form a straight line and therefore represent a high correlation. Figure 10-3 shows a positive moderate correlation, whereas Figure 10-4 illustrates a negative moderate correlation. Note the greater spread of data around the line of best fit in the latter two figures.

When data are weakly related or correlated, little or no apparent pattern is obvious. One would have difficulty judging whether the data are aligned in a positive or negative direction. Figure 10-5 portrays a weak correlation.

Figure 10-3.    Moderate positive correlation.

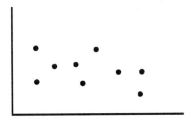

Figure 10-4    Moderate negative correlation.

## Scattergrams

Scattergrams are a useful way to depict data dealing with relationships. Some guidelines are presented here to facilitate producing them. Computer software is also available to construct scattergrams.

1. Make the vertical (*Y*) axis three-fourths the length of the horizontal (*X*) axis. This allows a good spread of the data, which facilitates interpretation.
2. Place the title below the figure.
3. Label each axis and the unit of measure.
4. Provide a key or legend to identify symbols.
5. Use a break mark if not starting at zero. This eliminates having large portions of a figure void of any data. For example, if body weight is one variable, values for that axis would start a bit below the lightest weight plotted.

## Assumptions

Use of any of the statistics in this chapter requires that data be interval or ratio level. They must also be linearly related, normally distributed, and have similar variances.

## PEARSON CORRELATION

The Pearson product moment coefficient of correlation, or Pearson *r*, is used to measure how well two variables are related to each other. Researchers can use the Pearson *r* to assess relationships between vertical jump and leg strength,

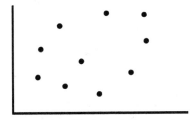

Figure 10-5    Weak positive correlation.

cholesterol level and incidence of cardiovascular disease, score on an exam in a health unit on nutrition and percent of calories consumed from fat, batting average and IQ, and so on.

The formula for calculating a Pearson $r$ is

$$r = \frac{N \Sigma XY - (\Sigma X)(\Sigma Y)}{\sqrt{(N \Sigma X^2 - [\Sigma X]^2)(N \Sigma Y^2 - [\Sigma Y]^2)}}$$

The steps in a sample problem are summarized in Table 10-1. In the problem a researcher wishes to measure the relationship between pull-ups and push-ups. The score for each variable is recorded under the $X$ and $Y$ columns. Either variable can be $X$ or $Y$. The values are squared, summed, and cross-multiplied with the appropriate values substituted into the equation. Note that $N$ refers to the number of subjects.

## Interpretation

The researcher usually wishes to know three things about a correlation: whether it is positive or negative, whether it is significant, and how strong it is. Correlation coefficients range from −1.00 to +1.00. As correlations approach either −1.00 or +1.00, they are said to be strong or high, whereas correlations approaching 0 are weak or low. A perfect correlation is one that is either −1.00 or +1.00. Perfect correlations rarely occur, as we shall see a bit later. A correlation of

**TABLE 10-1**  Calculation of the Pearson $r$

| Subject | Pull-ups $X$ | Push-ups $Y$ | $X^2$ | $Y^2$ | $XY$ |
|---------|--------------|--------------|-------|-------|------|
| A | 8 | 17 | 64 | 289 | 136 |
| B | 5 | 12 | 25 | 225 | 60 |
| C | 7 | 11 | 49 | 121 | 77 |
| D | 12 | 26 | 144 | 676 | 312 |
| E | 2 | 4 | 4 | 16 | 8 |
| $N = 5$ | $\Sigma X = 34$ | $\Sigma Y = 70$ | $\Sigma X^2 = 286$ | $\Sigma Y^2 = 1246$ | $\Sigma XY = 593$ |

$$r = \frac{N \Sigma XY - (\Sigma X)(\Sigma Y)}{\sqrt{(N \Sigma X^2 - [\Sigma X]^2)(N \Sigma Y^2 - [\Sigma Y]^2)}}$$

$$r = \frac{5(593) - (34)(70)}{\sqrt{(5[286] - 34^2)(5[1246] - 70^2)}}$$

$$r = \frac{2965}{\sqrt{(1430 - 1156)(6230) - 4900)}} = .969$$

0 means that absolutely no relationship exists between two variables. This is also quite unlikely to occur.

***Positive or Negative*** The operation sign indicates whether the correlation is positive or negative. The correlation calculated in the sample problem is positive, so we know that as performance in one variable increases so does performance in the other variable.

***Significance*** A correlation significantly different than zero indicates that it really exists and most likely is not attributable to chance or sampling error. The $r$ of .969 is nearly a perfect positive relationship. Examining Appendix I, Table C, Critical Values of $r$, with *degrees of freedom* or $df = N - 2$ or $5 - 2 = 3$, $r$ must equal .878 or higher with a two-tailed test to be significant at the .05 level. The calculated $r$ exceeds that amount and so is judged to be a real relationship. Thus, in the sample problem, the null hypothesis is rejected and the alternative

**TABLE 10-2** Steps in a hypothesis test

1. State the null and alternative hypotheses.
   $H_0: r = 0$
   $H_A: r \neq 0$
2. Set the significance (alpha) level.
   .05
3. Determine the appropriate statistic.
   Pearson $r$
4. Determine the critical statistic value.
   Critical value = .878 with 3 $df$ ($df = N - 2$)
5. Place the critical values on a curve and determine the areas of "do not reject" and "reject."
6. Calculate the statistic and place it on the curve.
   $r = .969$

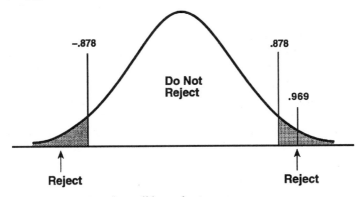

7. Do not reject or reject the null hypothesis.
   The null hypothesis is rejected.
8. Draw a research conclusion.
   It is 95% likely that the correlation between pull-ups and push-ups is real and there is a 5% possibility that it is due to chance.

hypothesis is accepted. Table 10-2 summarizes the steps in hypothesis testing for correlation.

The interpretation here is that subjects performing well in the pull-up test tended also to do well in push-ups, and subjects scoring low in one test tended to score low in the other. Thus performance in the two tests is well related. The relationship is not perfect, however, as there are exceptions to this overall trend.

When testing nondirectional hypotheses for correlation, a two-tailed test is used, as was done in the sample problem for pull-ups and push-ups. Hypotheses are usually stated in the null form when the sign of the correlation to be determined is uncertain. This is probably the case for pull-ups and push-ups. However, if reasonably certain that most pairs of data will be positive or negative, then a directional hypothesis would be used. An example might be the relationship between height and weight. Overall it would be strongly suspected that the variables are positively related to each other. Therefore the hypothesis would be stated directionally: $r > 0$. This allows use of the one-tailed column for critical values, which increases the likelihood of achieving significance because all of the rejection area appears on the positive end of the normal curve, which places the value closer to the middle. An example of an expected negative relationship would be incidence of cardiovascular disease and level of physical activity. Here, also, a directional hypothesis would be stated ($r < 0$) and a one-tailed test used.

*Strength*   The strength of a correlation is an entirely different factor than significance. Often, it is mistakenly thought that significance denotes strength. One means of judging the strength of correlations is a subjective rating based only on the size of $r$. The ratings apply to both positive and as negative correlations: .25 or lower is weak, .26 to .50 is moderate, .51 to .75 is fair, and .76 and higher is high. A common mistake in interpreting correlations is that a negative $r$ implies a weak relationship. This is not so, as is explained shortly. Weak, moderate, fair, and so on are descriptive in a general way but lack precision. Therefore these terms are best used to supplement more exact quantitative information, such as calculation of $r^2$.

The most meaningful and common way to assess the strength of $r$ is by calculation of the *coefficient of determination* ($r^2$), which is a measure of the variance shared by two variables. The calculation is easy: $r^2 \times 100$. The remaining variance is calculated as $(1 - r)^2 \times 100$ and is called the *coefficient of nondetermination*. These statistics indicate entirely different information than that provided by determining if the $r$ is significant. The fact that an $r$ value is significant only indicates that the confidence is high that a relationship really exists, but nothing is indicated about its strength. With a large $N$, a .20 correlation may be significant, yet the variance accounted for by the relationship is only 4% ($.20^2 \times 100 = 4$)! Therefore, when correlations are presented in research they should include information regarding both significance *and* strength. Remember, negative correlations do not infer weak relationships. When squaring a negative number, the result is positive and therefore negative correlations can explain just as much variance as do positive correlations.

The $r$ between the pull-up and push-up scores was .969. The variance shared by or common to the variables is 94% ($.97^2 \times 100 = 94$). Consequently, the two variables have much in common. Theoretically, what might be some of these common factors? They may include upper body strength and local muscle endurance, total body weight, percent body fat, previous practice and skill in the two tests, and the like. The coefficient of nondetermination is 6% ($100\% - 94\% = 6\%$). Thus 6% of the variance is not shared and is known as *specific variance*. Sources of specific or unique variance might include grip strength (more important in pull-ups than in push-ups), strength and local muscle endurance of the elbow flexors (more important in pull-ups), and elbow extensors (more important in push-ups). Figure 10-6 shows the degree of relationship by the degree of overlap of the two circles. The degree of overlap represents the variance common to both variables; the portions of each circle not overlapping represent variance specific to each variable. Such a depiction is a useful conceptual aid.

## CAUSE AND EFFECT RELATIONSHIPS

Researchers are often interested in determining if one variable causes a change in a second variable. For example, medical researchers carry out research to test the effectiveness of various drugs. By nature of the purpose and design of a study, some research attempts to establish cause and effect—that is, variable A causes a change in variable B. Correlation by itself does not examine cause and effect. Yet the most common misconception about correlation is that a cause–effect relationship exists. Some variables may well have a cause–effect relationship, but a Pearson $r$ by itself does not determine this. For example, decades ago, epidemiologists in a number of studies found high positive correlations between cholesterol level and incidence of cardiovascular disease. Could they infer that high cholesterol caused cardiovascular disease? They most certainly could not! Only experimental studies where intake of dietary fat was controlled could produce scientific evidence that excess cholesterol in the diet or blood caused the disease. Because of this limitation to the use of correlation, it is often used as a preliminary stage of knowledge development. The study of lifestyle and disease is often initiated by examining relationships between how people live and the in-

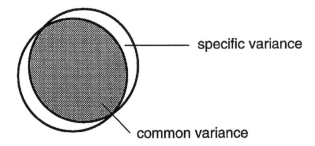

Figure 10-6   Percent common and specific variance.

cidence of disease. Correlation is the statistic of choice because if significant and strong relationships are found, then experimental studies can be done to determine actual causes of disease.

So don't be a sucker and assume cause and effect relationships are justified from using correlation. Here are several examples of such "leaps in logic": A researcher found a significant negative $r$ of $-.78$ between the amount of tea consumed in three countries and incidence of osteoporosis. It was concluded that drinking tea reduces osteoporosis. In another study a researcher noted that as Halley's comet approached closer to earth over several weeks, inflation rose significantly. It was concluded that Halley's comet not only was causing inflation but that as it passed by the earth inflation would gradually drop. In a third study a noted dermatologist researcher noted that as more cases of severe sunburn occurred during an especially hot summer, the sales of ice cream also rose. He concluded that ice cream increases susceptibility to sunburn and that fair-skinned people should eat ice cream in limited amounts. Aren't statistics wonderful— and sometimes misleading!

## CORRELATION MATRIX

A common way to present a number of correlations is to put them in a table called a *correlation matrix*. Reading numerous correlation coefficients and the associated variables is tedious when in text form. A table greatly facilitates comprehension. Table 10-3 is an example of a correlation matrix. Each variable is numbered in column 1 and the same variables are listed as column headings without being written out. No value is given under column 1, row 1, because this value would represent the $r$ of height with itself, which of course would be 1.00. Therefore the $r$ of each variable with itself is deleted in the table. Each $r$ is read where two variables intersect in the table. The $r$ between height and weight is .70; the $r$ between wrist circumference and weight is .40. Half of the values in the table appear to be missing. These values are not needed because the values to the left of an imaginary line running diagonally through the table are identical with the values already in the table. Thus half of the table is a mirror image of the other half.

## OTHER USES OF CORRELATION

The Pearson $r$ is used for several purposes besides examining relationships. Several of these are described here.

**TABLE 10-3** Correlation matrix

| Variable | 1 | 2 | 3 | 4 |
|---|---|---|---|---|
| 1. Height, cm | — | .70 | .80 | .40 |
| 2. Weight, kg | | — | .50 | .40 |
| 3. Leg length, cm | | | — | .20 |
| 4. Wrist circumference, cm | | | | — |

*Reliability* *Reliability* refers to the consistency of measurements. For example, in assessing nutritional status, subjects may be instructed to record all food and drink consumed for several days. The reliability of the measurement can be determined by assessing food intake a second occasion in the same subjects and performing a Pearson *r* between the two measures. If protein intake is the variable of interest, then the *r* between protein intake on each occasion is calculated. The higher the correlation, the higher the reliability.

*Objectivity* *Objectivity* is the reliability or consistency of measurement between different test administrators. A high *r* between two researchers measuring blood pressure in the same people indicates a good consistency in the measurements.

*Validity* *Validity* indicates how well a test measures what is intended to be tested. Researchers typically validate tests by correlating the results of a new test with the results obtained from the best accepted test known as the "gold standard test." A high *r* between the results of the two tests indicates a good level of agreement, which is desirable.

## PREDICTION: SIMPLE LINEAR REGRESSION

Most of us from time to time are involved in predictions. Your acceptance in graduate school may have depended on your score on an achievement test used to predict academic success. Fitness evaluations typically are based on field tests that predict the score you would have achieved on a more sophisticated test in a laboratory. Economists predict unemployment and business trends.

*Simple linear regression* is used to make a prediction of a variable based on the correlation between the two variables. It is the simplest form of prediction.

### Linear Regression Equation

The linear regression equation is based on the formula for a straight line ($Y' = a + bX$ or $Y' = bX + a$) and predicts a $Y$ value from one value of $X$. Because $a$ and $b$ in the equation for a straight line must each be calculated, a one-step formula for simple linear regression becomes:

$$Y' = bX + a$$

where:

$Y'$ = predicted score or dependent variable
$b$ = slope of the regression line = $r (S_Y / S_X)$
$a$ = $Y'$ intercept = $M_Y - bM_X$
$X$ = score for the independent variable
$M_Y$ = mean of $Y$ scores
$M_X$ = mean of $X$ scores

The slope or steepness of the regression line, $b$, can be positive (line running up-hill) or negative (running downhill). It represents the change in the $Y$ variable for each unit change in $X$. If $X$ increases one while $Y$ increases four, then the slope is four. The second part of the equation, $M_Y - bM_X$, represents $a$, the $Y$ intercept or point on the $Y$ axis where the regression line intersects. $X$ represents the known value of the $X$ variable used to predict $Y$; that is, you know the score on variable $X$ and will use it to predict the $Y$ score.

A sample problem appears in Table 10-4 in which a researcher wishes to predict the heaviest lift one can make in the bench press ($Y$). The independent variable ($X$) is the maximum number of push-ups one can do in 30 seconds.

The equation can now be used to predict the maximum bench press lift for other participants from the same population. Suppose we wish to predict the bench press for John Doe. He performs the 30-second push-up test and completes 25 push-ups. Twenty-five is the $X$ value in the regression equation developed. By substitution into the equation for a straight line, his bench press maximum is estimated:

$$Y' = a + bX = 104 + 3.2(25) = 104 + 80 = 184 \text{ lb}$$

Therefore, John's estimated bench press is 184 lb. Such a prediction may be useful here if a person was not able to perform maximal lifting due to injury or because the instructor didn't want to expose people to the risk of maximal lifting. Furthermore, an instructor of a weight training class may wish to predict maximal scores simply to save time. Performance of a 30-second push-up test could be accomplished by an entire class in minutes, whereas weight training performance of warm-up sets and gradually increasing loads up to maximum would take considerably longer.

### Line of Best Fit and Scattergram

A scattergram is often constructed to aid interpretation of the prediction line calculated. The point where each subject's scores fall is plotted on a graph. After the regression equation is calculated, the line of best fit may be drawn. Start at the $Y$

**TABLE 10-4** Simple linear regression

$r = .80$ between push-ups and maximum bench press
$M_Y$ (bench press) = 200 lb
$S_Y = 20$
$M_X$ (push-ups) = 30
$S_X = 5$

Therefore:

$b = r(S_Y)/S_X = .80(20/5) = .80(4) = 3.2$

$a = M_Y - bM_X = 200 - 3.2(30) = 200 - 96 = 104$

$Y' = a + bX = 104 + 3.2X$

intercept, which is *a* in the regression equation. Substitute a large value of *X* into the regression equation, for example, 50 push-ups, and calculate *Y'*. Make a mark where these *X* and *Y* scores fall and draw a straight line between the *Y* intercept and this point. This line of best fit passes through the mean of the *X* and *Y* scores. Figure 10-7 depicts the regression line for data on the 30-second push-up test and maximum bench press. Note that the line of best fit can be used visually to predict any *Y* score by plotting the point on the regression line that intersects with the *X* score. The best predicted *Y* score is that value that intersects with the regression line at the same point as the associated *X* score.

The scattergram in Figure 10-8 depicts a line of best fit from the equation $Y = -3X + 10$. Note that the slope is negative (a slope of −3 means a descent of −3 for *Y* for each unit change of *X*) and that the line intersects the *Y* axis at positive 10.

### Accuracy of an Estimate

Although it is helpful to be able to predict something, the prediction is limited unless it is reasonably accurate. Nearly all prediction equations are in error to some extent unless they were generated from variables perfectly correlated. This is rarely, if ever, the case, however. The *standard error of estimate* (*SEE*) is the average error in a prediction equation. Statistically, it is the standard deviation of actual scores around the prediction line. For example, several subjects may have performed the same number of push-ups (*X*), yet their bench press scores (*Y*) are not the same. The difference between each person's actual score and the score

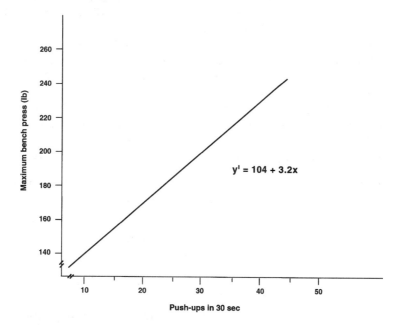

Figure 10-7   Simple linear regression equation and line of best fit.

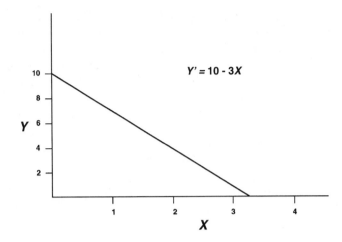

Figure 10-8   Simple linear regression equation and line of best fit.

predicted from the regression line is an estimation error or a *residual*. The SEE quantifies the size of this error, and therefore is a measure of the accuracy of a prediction equation or prediction line. It is calculated as follows:

$$SEE = S_Y\sqrt{1-r^2}$$

A small SEE indicates greater accuracy of prediction and occurs when two variables are highly correlated with each other. Actually, if $r = 1.00$, the SEE = 0. One would not expect to obtain much accuracy in prediction if using finger length to predict bone density, because as far as we know the two variables are not related to each other. Thus, when examining scattergrams, unless the data are reasonably close to the regression line, the correlation is probably not particularly high, and one variable would not be a strong predictor of the other—that is, the SEE would be relatively large.

Typically, about 68% of all predicted scores fall within one SEE of the prediction line, about 95% of scores lie within 1.96 SEEs, and nearly all scores fall within 2.58 SEEs. These represent the 68%, 95%, and 99% *confidence intervals*, respectively. For example, using data from the example on push-ups and bench press, the SEE = $S_r\sqrt{1-r^2} = 20-1-.80^2 = 20(.6) = 12$ lb. The confidence intervals for a predicted bench press score of 180 lb would be:

$$68\% = 180 \pm 1(12) = 168 \text{ TO } 192 \text{ lb}$$
$$95\% = 180 \pm 1.96(12) = 156.5 \text{ TO } 203.5 \text{ lb}$$
$$99\% = 180 \pm 2.58(12) = 149 \text{ TO } 211 \text{ lb}$$

Thus we would expect about 68% of participants whose predicted score was 180 to be within one SEE, or 12 lb of their actual value.

Researchers wishing to accurately predict a variable should strive to use variables as highly correlated as possible and to use a reasonably large sample size because $N$ size tends to improve the correlation and shrink the standard deviation. The SEE should be a primary factor in deciding if a prediction is accurate enough to use. Would you use an equation to predict cholesterol level if the SEE was 40 mg/dl? This would mean that about two-thirds of people tested would be within 40 units of their actual cholesterol. Some people may be as much as about three SEEs from the actual value, in which case the error would be 120 units! The predictive error associated with this equation would not allow its use. The point to be emphasized here is that the size of the SEE should be considered when selecting measurements to use in the professional setting. To do otherwise is to shirk professional responsibility.

## PREDICTION: MULTIPLE REGRESSION

*Multiple regression* is a means of making a prediction from two or more variables. It is typically more accurate than simple linear regression because more information is used in making the prediction. Examples are predicting academic success from socioeconomic level, IQ, and score on a standardized test; predicting body fatness from skinfold thickness at three sites; and predicting participation in high-risk outdoor adventure activities from birth order, participation in interscholastic sport, and socioeconomic level.

The concept of adding variables to improve prediction is intuitively logical. If a coach was considering recruiting a football player, more than one bit of information would be used in predicting the possible value of this player to the team. The coach may view game films from high school, request performance data from the high school coach such as 40-yard dash time, strength, and agility, and even watch the player in a game. The sum of the information would tend to allow the coach to predict better whether or not a scholarship should be offered than if only one piece of information was known.

The calculation of a multiple regression equation is an extension of the equation for a single straight line or regression line. The equation is:

$$Y' = a + bX_1 + bX_2 + bX_3 + \ldots$$

For each predictor variable, a $bX$ component is added to the equation. Each predictor variable contributes some information to the equation. Because the number of steps in the equation is proportional to the number of predictor variables, the mathematics of calculating a multiple regression equation become lengthy. Computer software readily handles this chore. Therefore a problem showing all of the steps is not covered here.

The following is an example of a multiple regression equation used to predict the risk of coronary heart disease (CHD). Consequently, CHD is the dependent variable or variable being predicted.

$$Y' = 34.77 + .97X_1 - .02X_2 + .07X_3 + .45X_4$$

where:

$X_1$ = smoking
$X_2$ = physical activity
$X_3$ = stress rating
$X_4$ = abdominal girth

A computer program first correlates (Pearson $r$) each predictor or independent variable with CHD. Variables are selected that account for the most variance and in the sequence of the strongest to the weakest predictor. In the above equation, smoking accounted for the most variance and abdominal girth the least. As more variables are added to the prediction, more variance is explained. The *multiple correlation*, $R$, is the correlation of two or more variables together with the dependent variable. The effect of each variable in explaining more variance is often summarized in a table, such as Table 10-5.

The $r$ between smoking and CHD was .50, which explains 25% of the variance in CHD ($.50^2 = 25\%$). The addition of the second best predictor, physical activity, increased the multiple $R$ to .60, which increased the explained variance to 36%. The third and fourth variable each increased the $R$ and explained a bit more variance. Realize that the improvement in explained variance is due to the pooled correlation of variables with CHD. Thus, in step 2, smoking and physical activity *together* have an $R$ of .60 with the criterion and *together* explain 36% of the variance in CHD.

An interesting question concerning prediction deals with the number of predictor variables: How many variables are needed to obtain a good prediction? Is there a point at which little or no improvement in predictive accuracy occurs by adding more variables to an equation? The answer is twofold. Researchers typically measure a number of factors that previous research indicates are good predictors. Others may be added because they logically appear to be related. The computer sorts through the individual Pearson correlations and develops an equation that explains the most variance. When no significant improvement in explaining variance is made by adding more variables, then a predictive equation developed at this point is the best equation. Interestingly, the most useful predictors after the first one or two are usually not well correlated with any of the other predictors. This happens because they are measuring something unique or not measured by the other variables. Thus it contributes

**TABLE 10-5**   Multiple correlation

| Variable | R | R² |
|---|---|---|
| Smoking | .50 | 25% |
| Physical activity | .60 | 36 |
| Stress | .65 | 42.2 |
| Abdominal girth | .68 | 46.2 |

something new in the way of variance, thereby enhancing the accuracy of prediction.

How many variables are needed to provide an accurate prediction? The best answer is that variables should be added until further addition no longer significantly adds explained variance. One important exception is that at least three or four subjects per variable or about one-tenth the sample size are needed in order for an equation to be reasonably accurate. Ten to 20 subjects per variable provides even greater accuracy (Kerlinger & Pedhazar, 1973). Great departure from this ratio tends to raise the correlation spuriously, which produces falsely high multiple correlations. This is a common limitation seen in published literature. For this reason, researchers usually limit the number of predictor variables to only those that have some logical basis for inclusion.

The plus and minus signs in the equation denote whether or not the correlation between each predictor variable and the dependent variable was positive or negative. The positive signs before smoking, stress rating, and abdominal girth indicate that each was positively associated with increased risk of CHD. The only negative correlation was with physical activity, which is logical: As physical activity increased, risk of CHD fell.

## SPECIFICITY OF PREDICTION

The last point to be made in our discussion of prediction is that a prediction equation is only sound or valid for subjects with nearly identical traits as the subjects used in the development of the equation. This concept is expressed by the term *population specificity*. A good example deals with the many equations that use skinfold thickness to estimate body fatness. Because nearly all studies that developed equations were based on small sample sizes of athletes of one gender in one sport in one small age range, perhaps as many as 100 different prediction equations evolved. Each, however, was valid only for people with the identical sex, age range, and sport as those of the subjects in the original investigation. Each equation was thus population specific.

In order to develop prediction equations for a broader range of the population, many more subjects with diversity of traits must be used in the development of the equation. For example, a general equation to predict percent body fat from skinfold thickness in females in their midteens to beyond age 60 was developed by Jackson, Pollock, and Ward (1980). They used several hundred female subjects in this age range with a wide variety of body fatness levels to formulate the equation.

## PARTIAL CORRELATION

A *partial correlation*, $r_{12.3}$, determines the relationship between two variables with the variance of a third variable removed or "partialled out" or held constant. The purpose is to derive a correlation that is purer or less tainted than using the Pearson $r$. Most phenomena studied by researchers are multifactorial. A limitation of using a Pearson $r$ is that the influence of other variables can easily be overlooked. For example, suppose a researcher wishes to assess the relationship between time running the marathon and maximum oxygen uptake. However, the researcher realizes that body fatness probably has something to do with the relationship; that is, leaner people tend to have higher maximum oxygen uptakes and tend to run the marathon faster.

Partial correlation can be used to eliminate the effect that body fatness has on this relationship. This statistical adjustment usually but not always reduces the Pearson $r$ because variance is removed. Therefore partial correlations are usually smaller than Pearson correlations. The following values illustrate this effect:

$$\text{PEARSON} \quad r_{12} = .60, \quad r_{12}^2 = 36\%$$
$$\text{PARTIAL} \quad r_{12.3} = .50, \quad r_{12.3}^2 = 25\%$$

The correlation decreased, which also reduces the explained variance ($r^2$). The .25 partial $r$ provides a better understanding of the actual relationship between the two variables than does the Pearson $r$.

A good example of the use of partial correlation occurred some years ago with studies that found a significant correlation between coffee consumption and incidence of cardiovascular disease. However, when researchers in later studies used partial correlation to hold the effects of smoking constant, the relationship dwindled to insignificance.

Researchers sometimes wish to control the association of several variables on a relationship rather than just one. This is done using first-, second-, or even third-order partial correlation. The result is an especially "clean" correlation because the variance of other variables is adjusted for.

## FACTOR ANALYSIS

*Factor analysis* is a method using correlation to determine the commonality in a large number of measures. It has been used in HPER to determine the number and kinds of test items to use when a large number of possible tests is available. For example, hundreds of test items that measure physical fitness have been used by physical educators in the last 100 years. The problem for the practitioner in the school setting has been knowing which tests to use. Fleishman (1969) used factor analysis to identify different components of fitness. The procedure involved correlating all the tests with each other. Those that were highly intercorrelated he analyzed to determine what they had in common. By noting the common feature, he was able to use a descriptive word or term to describe a cluster of tests. Thus evolved three areas of strength he termed explosive strength (short sprints, hops, jumps, ball throws), static strength (isometric contractions using strength measuring devices called dynamometers), and dynamic strength (pull-ups, push-ups, rope climb, dips on parallel bars). Because the tests within one cluster were well intercorrelated, a practitioner might select just one or two tests within each cluster or factor rather than using a much larger number in a haphazard manner of selection. Thus one test from each cluster would measure a different type of strength. The same procedure was used to develop groups of tests measuring local muscle endurance, cardiovascular endurance, flexibility, and so on.

A factor is a group of measures which hypothetically have something in common. Factors of human intelligence often include verbal ability, quantitative ability, abstract reasoning, spatial perceptiveness, etc. Recreation behavior could similarly be classified using factor analysis with the result that a number of distinct entities might exist such as intellectual development, physical development, social interaction, stress reduction, etc.

## SUMMARY

The Pearson $r$ correlation coefficient is used to determine the relationship between two variables. The relationship is evaluated by the significance level as well as strength. Care must be taken not to infer that significant relationships are causal: They may or may not be, but only experimental research can confirm cause. Pearson $r$ is the basis for prediction based on one independent variable (simple linear regression) or two or more independent variables (multiple regression). The accuracy of a prediction equation is expressed by the standard error of estimate (SEE). Correlations can also be made among several variables pooled together (multiple correlation) and with the variance of a third variable removed (partial correlation). Correlation is used in factor analysis to determine similarities among various tests or measures.

## STATISTICS EXERCISES

1. A health official wished to know the relationship between health care cost per family member per year and years of education. Using the following data, calculate a Pearson $r$ between the two variables. Determine whether or not the $r$ is significant at the .05 level and the percent common and specific variance.

| Health Care Cost per Family Member | Years of Education |
|:---:|:---:|
| $1200 | 13 |
| 1400 | 14 |
| 900 | 11 |
| 1100 | 12 |
| 1500 | 17 |
| 1400 | 14 |
| 1100 | 16 |
| 1300 | 15 |
| 1700 | 19 |
| 1500 | 16 |

2. A physical education teacher administered a trunk curl test to a group of students and wanted to know how reliable the scores were. Calculate a Pearson $r$ to express reliability.

| Test 1 | Test 2 |
|--------|--------|
| 24 | 23 |
| 23 | 23 |
| 22 | 20 |
| 22 | 25 |
| 19 | 18 |
| 17 | 19 |
| 17 | 18 |
| 17 | 16 |
| 16 | 20 |

3. A recreator examined the relationship between the number of summers children attended an outdoor adventure camp and their grade point average. Calculate a Pearson $r$ to determine if the relationship was significant and calculate the percent explained variance.

| Number of Summers | Grade Point Average |
|-------------------|---------------------|
| 2 | 3.11 |
| 1 | 3.87 |
| 4 | 2.95 |
| 2 | 3.10 |
| 3 | 3.02 |
| 4 | 2.75 |
| 3 | 2.86 |
| 3 | 3.00 |

4. The following data were collected by an exercise physiologist who wanted to derive a simple test not requiring laboratory equipment to predict overall body strength. The following data were collected:

| Grip strength (kg) X | Overall strength (kg) Y |
|----------------------|-------------------------|
| 13 | 43 |
| 16 | 44 |
| 17 | 45 |
| 13 | 41 |
| 18 | 40 |
| 15 | 43 |
| 14 | 46 |
| 10 | 38 |
| 9 | 37 |
| 10 | 36 |

    a. Calculate the linear regression equation.

    b. Calculate the standard error of estimate.

    c. Calculate the predicted score if grip strength ($X$) = 13 kg.

5. A physical educator conducted a study examining the relationship between $VO_2$ max ($Y$) and 1.5-mile run times ($X$). A statistical analysis resulted in the following: $M_Y$ = 45.0 ml/kg/min, $M_X$ = 12.0 min, $S_Y$ = 4.0, $S_X$ = 3.0, $r$ = −.85.

    a. Calculate the linear regression equation and SEE.

    b. Calculate the predicted $VO_2$ max ($Y'$) and 68% confidence interval if the run time was 11 min ($X$).

6. A park official studied the relationship between the number of people who used the lake area of a park ($Y$) and the number who used a certain trail ($X$). Data revealed that $M_Y$ = 400 people, $M_X$ = 140 people, $S_Y$ = 80, $S_X$ = 30, $r$ = .70.

    a. Calculate the linear regression equation and SEE.

    b. Calculate the predicted use of the lake area ($Y'$) and 95% confidence interval if the use of the trail ($X$) was 160 people.

# CHAPTER 11

# COMPARING MEAN SCORES

$A$ common research problem is assessing the effect of one or more independent or experimental variables on a dependent variable. Performance on the dependent variable is measured before and after a treatment period, and the change in performance for each group is compared. When only two mean scores are compared, and if the data are interval or ratio, then two types of *t tests* can be used for the comparisons. If more than two mean scores are compared, then the most common type of statistic used is *analysis of variance*, or *ANOVA*. Each of these statistics is discussed in this chapter.

## Statistical Assumptions

Before using a statistical test, a researcher should examine the criteria for using the test. The criteria for using any $t$ test or ANOVA are

1. Data are drawn from normally distributed populations.
2. Data represent random samples from the population.
3. Variance in each group is similar. If variance in one group greatly exceeds that of another group, the within-groups variance or denominator of a $t$ or $F$ ratio is inflated. As will be seen

$$t \text{ and } F = \frac{\text{Variance between groups}}{\text{Variance within groups}}$$

Therefore a larger within groups variance reduces the $t$ or $F$ ratio, which in turn reduces the likelihood of significance occurring.

4. Data are interval or ratio. The data must be continuous and have equal intervals.

The first several assumptions do not have to be strictly met. Kerlinger (1964) supports the opinion of others that the normality and equality of variance criteria are probably overrated. Furthermore, he advocates that unless there is good reason to believe the data are not normal or do not have equal variance, use of a nonparametric test instead of a parametric one, such as a $t$ test or ANOVA, is not recommended. Nonparametric tests are less powerful, meaning that attaining significance is more difficult, and therefore, whenever possible, parametric tests should be used. The researcher must use some judgment in the matter. A student researcher would be wise to discuss the issue with an experienced faculty researcher.

## Significance and Magnitude

Typically one expects to find the published results of a study expressed in terms of significant findings. Although this is important, it should not be the only interest of the reader regarding the results. Too often it is. Significance deals only with the confidence in the results, that is, whether or not they likely occurred due to chance or sampling error or an experimental effect. However, the magnitude of the effect should also be discussed. Magnitude can be quanti fied in several ways and will be demonstrated in this chapter. For now, we wish merely to emphasize that it should be addressed in every research paper.

## CORRELATED OR DEPENDENT *t* TESTS

The purpose of the correlated or dependent *t* test is to compare two mean scores that are related or correlated. The analysis typically involves pre- and posttest data within one group or comparison of two groups that are matched on a key trait. In either case, the scores are correlated. Examples of comparisons within a group are assessing change in body weight before and after 10 weeks of walking and comparing resting blood pressure before and after a month of meditation.

$$ t = \frac{\sum D / N}{1 / N \sqrt{\left[ N \sum D^2 \right] - \left( \sum D \right)^2 / (N-1)}} $$

where:

$D$ = pretest – posttest score for each subject

$N$ = number of subjects

For example, suppose a coach wished to determine if shooting free throws in basketball 30 minutes a day twice a week improves free-throw shooting skill after 4 weeks. There are 10 subjects each with a pre- and post-test score. The steps used to calculate the *t* ratio are summarized in Table 11-1. The negative ratio occurred because the calculation of $\sum D$ requires subtracting the second score from the first. Note that the mean score improved with practice from 16.2 to 17.3. Consequently, here the negative sign does not indicate a decrease in performance.

The *df* is $N - 1$. Therefore, *df* = $10 - 1 = 9$. Consult Appendix I, Table D Critical Values of *t* to determine if the *t* ratio is significant using a one-tailed test. (The selection of the one-tailed test is explained shortly.) The *t* ratio $-1.94$ is significant at the .05 level, and it is concluded that practice improved free-throw performance. Table 11-2 summarizes the steps in hypothesis testing for this experiment.

### Interpretation of Results

Note that researchers employing correlated *t* tests often are quite sure that the direction of change will be beneficial. In the study described here it is assumed that free-throw practice will improve skill, but it is unknown how much. In such a case, one would logically use directional hypothesis testing. Thus the hypothesis to be tested is $H_0: \mu_{Pre} \geq \mu_{Post}$. If this hypothesis is rejected, then the following hypothesis is accepted: $H_A: \mu_{Pre} < \mu_{Post}$. Directional hypothesis testing allows use of the one-tailed column, which increases the likelihood of detecting a significant effect. Therefore it is to the researcher's advantage to use directional testing when the direction of change is obvious. Other examples of obvious direction

**TABLE 11-1** Calculation of dependent *t* test

| Subject | Pretest | Posttest | D | $D^2$ |
|---------|---------|----------|-----|-------|
| 1 | 19 | 20 | −1 | 1 |
| 2 | 17 | 15 | 2 | 4 |
| 3 | 19 | 20 | −1 | 1 |
| 4 | 14 | 16 | −2 | 4 |
| 5 | 13 | 17 | −4 | 16 |
| 6 | 16 | 16 | 0 | 0 |
| 7 | 16 | 15 | 1 | 1 |
| 8 | 17 | 18 | −1 | 1 |
| 9 | 17 | 19 | −2 | 4 |
| 10 | 14 | 17 | −3 | 9 |
| Σ | 162 | 173 | −11 | 41 |
| M | 16.2 | 17.3 | | |

$$t = \frac{\Sigma D / N}{1/N\sqrt{[N\Sigma D^2] - (\Sigma D)^2 / N - 1}} = \frac{-11/10}{1/10\sqrt{[10(41)] - (-11)^2 / 10 - 1}}$$

$$= \frac{-1.1}{.10\sqrt{(289/9)}} = \frac{-1.1}{.567} = -1.94$$

$$df = 10 - 1 = 9$$

$t(9) = -1.94$, $p \leq .05$ for a one-tailed test

change are comparison of weight loss in a control group versus a jogging group and reduction in cholesterol in nonexercisers versus regular exercisers.

A second useful tool in interpreting the result of statistical tests is to determine the magnitude of change as a result of a treatment. This can be done simply by calculating the percent change in pre- to posttest mean scores. In the example here, the percent change equals

$$100 = \frac{M_{Post} - M_{Pre}}{M_{Pre}}$$

$$= 100 \frac{16.2 - 17.3}{16.2}$$

$$= 100(1.1/16.2) = 6.8\%$$

Thus performance improved 6.8%.

With other statistics, formulas are available to calculate the percent of variance or change due to the experimental variable, which is something most readers of research are concerned with. A technique to do this is not available

**TABLE 11-2**    Hypothesis testing for dependent $t$ test

1. State the null and alternative hypotheses.

   $H_0: \mu_{Pre} \geq \mu_{Post}$

   $H_A: \mu_{Pre} < \mu_{Post}$

2. Set the significance (alpha) level.

   .05

3. Determine the appropriate statistic.

   Dependent $t$ test.

4. Determine the critical statistical value.

   Critical value for a one-tailed test with 9 $df$ is –1.833.

5. Place the critical value on a curve and determine the values of "do not reject" and "reject."

6. Calculate the dependent $t$ ratio and place it on the curve.
   t = 1.94

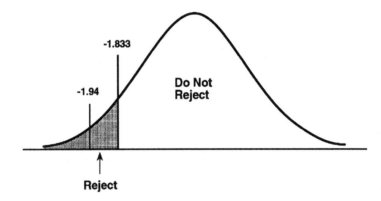

7. Do not reject or reject the null hypothesis.

   The null hypothesis is rejected.

8. Draw a research conclusion.

   It is concluded that free-throw performance did improve. The change was likely due to practice.

---

for correlated $t$ test (Thomas & Nelson, 1990), so the magnitude of the independent variable can at least be expressed by the percent change.

## INDEPENDENT $t$ TEST

This version of the $t$ test determines if the means from two different groups are significantly different. An example of such research, assuming that one experimental group and a control group are involved in the design of each study, would be the effect of videotape feedback on acquisition of a novel skill. Another would be the difference in dollars spent on recreation in coastal versus non-coastal states.

$$t = \frac{M_1 - M_2}{\sqrt{\left[\dfrac{(N_1 - 1)S_1^2 + (N_2 - 1)S_2^2}{N_1 + N_2 - 2}\right]\left[\dfrac{N_1 + N_2}{N_1 N_2}\right]}}$$

Suppose that a researcher wanted to compare the percent body fat between wrestlers and football players. The means were 9% and 13%, respectively. Twenty athletes from each sport are randomly sampled. A summary of the calculations appears in Table 11-3.

After calculating the $t$ ratio, refer to Appendix I, Table D, Critical Values of $t$, to determine if the $t$ ratio of 4.96 is significant. Because there are two independent groups in this comparison, $df = N - 2$ or $(20 + 20) - 2 = 38$. Table T does not indicate a critical value for exactly 38 $df$. In such a case, one may use the next highest value in the table, which is 40. This is acceptable because the critical values change only slightly. Note that the critical value for 30 $df$ at the .05 level using a two-tailed test is 2.042, and for 40 $df$ it is 2.021. The $t$ ratio is significant not only at the .05 level but also at the .01 level (critical value = 2.704) as well. Therefore we are at least 95% confident (alpha of .05) that the difference in percent body fat between the two groups is real with only a 5% probability that the

**TABLE 11-3** Summary of independent $t$ test

|  | Football Players | Wrestlers |
|---|---|---|
| $M$ % body fat | 13 | 9 |
| $SD$ | 3 | 2 |
| $N$ | 20 | 20 |

$$t = \frac{M_1 - M_2}{\sqrt{\left[\dfrac{(N_1 - 1)S_1^2 + (N_1 - 1)S_2^2}{N_1 + N_2 - 2}\right]\left[\dfrac{N_1 + N_2}{N_1 N_2}\right]}}$$

$$t = \frac{13 - 9}{\sqrt{\dfrac{(19)3^2 + (19)2^2}{20 + 20 - 2}\left[\dfrac{20 + 20}{(20)(20)}\right]}} = \frac{4}{\sqrt{.65}} = 4.96$$

$df = (N_1 + N_2) - 2 = (20 + 20) - 2 = 38$
$t(38) = 4.96, p \leq .05$

difference is due to chance and sampling error. With an alpha level of .01, we are 99% confident that a real difference exists with only a 1% likelihood that the difference is due to chance and sampling error. The null hypothesis is therefore rejected and the alternative hypothesis accepted.

## Omega Squared

Although a high level of confidence exists that the difference between the two groups used in the example is significant, how much of the difference can actually be attributed to the participation in the two sports? This information is just as important as knowing whether or not significance occurs. Remember that with the Pearson $r$, $r^2$ was used to determine the variance common to two variables. Thus $r^2$ was used as a measure of the strength of the correlation. Similarly, a procedure is needed to determine the strength of the treatment or experimental variable. The statistic that does this is known as *omega squared* ($\Omega^2$) (Tolson, 1980). Fortunately, the formula is short and simple:

$$\Omega_2 = \frac{t^2 - 1}{t^2 + N_1 + N_2 - 1}$$

The answer, .36%, means that 36% of the variance or difference in percent body fat between the two groups is due to the effect of the variable tested (i.e., being a wrestler or a football player) and the rest of the difference is caused by other factors. Table 11-4 summarizes the steps in calculating omega squared.

It should be emphasized that two statistics are needed to effectively assess the results of the study: an independent $t$ test to determine if there is a difference in the means and omega squared to measure the size or magnitude of the difference.

Omega squared is infrequently used simply because even researchers often confuse significance with magnitude of the treatment effect. Significance does not infer a large treatment effect. Remember that as sample size increases, smaller $t$ ratios may be found significant. For example, with an $N$ of 122, a $t$ ratio of 1.980 is significant at the .05 level with a two-tailed test. With an $N$ of 12, 2.228 is significant. The difference in mean scores between two groups may not have to be great in order for significance to occur. When testing the effectiveness of new medications, pharmaceutical companies use very large sample sizes in order to boost the probability that significant differences will be found with

**TABLE 11-4**   Summary of omega squared

$$\Omega^2 = \frac{t^2 - 1}{t^2 + N_1 + N_2 - 1} = \frac{4.96^2 - 1}{4.96^2 + 20 + 20 - 1}$$

$$\Omega^2 = \frac{23.6}{65.6} = .36 \times 100 = 36\%$$

other medications. If a medication is found significantly better than another, we have confidence that the difference is probably real. However, the size of the difference should always be addressed. A difference could be real statistically without having a great impact on people's health.

Suppose that a piece of exercise equipment used to build strength is found to be significantly better ($p < .001$) than the standard barbell. Should weight trainers necessarily switch to the new piece of equipment? If the mean difference in strength development is 3% across a number of basic exercises, is the switch justified in order to gain 3% more strength? For serious weight trainers and competitive lifters, the small difference may justify a switch, but the average fitness enthusiast may not think the difference is noteworthy.

## ANALYSIS OF VARIANCE

Analysis of variance (ANOVA) is used to compare more than two mean scores. Several types of ANOVA exist and they are discussed in the remainder of this chapter.

### One-Way ANOVA

The purpose of one-way ANOVA is to compare two or more means on one dependent variable. An example of the use of one-way ANOVA is comparison of the effect of three ball colors on ball-catching skill. Another is comparison of lecture, small-group discussion, and role playing on smoking behavior. Comparing the groups in pairs—that is, group 1 with group 2, group 1 with group 3, and so on—with a number of independent $t$ tests is invalid because it violates an assumption regarding the alpha level. An alpha level of .05 means there is a 5 in 100 probability that a difference could occur due to chance if the groups compared are independent and random. In this case, the groups are not independent because each group is compared more than once with every other group. ANOVA allows making any number of group comparisons without violating the alpha level. We discuss this topic in more detail later.

Students studying statistics usually do quite well comprehending the math as well as concepts until they confront ANOVA. In the authors' opinion much of this is due to the rather lengthy number of steps involved in calculating ANOVA. Each of the steps is actually easy mathematically and could be mastered by junior high school students. However, the number of steps tends to make students so concerned with the accuracy of their math that they lose sight of the big picture and how to readily interpret ANOVA. Computer software is now used to calculate the numerous steps so quickly that spending much time on the mathematics by hand seems fruitless. Therefore many of the computational steps are not presented here.

The results of an ANOVA are often summarized in a table. For an example, see Table 11-5. *SS* refers to sum of squares. In calculating the *F* ratio, the statistic for ANOVA, each subject's score is squared and the sum of the squared values is used in several steps to determine the sum of squares for *treatment variance*, *error variance*, and *total variance*. Sometimes the term *within-group vari-*

**TABLE 11-5**   Summary of one-way ANOVA

| Source of Variance | SS | df | MS | F ratio |
|---|---|---|---|---|
| Treatment or between groups | 100 | 2 | 50 | 12.5* |
| Error or within | 80 | 20 | 4 | |
| Total | 180 | 22 | | |

*$p \leq .01$.

*ance* is used to describe error variance. Then each *SS* is divided by the appropriate number of *df* to calculate the *mean square (MS)* for treatment and error. A mean square is a measure of variance. The *df* are determined as follows:

> Treatment *df* = $k - 1$, where $k$ = the number of groups
> Here $k = 3$, so treatment *df* = 2
> Error *df* = $N - k$, where $N$ = the total number of subjects in the study
> Here $N = 23$ and $k = 3$, so error *df* = $23 - 3 = 20$
> Total *df* = $N - 1$
> Here $N = 23$, so total *df* = $23 - 1 = 22$

The *F* ratio is the answer calculated in analysis of variance. It represents the ratio between variance due to the treatment or experimental variable and the variance due to error, the latter representing chance and sampling error. Thus mathematically the *F* ratio may be expressed as follows:

$$F = \frac{\text{Treatment variance}}{\text{Error variance}}$$

A large *F* ratio indicates that a good portion of the variance is due to the treatment used in a study, whereas chance and sampling error are secondary sources in causing the mean scores to vary. Conversely, if the *F* ratio is less than 1.00, less than half of the variance is due to the treatment. If *F* is 1.00, then the treatment and error have an equal effect in causing scores to vary. For example, an *F* ratio of 5.0 means treatment variance was five times greater than error variance. *F* ratios less than 1.00 are never significant, as they infer that the effect of error exceeded the effect of the treatment in causing mean scores to vary.

The *F* ratio is calculated by dividing treatment *MS* by error *MS*. Even without calculating the *F* ratio, we already know that the treatment *MS* greatly exceeds the error *MS* in the sample problem, which indicates that *F* will be well over 1.00. The larger the *F* ratio, the greater the proportion of total variance due to the treatment and therefore the greater the probability that *F* will be significant.

The sample problem here is a comparison of one, two, and three sets of weight training on strength development. The null hypothesis in a study comparing three group means is stated as follows: $H_0: \mu_1 = \mu_2 = \mu_3$. The alternative hypothesis is $H_A: \mu_1 \neq \mu_2 \neq \mu_3$.

To determine significance, consult Appendix I, Critical Values of $F$ Table E with 2 and 20 *df*, the *df* associated with the treatment and error $MS$, respectively. The table is read by first locating the *df* for the greater $MS$ on the horizontal axis. In our example, the $MS$ for treatment is larger than the $MS$ for error and the associated *df* is 2. Two *df* is located on the horizontal axis. Then the *df* for the smaller $MS$ error, which is 20, is located on the vertical axis. The $F$ ratio for significance at the .05 level is 3.49 and 5.85 for the .01 level. The .05 level is the first value given at each *df*. Consequently, the $F$ ratio 12.50 is significant at the .01 level.

The significant $F$ means that the null hypothesis is rejected and the alternative hypothesis accepted. We are 99% confident that a difference exists among one, two, and three sets in building strength.

## Post Hoc Tests

A question arises, however. Which of the means are significantly different from each other? The significant $F$ only indicates that at least one pair of means is different, not which pair or pairs are different. All three scores could be different or perhaps only one pair of means. A second statistical test is required to identify the differences when $F$ is significant. Several terms are used to describe the second test: *follow-up, multiple comparison, post hoc,* and *a posteriori.* Implicit in each of these is the fact that they are used after an initial test to determine the $F$ ratio. Thus a follow-up test follows the ANOVA; a multiple comparison test compares each group mean with every other group mean; and both post hoc and a posteriori imply a test done "at the end."

Several post hoc tests are available. They perform the same function as a *t* test in comparing each group with every other group, and they give similar but not identical results. These tests vary in their likelihood of producing a significant difference. Liberal tests are more likely than conservative or stringent tests to yield significance. We list several of these tests in order from very liberal to very conservative (Winer, 1962): Duncan Multiple Range, Newman-Keuls, Fisher's Least Significant Difference, Tukey's Honestly Significant Difference (HSD), and Scheffé. Thus use of the Duncan Multiple Range test would more likely produce a significant difference than any of the other multiple comparison tests when mean-by-mean comparisons are made. The Scheffe test would be least likely to yield significance.

Does it make a difference which test is selected? Is it unfair to use the most liberal test? The decision lies with the researcher, but it should be experimentally defensible. For example, if the study dealt with medications for patients with AIDS, a researcher may be wary of proclaiming that one medication is more likely to be of value than others unless he made it as difficult as possible for significance to be detected. In such a case, the Scheffe test would be justified and the researcher could claim that statistical decisions were made to minimize the chance of Type I error occurring (falsely rejecting the null hypothesis).

Most research in the fields of health, physical education, and recreation, as well as most academic disciplines, does not address issues of life and death. If a researcher in HPER chose a Duncan Multiple Range test and significant results were obtained but they would not have been with the conservative Scheffe test, the impact would probably not be great. As a matter of fact, researchers are rarely if ever questioned about the rationale for selecting a particular post hoc test. Most researchers probably select a test that is most likely to support their hypothesis. The actual differences among the tests is small anyway.

## Limitations of the *t* Test as a Post Hoc Test

One may ask why independent *t* tests could not be used to make group-by-group comparisons. The *t* test is appropriate *only* for comparing two means on a single dependent variable. If the group training with one set was compared with the groups using two and three sets, the chance of falsely finding significant differences or making a Type I error is increased. If a statistic is significant at the .05 level, a 5% probability exists that it may not really be significant. One can be only 95% confident when $\alpha = .05$. With two *t* tests used with the same dependent variable, the chance of finding significance by chance alone increases to 10%. If three *t* tests were used, as would be the case here, the probability of Type I error rises to 15%. Obviously, this poses a problem because while more significant findings would tend to occur, the researcher would lose confidence that any one finding is truly significant. The multiple comparison tests avoid this problem because the calculated statistic takes the number of comparisons into account. Thus no sacrifice in confidence of the findings occurs and the chance of making decision errors is not affected.

## Reporting Results

The results of a multiple comparison test are expressed in several ways. If only three mean scores are compared, the results may be explained in a sentence or two, for example, "Three sets was found to be significantly greater than either one or two sets, but no difference was observed between one and two sets." However, as more means are compared, results become more difficult to understand because a large number of comparisons are made. To facilitate communicating the results of a large number of comparisons, the information is often put in tabular form. Table 11-6 demonstrates how this can be done. Imagine that five groups for number of sets were used in a study rather than three: one set, two sets, up to five sets. Group means are arranged according to size from small to large. Lines appear below means that are *not* significantly different. Therefore means not underlined by the same line are significantly different. In the exam

**TABLE 11-6**   Reporting results of multiple comparisons: The underlining method

| 1 set | 2 sets | 3 sets | 4 sets | 5 sets |
|-------|--------|--------|--------|--------|
| 10.2  | 11.8   | 15.1   | 15.9   | 16.4   |

**TABLE 11-7**   Reporting results of multiple comparisons:
The matrix method

|  | 1 | 2 | 3 | 4 | 5 |
|---|---|---|---|---|---|
| *Group* | *10.2* | *11.8* | *15.1* | *15.9* | *16.4* |
| 1 | 10.2 | 1.66 | 3.71[a] | 3.98[a] | 4.11[a] |
| 2 | 11.8 | | 3.30[a] | 3.56[a] | 4.02[a] |
| 3 | 15.1 | | | 1.34 | 1.46 |
| 4 | 15.9 | | | | .89 |
| 5 | 16.4 | | | | |

[a]Significant at $p \leq .05$.

ple, the mean gains for groups 1 and 2 are not significantly different, whereas the scores for groups 3, 4, and 5 are significantly higher than those of both groups 1 and 2. Groups 3, 4, and 5 are not significantly different. This technique is known as the *underlining* method.

A *matrix* is a second means of indicating results from a number of comparisons. A sample is given in Table 11-7. It is a matrix and read the same as a correlation matrix covered earlier. The means are arranged according to magnitude of change. The numbers in the matrix such as 1.66, 3.71, and so on, are the statistics calculated in comparing each group with another. A superscript denotes where significant differences occurred. The significance or *p* level denoted by a superscript is indicated at the bottom of the table.

Most people find reading a table faster and easier than trying to extract the same information from a paragraph. Both types of tables provide the key results in abbreviated form, particularly the table using the underlining method.

### Magnitude of the Treatment Effect

If a *t* test is significant, the only meaning implied deals with the confidence that a difference is likely to be real rather than due to chance, or sampling error. However, no quantitative analysis is made regarding how much of the variance is due to the experimental variable. One means of doing this is by calculating the proportion of the total variance that is explained by treatment variance. This provides an estimate, but a more precise means of determining percent of variance due to the treatment variable is omega squared ($\Omega^2$) (Tolson, 1980). Its formula, a

$$\Omega^2 = \frac{F(k-1)-(k-1)}{F(k-1)+(N-k)+1}$$

variation of the one used for the independent *t* test, is
where:

$F$ = *F* ratio
$k$ = number of groups
$N$ = total number of subjects in all groups

Using the values from the ANOVA summary table (Table 11-7), we find $F = 12.5$, $k = 3$, and $N = 23$. Therefore

$$\Omega^2 = \frac{12.5(2)-2}{12.5(2) + (23-3) + 1} = \frac{23}{46} = .50$$

A value of .50 means that 50% of the variance in mean scores is accounted for by the treatment or independent variable and the remaining 50% of the variance is due to other factors. Dividing total $SS$ by treatment $SS$ ($100/180$) $\times$ 100 we get 55.6%. Here the estimate agrees fairly well with the calculated $\Omega^2$ value. In reading journal articles where $\Omega^2$ is not reported, which is the great majority of cases, the insightful reader can easily calculate or roughly estimate the percent variance due to the treatment if a summary ANOVA table is included.

It should be understood that statistics can be significant without explaining a high percentage of the variance. Too often students and researchers indicate which comparisons are significantly different but then provide no information as the size of the treatment effect. Most of us are (or should be!) just as concerned with the latter as we are the former.

## Randomized Blocks ANOVA

Randomized blocks ANOVA is used to equate groups on the basis of pretest data. The procedure reduces the error mean square, which increases the F ratio and the likelihood of significance. In the strength training programs we used to illustrate the one-way ANOVA a researcher will carry out the same study but use the blocking procedure. Subjects are ranked according to performance on the dependent variable. If more than one dependent variable exists, which normally is the case, the most important variable that theoretically may affect the results of the study is selected. For example, if a researcher wished to study strength development, pretest performance on the dependent variables bench press, curl, and leg press may be used to equalize the groups.

Then *blocking* is done. The procedure is similar to choosing sides before playing a game. If three groups were to be formed, then the three subjects having the best total or sum of the three lifts would compose block 1. They are each randomly assigned to one of the three groups. The next block of three strongest subjects are also each randomly assigned to a group. The blocking and random assignment continue until all subjects have been placed in a group. The process of randomly assigning subjects based on their rank on one or more key dependent variables makes the groups initially as equal as possible.

## Interpretation of Randomized Blocks ANOVA

A summary table for randomized blocks ANOVA is identical to that of the simple one-way ANOVA except that one additional source of variance is accounted for. Table 11-8 illustrates a summary of randomized blocks ANOVA.

The variance due to blocking was more than 10% of the total variance ($16/150 \times 100 = 10.7\%$). Had blocking not been used, the error $SS$ would have been enlarged by 16. This would have resulted in a smaller $F$ ratio because $F$

**TABLE 11-8**  Summary of randomized blocks ANOVA

| Source of Variance | SS | df | MS | F ratio |
|---|---|---|---|---|
| Treatment | 70 | 2 | 35 | 8.75* |
| Blocks | 16 | 8 | | |
| Error | 64 | 16 | 4 | |
| Total | 150 | 26 | | |

*$p \leq .01$ level.

equals treatment variance divided by error variance. With 2 and 16 *df* for the greater and lesser mean square, respectively, *F* is significant at the .01 level. The null hypothesis is rejected and the alternative hypothesis accepted. We can be 99% confident that there is a real difference in mean scores. To identify which means are different, a multiple comparison test would be used.

How much of the variance in the dependent variable can be attributed to the treatment or experimental variable? As a quick estimate, treatment *SS* divided by total *SS* = 70/150 = 46.7%. Therefore, approximately 47% of the variance is due to the experimental variable. This is a practical and easy technique to use when reading journal articles and one doesn't have easy access to a calculator. The computation of omega squared equals 43.7% for these data, illustrating that the estimation method is reasonably accurate.

## Two-Way ANOVA

Two-way ANOVA is used to examine the effect of two independent variables on a dependent variable. This provides a realistic analysis because rarely if ever does one independent variable completely determine a dependent variable. Examples include comparing the effects of two types of feedback and age on dental care (type of feedback and age are the independent variables and dental care is the dependent variable) and comparing two exercise intensities and two durations on swimming performance (exercise intensity and duration are each independent variables and swim performance is the dependent performance).

Although either study could be performed with a one-way ANOVA on each independent variable, the combined or synergistic effects of the two independent variables working together could not be assessed. In many professional situations, we do not limit our choices to a single factor. For example, when a teacher examines textbooks for classroom use, many factors are considered in making a decision: age of the children, reading level, socioeconomic status, psychological maturity. Two-way ANOVA permits the integrated effect of different variables on some type of behavior to be studied. In research this is termed *interaction*.

A two-way ANOVA research design allows at least two questions to be asked: (1) Does each independent variable have a significant effect? (2) Is there an interaction between the independent variables? Therefore, these two-way, or

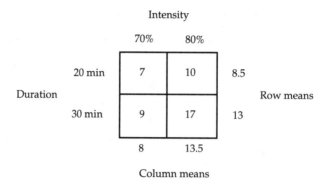

Figure 11-2   Summary of a two-way ANOVA.

two-factor, designs permit a more complete research design and assessment of the effects of two or more experimental variables than do studies examining a single independent variable. Consequently, more findings and conclusions can be drawn.

Suppose a researcher wished to study the effects of exercise intensity and exercise duration on swim performance. The independent variables are intensity of exercise, expressed as a percent of maximum heart rate, and duration of exercise at target heart rate. The dependent variable is swim performance. It is helpful to sketch the design of a *factorial* study because it aids understanding how many *levels* of each independent variable are used, as well as the number of groups needed to carry out a study. See Figure 11-2. There are two levels of each independent variable in this study: 20 and 30 minutes for duration and 70% and 80% for intensity. Each independent variable is also known as a *main effect*. It assesses the effect of one independent variable with the effect of the other independent variable held constant. Thus the study is investigating two main effects and the possible interaction of the main effects on swimming performance. The type of factorial ANOVA used to examine the results of a study with two main effects or independent variables is called a *two-way ANOVA*. If three main effects were studied, a three-way ANOVA would be used and so on.

The sketch indicates the number of groups to be used in this study. Each of the four boxes in the table depicts one group. Therefore two groups will swim for 20 minutes, one at 70% of maximum heart rate and one at 80%; the other two groups will swim for 30 minutes, one at 70% and one at 80%. Because two levels are found for each independent variable, this could be called a *2 × 2 ANOVA* or *design*. It would be a 2 × 3 ANOVA or design if there were three levels of one of the independent variables, for example, if a 40-minute level was added. Three hypotheses will be tested. One will examine the main effect duration ($H_0$: 20 minutes = 30 minutes; $H_A$: 20 minutes ≠ 30 minutes); a second will test the main effect intensity ($H_0$: 70% = 80%; $H_A$: 70% ≠ 80%); and the third will test the interaction between the main effects: $H_0$: $\mu_1 = \mu_2 = \mu_3 = \mu_4$; $H_A$: at least two of the groups are different.

The main effects are tested by comparing the two row means and the two column means. The row means for improvement in swim performance, 8.5 and 13 seconds, represent the averages for the two levels of exercise duration. Thus the mean improvement of 8.5 is the average for both groups exercising for 20 minutes. This mean will be compared to the mean improvement for the two groups exercising for 30 minutes, which was 13 seconds. An *F* ratio is calculated and compared to the critical value for *F* to determine if the *F* ratio for row means is significant. In Table 11-9, the *F* ratio for the rows, representing duration, is 16.0 with 1 and 16 *df*. This ratio is significant both at the .05 and .01 levels with critical values of 4.49 and 8.53, respectively.

Similarly, an *F* ratio is calculated for the main effect intensity. The mean of column 1, averaged across both durations, is 8 seconds. The mean improvement in column 2, averaged across the two groups exercising for 20 and 30 minutes, is 13.5 seconds. The ANOVA thus compares the mean improvements of 8 and 13.5 seconds. The resulting *F* ratio is compared to the critical value to determine if the difference is significant. The *F* ratio of 16.0 with 1 and 16 *df* is significant at .05 as well as .01.

A summary table of the two-way ANOVA (Table 11-9) shows that it is identical to the one-way ANOVA table except that it includes a second main effect and interaction as sources of variance. The table indicates that both independent variables were significant. Because there are only two levels of each variable, a follow-up test is not needed. We know that the larger row or column mean is significantly greater than the smaller one. So we reject the null hypothesis for intensity and accept that training at 80% maximum heart rate is superior to training at 70%. We also reject the null hypothesis for duration and accept the alternative hypothesis that 30 minutes is superior to 20 minutes of training.

The table also indicates that interaction between the two main effects was significant. Interaction means that some combination of the two variables elicited a particularly strong effect on performance. The improvement in swim performance for the two groups training at 70% is fairly similar, 7 and 9 seconds. However, a greater disparity in results occurred in the groups training at 80%, 10 and 17 seconds. A multiple comparison test is used to compare either the four group means or the four row/column means. Let us assume that a Newman-

**TABLE 11-9** Summary of two-way ANOVA

| Source of Variance | SS | df | MS | F ratio |
|---|---|---|---|---|
| Intensity (column) | 6000 | 1 | 6000 | 16.00** |
| Duration (row) | 6000 | 1 | 6000 | 16.00** |
| Interaction | 2000 | 1 | 2000 | 5.33* |
| Error | 6000 | 16 | 375 | |
| Total | 20,000 | 19 | | |

*$p \leq .05$.
**$p \leq .01$.

Keuls multiple comparison test is used (p = .05). The results are depicted here using the underlining method.

| 20 min at 70% | 30 min at 70% | 20 min at 80% | 30 min at 80% |
|---|---|---|---|
| 7 | 9 | 10 | 17 |

The table indicates that the group improving by 17 seconds gained significantly more than the groups improving by 7, 9, and 10 seconds, and that the differences of 7, 9, and 10 were not significant. Thus 30 minutes of training at 80% maximum heart rate is an especially effective combination of the variables studied. The existence of a special combination of variables illustrates interaction.

When significant interaction occurs, plotting the results greatly aids interpretation, and a figure normally accompanies the text. Figure 11-3 illustrates significant interaction of the results discussed. When interaction is significant, the lines are not parallel. Significant departure from parallelism means that a greater effect on the dependent variable occurs with a particular combination of variables. If the lines are fairly parallel, no special or disproportionate effect occurs under any of the combinations examined in the study. (See Figure 11-3)

Interpretation of the results of factorial studies should not be limited to the main effects because an erroneous conclusion might be drawn. In some studies neither main effect is significant but interaction is. One should not conclude that the independent variables do not affect the dependent variable. What the results mean is that alone they may not, but together they do. In reality, few things in life depend solely on one factor. Rather, combinations of variables determine the outcome. Consequently, it is important to analyze the impact of interaction.

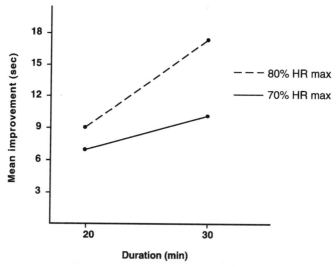

Figure 11.3   Interaction of exercise intensity and duration.

## Other Types of Factorial ANOVA

If the effect of three independent variables was studied, the result would be a *three-way ANOVA*. For example, if two curricula (first independent variable) in health education were compared in three grade levels (second independent variable) in low and middle socioeconomic levels (third independent variable), the result would be a three-way ANOVA or more specifically, a $2 \times 3 \times 2$ factorial ANOVA . Such designs require a large number of subjects and they are complex to interpret. Studies examining the effect of more than three independent variables are not often used in HPER.

## ANOVA with Repeated Measures

A *repeated measures design* means that the same subjects are tested several times for a measure of an independent variable. Use of the same subjects reduces the problem of obtaining an adequate number of subjects and for this reason alone is a widely used design in HPER. The procedure also reduces the component of error variance due to differences among individual subjects, thereby increasing the likelihood of detecting significant differences. ANOVA is also frequently used to assess changes in a variable over time such as changes in cholesterol level with aging or changes in locomotor skills at different levels of maturity. Another example is measuring reaction time in the same subjects at three levels of arousal. Repeated measures designs may use any number of independent variables and so may use one-way ANOVA, two-way ANOVA, and so on. Table 11-10 is an example of a summary of a repeated measures ANOVA.

Subjects in repeated measures studies should be exposed to each independent variable on a random basis to prevent an order effect. An *order effect* is a change in behavior due to the sequence of activities in a study. For example, if all subjects were observed doing the activities listed for a social contact study in the order given, subjects may become better acquainted and more familiar with each other as they proceed from the first to the last activity. This could increase the number of social contacts made. If the activities are randomly sequenced for each subject, the effects of order are eliminated. Other examples of order effects include fatigue, boredom, or discomfort on one test affecting performance on ensuing tests.

**TABLE 11-10**   Summary of one-way ANOVA—repeated measures

| Source of Variance | SS | df | MS | F ratio |
|---|---|---|---|---|
| Between subjects | 760 | 4 | 190 | 5.9* |
| Within subjects | 480 | 15 | 32 | |
|    Treatments | 360 | 3 | 120 | 12.0* |
|    Error | 120 | 12 | 10 | |
| Total | 1720 | 19 | | |

*$p \leq .05$.

## ANALYSIS OF COVARIANCE

Analysis of covariance (ANCOVA) is a special version of ANOVA that statistically adjusts the means of groups when they may be different at the onset of a study. This occurs fairly frequently in research. Adjustment for differences makes comparisons more valid because the degree of change in studies is often related to the initial score. For example, if the mean sprint speed of professional football players is compared to the mean of college students who are not athletes enrolled in a track and field class, a sizable difference would be expected. Suppose both groups were to train in order to improve sprint speed. The professional athletes would probably show little or no progress, whereas the college students would likely demonstrate a significant training effect. ANCOVA, by adjusting initial sprint times, would provide a better comparison than a *t* test or one-way ANOVA. The variable adjusted is termed the *covariate*. The pretest score for the dependent variable often serves as the covariate. Table 11-11 is an example of a summary of ANCOVA.

There are times when random assignment may be difficult and therefore initial group scores may be different. For example, a health researcher may wish to have different classes remain intact as each class receives some treatment in a study. In comparing teaching techniques, it is easier for each class to be exposed to a specific treatment rather than randomly to assign each student to a class receiving a treatment. The latter would disrupt a school schedule and be difficult to carry out. Research in the field or clinical setting frequently precludes random assignment, which makes ANCOVA the preferred statistical tool. Research comparing the response to training of males and females often is corrected for basic gender differences such as percent body fat, weight, and height using ANCOVA.

Sometimes differences in initial mean scores occur because of subjects dropping out of a study. They may have been initially equal, but at the end of a study are not. ANCOVA could be used to equalize the groups by adjusting the pretest score (covariate).

ANCOVA is also used to eliminate the effect of an extraneous variable on a dependent variable. For example, in a study assessing the effect of diet on cholesterol level in men and women, women's values may vary because of the difference in body composition (i.e., greater percent fat and smaller percent muscle). The differences in body composition can be controlled using ANCOVA,

**TABLE 11-11**   Summary of ANCOVA

| Source of Variance | Adj. SS | df | Adj. MS | F ratio |
|---|---|---|---|---|
| Between | 1289.2 | 2 | 644.6 | 93.4* |
| Within | 76.4 | 11 | 6.945 | |
| Total | 1365.6 | 13 | | |

*$p \le .001$.

thus eliminating an extraneous variable. Researchers sometimes will perform several ANCOVAs using different extraneous variables as covariates. This allows determining the effect of different extraneous variables when making comparisons. For example, in the diet-cholesterol study, if none of the $F$ ratios from ANCOVAs using different covariates is significant, the researcher has achieved a better understanding of the phenomenon. Had only an independent $t$ test been used, the researcher could only wonder if differences in body composition or some other extraneous variable made a difference.

## SUMMARY

Much research involves comparison of mean scores. When only two means are compared, either a correlated $t$ test (pre-post differences within one group) or independent $t$ test (two different groups) is used. ANOVA is used to compare more than two mean scores. A one-way ANOVA examines the effect of one independent variable, and a two-way ANOVA determines the effect of two independent variables. Several levels of an independent variable are often compared in studies, so that a two-way ANOVA might also be termed a $2 \times 3$ ANOVA if two and three levels, respectively, of each independent variable exist. The combined effect or interaction of two independent variables can be assessed with factorial ANOVAs. If mean scores of a dependent variable are different at the onset of a study, ANCOVA may be used to adjust the means statistically, thereby providing a more valid comparison of a treatment effect.

Criteria called assumptions must be satisfied in selecting an appropriate statistical test. They are based primarily on type of data and the normality and variance of data. Although nearly all studies report whether or not significant results occurred, often information regarding the magnitude of the results is omitted. The size of the treatment effect is of vital concern in any study and should be quantified in some way such as use of omega squared.

## STATISTICS EXERCISES

1. A health researcher examined the influence of a stress management program on systolic blood pressure.

   Initial scores (mm Hg): 120, 124, 132, 148, 160, 144, 124, 136

   Postscores (mm Hg): 120, 118, 118, 140, 124, 140, 124, 126

   a. Calculate a two-tailed correlated $t$ test.

   b. Did the program significantly ($p < .05$) reduce systolic blood pressure?

2. A recreation researcher compared the expenditures for families over one year for outdoor recreational activities in several Sunbelt states with several states bordering Canada.

   Sunbelt states ($): 300, 450, 600, 400, 200, 350

   States bordering Canada ($): 200, 250, 400, 300, 350, 350

   a. Calculate an independent $t$ test.

   b. Is the difference significant at the .05 level?

3. A fitness director for a company compared the sit and reach flexibility of men and women in an adult fitness program.

     Flexibility for women (cm): 7, 3, 4, 9, 2, 8, 10, 5, 12, 13

     Flexibility for men (cm): 2, 3, 9, 4, 1, 3, 6, 2

     a. Calculate an independent *t* test to determine if a significant difference at the .05 level existed.

     b. What conclusion can be made?

     c. Calculate omega squared and interpret its meaning in this study.

4. A researcher found that entry-level salaries of professionals in recreation were significantly higher than that of police officers. The independent *t* test was 3.6 and the sample sizes were 200 and 100, respectively.

     a. Calculate omega squared.

     b. Interpret what this means.

5. You are interested in comparing percent body fat for a select group of Junior Olympic female volleyball players and swimmers. Calculate an independent *t* test to determine if a significant difference exists at the .05 level.

     Percent fat for volleyball: 11, 15, 17, 16, 13, 14, 12, 9, 10

     Percent fat for swimmers: 21, 19, 18, 22, 17, 16, 20

6. Three groups of female athletes are compared by $VO_2$ max (ml/kg/min): track $n = 4$, $M = 61.0$; basketball $n = 5$, $M = 45.0$; volleyball $n = 7$, $M = 46.0$.

| Source | SS | df | MS | F |
|--------|-----|-----|-----|-----|
| Between | 725 | | | |
| Within | 150 | | | |
| Total | | | | |

     a. Complete the rest of the ANOVA summary table.

     b. Is the *F* ratio significant at the .05 level?

     c. If it is significant, what does this mean?

     d. If it is significant, what is the next step in the data analysis?

     e. Calculate omega squared and interpret the value.

7. The effect of different levels of estrogen replacement therapy on bone mineral content is compared in three groups of subjects. Each group consists of 50 subjects. The following ANOVA table appears in a journal article summarizing the results.

| Source | SS | df | MS | F |
|--------|-----|-----|-----|-----|
| Between | 100 | 2 | 50 | 12.5 |
| Within | 80 | 20 | 4 | |
| Total | 180 | 22 | | |

     a. Is the *F* ratio significant at the .05 level?

     b. Interpret the finding.

     c. If *F* is significant, what is the next step in the data analysis?

     d. Calculate omega squared and interpret the value.

# CHAPTER 12

# SELECTED NONPARAMETRIC STATISTICS

AFTER READING THIS CHAPTER, YOU SHOULD BE ABLE TO

- Calculate, interpret, and know when to use a one-way chi-square.
- Calculate, interpret, and know when to use a two-way chi-square.
- Calculate, interpret, and know when to use a Spearman $r$.
- Identify research situations that require the use of a nonparametric test and know which one to use.

So far we have discussed statistics used for data that are interval and ratio level. For most parametric statistics there are nonparametric alternatives that must be used when data are only nominal or ordinal level and when the assumptions underlying the parametric tests cannot be met. Sometimes these tests are also preferred when analyzing small sets of data. Overall, nonparametric are not as powerful as parametric tests. Power in this case is the ability to reject a null hypothesis when it should be, that is, when it is false. A wide variety of nonparametric statistics are available. Here we discuss a few of the more commonly used ones.

## CHI-SQUARE

The chi-square analysis ($\chi^2$, pronounced "ki," as in "kind") is a commonly used nonparametric test. It is utilized for data that are nominal level frequency counts. Frequency counts could be the number of boys and girls on a playground, the number of votes cast in an election, the number of Hondas in a parking lot, and so on. With a chi-square analysis, observations are made and counted in only one category. In this way the observations are said to be independent of one another. The premise behind the analysis is a comparison of what is expected to occur (theoretical probability) versus what is observed (empirical probability). We have discussed theoretical probability already, but what is empirical probability?

*Empirical probabilities* are derived from observations of certain events. Based on the frequency of occurrence, projections of future events can be made. Here is an example: Let's say that a recreation center director has observed and counted the number of men and women who have entered the facility in one week. She found that 200 men and 100 women have entered the building. Based on these "empirical" observations, what would be the probability that the next person who entered the center would be a man? The empirical probability would be $p = 200/300 = .67$, as 200 of the 300 participants in the past observations were men. The empirical probability for a woman entering the facility would then be $p = 100/300 = .33$. Of course, the theoretical probability for either a man or a woman entering would be $p = 1/2 = .50$. The chi-square analysis, then, is a test to determine if there is significant deviation from what is expected to occur in a theoretical fashion. There are several applications for this statistic. Let's look at some.

## ONE-WAY CHI-SQUARE

The *one-way chi-square* is used to determine if there is a significant difference between the frequency of observed (empirical) and expected (theoretical) observations in two or more categories. The equation for a one-way chi-square is

$$\chi^2 = \Sigma \frac{(O - E)^2}{E}$$

**TABLE 12-1** Chi-square analysis for bungee-cord jumping

| Category | Observed (O) | Expected (E) | O – E | (O – E)² | (O – E)²/E |
|---|---|---|---|---|---|
| Yes | 20 | 50 | –30 | 900 | 18.0 |
| No | 80 | 50 | 30 | 900 | 18.0 |
| Total | 100 | 100 | | | $\chi^2 = 36.0$ |

where $O$ is the observed frequency and $E$ is the expected frequency of a given category.

Suppose that a recreator polled 100 people to determine if they would partake in the high-risk leisure activity of bungee-cord jumping. Because of the recent popularity of this activity, he feels that many more people would want to try it than not. The categories in this case would be the "yes" and the "no" responses. The expected or theoretical frequencies would be 50 "yes" and 50 "no" answers. The recreator determined that there were actually 20 "yes" and 80 "no" observations. The basic question now becomes: Is a 20/80 observed frequency significantly different than a 50/50 expected frequency? To answer this question, a one-way chi-square analysis is performed. A summary of the analysis appears in Table 12-1.

### Interpretation of Chi-Square

In any chi-square analysis the totals for the observed and expected frequencies must equal each other. Now, with the $\chi^2$ value of 36.0, a hypothesis test is performed. The steps in this test are summarized in Table 12-2. The null hypothesis for a chi-square analysis is stated as $H_0$: $O = E$, which means that there is no difference in the observed and expected frequencies and that any observed difference would be attributed to sampling error. Conversely, the alternative hypothesis is $H_A$: $O \neq E$, which is interpreted as there is a significant difference between the observed and expected frequencies. Therefore sampling error would rarely produce a statistic that size, so something other than sampling error probably caused it. (Sounds familiar, doesn't it?)

The critical chi-square is referenced from Appendix I, Table A under the appropriate alpha level and degrees of freedom. Note that the degrees of freedom for a one-way chi-square is $r - 1$, where $r$ is the number of categories. The chi-square sampling distribution is one-tailed, because it contains only positive values, just like the $F$ distribution. For this example there is one degree of freedom (2 categories – 1 = 1), and at the .05 level the critical chi-square is 3.84. The calculated chi-square of 36.0 is greater than 3.84. Therefore we conclude that there is a significant difference between what was observed and what was expected. So the recreator's hypothesis of more people wanting to try bungee-cord jumping is not supported.

Another example might be if a university recreation director wanted to determine the composition of users of a campus exercise facility. She has heard reports that there may be a disproportionate number of freshmen and seniors using the complex, but doesn't believe that this is true. Data on users were col-

**TABLE 12-2**   Summary of a hypothesis test for bungee-cord jumping

1. State the null and alternative hypotheses.
   $H_0: O = E$
   $H_A: O \neq E$
2. Set the significance (alpha) level.
   .05
3. Determine the appropriate statistic.
   chi square
4. Determine the critical statistic value.
   $\chi^2 = 3.84$
5. Place the critical values on a curve and determine the areas of "do not reject" and "reject."

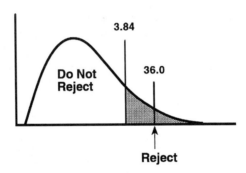

6. Calculate the statistic and place it on the curve.
   $\chi^2 = 36.0$
7. Do not reject or reject the null hypothesis.
   Reject the null
8. Draw a research conclusion.
   There is a significant difference ($p \leq .05$) between what was observed and what was expected.
   Therefore, more people than expected did not want to try bungee-cord jumping.

lected for a week with the following results for 400 participants in four categories. A summary of the analysis appears in Table 12-3.

The degrees of freedom would be $4 - 1 = 3$, and the critical value at the .05 level would be 7.82. Because the calculated chi-square of 7.50 is less than the critical value of 7.82, the null hypothesis is accepted, and it is concluded that there is no significant difference between what was observed and what was expected. Therefore the recreation director's hypothesis is upheld: Participation numbers are similar for all four categories.

Further interpretation of the chi-square analysis is possible by examining the summary and determining which category or categories make the greatest or least contribution to the total chi-square. In this example, the greatest contribution to the chi-square was the seniors' observed frequency departure from what was expected, $4.0/7.50 = .533$, or 53.3%, of the total chi square.

**TABLE 12-3** Chi-square analysis for recreation center users

| Category | Observed (O) | Expected (E) | O – E | (O – E)² | (O – E)²/E |
|----------|--------------|--------------|-------|----------|------------|
| Freshmen | 105 | 100 | 5 | 25 | 0.25 |
| Sophomores | 90 | 100 | 10 | 100 | 1.00 |
| Juniors | 85 | 100 | 15 | 225 | 2.25 |
| Seniors | 120 | 100 | 20 | 400 | 4.00 |
| Total | 400 | 400 | | | $\chi^2 = 7.50$ |

## Goodness of Fit Application

Another application of the one-way chi-square is to determine the goodness of fit of a set of data. *Goodness of fit* is actually a comparison of an observed set of data with expected values derived from some preexisting group of observations. Let's look at an example. A health educator reads a government report that shows typical cholesterol levels of adults in the United States. The document indicates that 30% of the population has low readings, 40% average, and 30% high values. A large-scale cholesterol screening was recently done in his community and he wants to know how well his town's values compare with the government report. He feels that many people in his town have healthy lifestyles and that they should have significantly better readings than the population at large. Cholesterol values for 500 people were used in the analysis and placed into three categories. Table 12-4 contains a summary.

The degrees of freedom would be 3 – 1 = 2, and the critical value at the .01 level would be 9.21. Because the calculated chi-square of 57.3 is greater than the critical value of 9.21, the null hypothesis would be rejected, and the researcher would conclude that there is a significant difference between what was observed and what was expected. Therefore the observed data from the health educator's community differ significantly from what was expected from the government report. It may be further concluded that there was not a good fit between the government's and researcher's data sets. Also, his hypothesis that the town would fare better is supported. Further inspection of the summary table shows that the largest difference from what was expected was 75 fewer, high readings (part of $\chi^2 = 37.5$).

## TWO-WAY CHI-SQUARE

The *two-way chi-square* is used to determine if there is a significant difference between the frequency of observed and expected observations in two or more categories with two or more levels. This arrangement is similar to the two-way

**TABLE 12-4** Chi-square analysis of cholesterol levels

| Category | Observed (O) | Expected (E) | O – E | (O – E)² | (O – E)²/E |
|----------|--------------|--------------|-------|----------|------------|
| Low (30%) | 200 | 150 | 50 | 2500 | 16.7 |
| Average (40%) | 225 | 200 | 25 | 625 | 3.1 |
| High (30%) | 75 | 150 | –75 | 5625 | 37.5 |
| Total | 500 | 500 | | | $\chi^2 = 57.3$ |

factorial ANOVA. The simplest version of a two-way chi-square employs a $2 \times 2$ table. Let's look at an application. A famous college football coach, who is also trained in research, feels that his team plays better on grass fields than they do on Astroturf. He is about to approach the booster club to ask for money to put a new surface in the stadium and wants some objective evidence to support his suspicions. (He also wants to win more games, keeping the boosters happy and thus keeping his job!) So he performs a two-way chi-square analysis on the won/lost frequencies of playing on natural and artificial surfaces for the previous 80 football games.

The two categories and levels are performance (won/lost) and surface type (artificial/natural). The first step in the analysis is to place the observed frequencies of each type of event in a *contingency table* and determine the expected values. As always, the expected and observed frequencies must equal each other. Therefore the marginal sums of the columns and rows must always equal the total number of frequencies. The $2 \times 2$ table appears in Table 12-5.

The expected values (in parentheses) in the table are easily determined from the marginal frequency sums for each column and row. The expected frequency for each cell is obtained by multiplying the row total by the column total and dividing by the total $N$. The expected values for this problem would be:

$$\text{Natural/won} = (60 \times 45)/80 = 33.75$$
$$\text{Natural/loss} = (20 \times 45)/80 = 11.25$$
$$\text{Artificial/won} = (60 \times 35)/80 = 26.25$$
$$\text{Artificial/loss} = (20 \times 35)/80 = 8.75$$

Once the expected frequencies are determined, we go about the business of calculating a two-way chi-square the same as we do a one-way. The summary appears in Table 12-6.

### Interpreting the Two-Way Chi-Square

In a hypothesis test, for a two-way chi-square the degrees of freedom are calculated as $(r - 1)(c - 1)$, where $r$ = the number of rows and $c$ = the number of columns in the contingency table. In this problem there are two rows and two columns, so the degrees of freedom are $(2 - 1)(2 - 1) = 1$. The critical value of chi-square at the .01 level is 6.64, which the calculated value of 7.47 exceeds. Therefore the observed performance/surface frequencies differ significantly

**TABLE 12-5**    $2 \times 2$ table for two-way chi-square analysis

| | | TYPE OF SURFACE | | | | |
| --- | --- | --- | --- | --- | --- | --- |
| | | Natural | | Artificial | | Marginal Total |
| | | O | E | O | E | |
| Performance | Won | 39 | (33.75) | 21 | (26.25) | 60 |
| | Lost | 6 | (11.25) | 14 | (8.75) | 20 |
| Marginal total | | 45 | | 35 | | 80 |

**TABLE 12-6**  Two-way chi-square analysis of football performance

| Category | Observed (O) | Expected (E) | (O − E)²/E |
|---|---|---|---|
| Natural/won | 39 | 33.75 | 0.82 |
| Natural/loss | 6 | 11.25 | 2.45 |
| Artificial/won | 21 | 26.25 | 1.05 |
| Artificial/loss | 14 | 8.75 | 3.15 |
| Total | 80 | 80 | $\chi^2 = 7.47$ |

from what was expected. The coach's hypothesis that the football team performs better on natural turf is supported. Further examination of the summary indicates that the greatest contribution to the total chi-square comes from more losses on artificial turf than expected (14 vs. 8.75 losses, part of total $\chi^2 = 3.15$). So, hopefully, now he can convince the boosters to put natural turf in the stadium!

### Other Two-Way Chi-Square Applications

The $2 \times 2$ is the most basic type of two-way chi-square, but it may be used for more than two levels of two categories. One could have a two-way chi-square such as $2 \times 3$, $3 \times 5$, $4 \times 4$, and so on. Here is an example of a $2 \times 3$ analysis.

An exercise physiologist is interested in determining the aerobic fitness habits of former collegiate athletes to see if there is a difference in adherence frequencies. Her hypothesis is that cross-country runners would be more compliant than the other athletes. She surveyed 150 former football, cross-country, and tennis athletes and determined if they conformed with the minimal recommendations for aerobic fitness as established by the American College of Sports Medicine (ACSM). Table 12-7 summarizes the observed and expected frequencies; the analysis is summarized in Table 12-8.

Because there are two rows and three columns, the degrees of freedom would be $(2 - 1)(3 - 1) = 2$, with the critical chi-square value at the .01 level being 9.21. The calculated chi-square of 43.01 exceeds the critical value of 9.21, so the null hypothesis is rejected. Therefore the observed ACSM standard/sport type frequencies differ significantly from what was expected. The research hypothesis that the cross-country runners would be more compliant than the others is upheld. Inspection of the summary indicates that the greatest discrepancies were in

**TABLE 12-7**  $2 \times 3$ table for two-way chi-square analysis

| | | SPORT | | | | | | Marginal Total |
|---|---|---|---|---|---|---|---|---|
| | | Football | | Cross-Country | | Tennis | | |
| | | O | E | O | E | O | E | |
| ACSM standard | Yes | 25 | (32) | 45 | (26.7) | 10 | (21.3) | 80 |
| | No | 35 | (28) | 5 | (23.3) | 30 | (18.7) | 70 |
| Marginal total | | 60 | | 50 | | 40 | | 150 |

**TABLE 12-8**    Two-way chi-square for exercise compliance

| Category | Observed (O) | Expcted (E) | $(O-E)^2/E$ |
|---|---|---|---|
| Football/yes | 25 | 32 | 1.53 |
| Football/no | 35 | 28 | 1.75 |
| Cross-country/yes | 45 | 26.7 | 12.54 |
| Cross-country/no | 5 | 23.3 | 14.37 |
| Tennis/yes | 10 | 21.3 | 5.99 |
| Tennis/no | 30 | 18.7 | 6.83 |
| Total | 150 | 150 | $\chi^2$=43.01 |

the frequencies of the cross-country runners, followed by the tennis players, whereas the football players where fairly close to what was expected.

## RESTRICTIONS AND ASSUMPTIONS FOR CHI-SQUARE

Certain conditions must be met in order to have a valid chi-square analysis. The primary assumptions and restrictions for its use include the following:

1. Data need to be nominal level frequency counts.
2. Observations need to be independent of one another.
3. Expected and observed frequencies need to equal each other.
4. $N$ size needs to be adequate. A one-way chi-square with only two categories must have expected frequencies of at least five. When there are more than two categories for one-way or two-way tables larger than the 2 × 2, no more than 20% of the categories or cells may have expected frequencies less than five or none of the categories may be less than 1. Also, a two-way chi-square using a 2 × 2 table cannot be used for $N$ less than 20.

## SPEARMAN *r*

The *Spearman r* (sometimes referred to as "rho") is the nonparametric version of the Pearson *r*. It is used when data are ordinal level or for problems with small data sets ($N < 30$). Parametric data may be used in this analysis if the observations are first converted to ranks. The equation for the Spearman *r* is

$$\text{Spearman } r = 1 - \frac{6(\Sigma D^2)}{N(N^2-1)}$$

where $\Sigma D^2$ is the sum of the squared differences in rank and $N$ is the number of pairs of observations. Let's look at an example.

A physical educator is interested in examining the relationship between the final season United Press International (UPI) ranking of NCAA Division I football teams and team scores of anaerobic power. Table 12-9 summarizes the Spearman *r* analysis. Ranks are assigned by giving the highest score a rank of 1, the next highest a rank of 2, and so on. Note that teams *E* and *H* have the same anaerobic power score and therefore share the average rank of the tied positions.

**Table 12-9** Relationship between team anaerobic power and UPI ranking

| Team | Power (kgm/sec) | Power Rank | UPI Rank | D | $D^2$ |
|------|-----------------|------------|----------|-----|-------|
| A | 220 | 1 | 1 | 0 | 0 |
| B | 195 | 4 | 2 | 2 | 4 |
| C | 210 | 2 | 3 | 1 | 1 |
| D | 200 | 3 | 4 | 1 | 1 |
| E | 185 | 6.5 | 5 | 1.5 | 2.25 |
| F | 182 | 8 | 6 | 2 | 4 |
| G | 190 | 5 | 7 | 2 | 4 |
| H | 185 | 6.5 | 8 | 1.5 | 2.25 |
| I | 180 | 9 | 9 | 0 | 0 |
| J | 175 | 10 | 10 | 0 | 0 |

$$\Sigma D^2 = 18.5$$

$$\text{Spearman } r = 1 - \frac{6(18.5)}{10(100-1)} = 1 - \frac{111}{990} = 1 - .112 = .89$$

These scores were competing for the ranks of 6 and 7, so the average rank would be $(6 + 7)/2 = 6.5$. The ranks of 6 and 7 are now "used up," so the next highest score receives the rank of 8. Because the UPI ratings are already in rank form, no conversion is necessary. The difference between the ranks is obtained and then squared and summed. As you can see, the Spearman $r$ is a quick and easy statistic to calculate.

### Interpreting the Spearman $r$

The Spearman $r$ is interpreted exactly the same way that the Pearson $r$ is. Therefore a Spearman $r = .89$ between the final ranking and anaerobic power suggests the higher the team anaerobic power, the higher the final ranking. In addition, a hypothesis test for $r = 0$ or $r \neq 0$ may be performed. There is a sampling distribution for Spearman $r$ values that may be seen in Appendix I, Table B, where $N$ is the number of pairs of observations. For this example the critical value of $r$ at .05 and .01 would be $r = .648$ and $r = .818$, respectively. Because the calculated $r = .89$ exceeds both of these critical values, it is concluded that $r \neq 0$ and that in this sample there is a relationship between final ranking and team anaerobic power.

One final word on the Spearman $r$: It can't be substituted for the Pearson $r$ in computations of the standard error of estimate or a regression equation. Also, if there are no tied ranks the value obtained with the Spearman $r$ will be almost identical to the Pearson $r$. However, if there are several tied ranks, the values will only approximate each other.

## SOME OTHER NONPARAMETRIC TESTS

The following are brief descriptions of some nonparametric tests that are the alternatives of the parametric *t* tests and ANOVAs. We provide no equations or sample problems for these statistics. The interested student may refer to Bartz (1988) or other statistics texts for more detail.

### Mann-Whitney U

The *Mann-Whitney U* is the nonparametric version of the independent *t* test. In order to use this statistic, data need to be ordinal level. Like the independent *t*, this statistic determines if two independent groups have been sampled from the same population. The basis behind the statistic is a comparison of the number of scores from each distribution that are larger than the other. If more scores are larger in one group than what would be expected due to sampling error, it would be concluded that the groups were not drawn from the same population and are significantly different from one another.

### Wilcoxon Matched Pairs

The *Wilcoxon matched pairs* is the nonparametric alternative to the correlated *t* and also requires that data be ordinal level. In this analysis the amount and sign of the difference between paired observations are determined. The size of the difference is then given a rank. The premise behind the statistic is there should be about the same number of small and large differences that are positive and negative values. This would be determined by taking the sum of the ranks of the positive and negative differences and comparing them to one another. If there is too great a disparity in these sums that could be attributed to sampling error, a significant difference exists between the paired observations.

### Kruskal-Wallis ANOVA

The *Kruskal-Wallis ANOVA* is used for ordinal data and is the nonparametric equivalent to the one-way ANOVA. It would be the statistic of choice when comparisons of more than two independent groups need to be made. Essentially all of the observations in the analysis are given a rank, then the sum of the ranks for each group is determined. If there is no significant difference among the groups, the sum of the ranks for each group should be similar to one another. If the difference in the sums are greater than what would be attributed to sampling error, it is concluded that they were drawn from separate populations and are significantly different.

### Friedman's ANOVA

*Friedman's ANOVA* is similar in theory to the Kruskal-Wallis test. It is used when more than two repeated measurements have been made on the same subjects. Therefore Friedman's ANOVA is the nonparametric version of the one-way ANOVA for repeated measures.

**TABLE 12-10**   Selected parametric and nonparametric tests

| Purpose | Parametric | Nonparametric |
|---|---|---|
| Compare the expected vs. observed frequency counts | None | Chi-square |
| Compare two independent groups | Independent *t* | Mann-Whitney *U* |
| Compare two related groups | Correlated *t* | Wilcoxon matched pairs |
| Compare more than two independent groups | One-way ANOVA | Kruskal-Wallis ANOVA |
| Compare more than two related groups | One-way ANOVA repeated measures | Friedman's ANOVA |
| Relationship between two variables | Pearson *r* | Spearman *r* |

## SUMMARY

In this chapter we have examined a variety of nonparametric statistics that must be used when data are nominal or ordinal level and when the assumptions for parametric analyses can't be met. Overall, nonparametric tests are not as powerful as their parametric counterparts. In addition to the chi-square analysis for nominal frequency data, there are nonparametric versions of correlation coefficients (Spearman *r*), *t* tests (Mann-Whitney *U* and Wilcoxon), and ANOVAs (Kruskal-Wallis and Friedman). A summary of these statistics appears in Table 12-10.

## STATISTICS EXERCISES

1. A physical educator is interested in comparing exercise habits, using standards for minimal activity of former varsity athletes (softball players, cross-country runners, and golfers). The following table summarizes the findings:

   | Minimal Standard | Softball | Cross-country | Golf |
   |---|---|---|---|
   | Yes | 20 | 45 | 10 |
   | No | 30 | 5 | 40 |

   Perform a chi-square analysis and provide a practical conclusion.

2. A recreator studied a group of men and women to determine their approval/disapproval of contact sports. The following table summarizes the results of the survey:

   | Gender | Approve | Disapprove |
   |---|---|---|
   | Men | 50 | 10 |
   | Women | 22 | 38 |

   Perform a chi-square analysis and determine if men and women differ on their approval of contact sports. Provide a practical conclusion.

3. An athletic trainer is interested in determining if there is a relationship between the type of playing surface and injury status. The following table summarizes the results of the research:

| Surface | Injured | Not Injured |
|---------|---------|-------------|
| Artificial | 41 | 59 |
| Natural | 27 | 73 |

Perform a chi-square analysis and determine if any relationship exists. Provide a practical conclusion.

4. The following data represent team ranking at the beginning and end of the season. Calculate a Spearman $r$, perform a hypothesis test, and provide a conclusion.

| Team | Beginning Rank | End Rank |
|------|----------------|----------|
| A | 5 | 8 |
| B | 1 | 2 |
| C | 2 | 1 |
| D | 4 | 3 |
| E | 6 | 5 |
| F | 7 | 7 |
| G | 3 | 4 |
| H | 8 | 6 |

5. The following data represent the finish time in a 10-km road race and maximal oxygen uptake ($VO_2$ max) scores for a group of runners. Calculate a Spearman $r$, perform a hypothesis test, and provide a conclusion.

| Runner | Time (min) | $VO_2$ max (ml/kg/min) |
|--------|------------|------------------------|
| A | 39 | 62 |
| B | 44 | 52 |
| C | 31 | 68 |
| D | 32 | 68 |
| E | 40 | 58 |
| F | 43 | 50 |
| G | 41 | 60 |

CHAPTER 13

# MEASUREMENT AND DATA COLLECTION CONCEPTS

KEY CONCEPTS

Validity
Logical validity: face and
  content
Statistical validity:
  criterion-based,
  concurrent, predictive,
  construct

Reliability: stability,
  equivalence,
  internal
  consistency
Objectivity
Measurement error

AFTER READING THIS CHAPTER, YOU SHOULD BE ABLE TO

- Describe the concepts of validity, reliability, and objectivity.
- Differentiate among the different categories and types of validity and reliability.
- Give examples and uses of various types of validity and reliability.
- Describe the concept of measurement error and explain how it may be minimized.
- Discuss how validity and reliability coefficients are interpreted.

$A$ researcher must carefully and logically consider the blueprint or design of a study so that it will yield meaningful and accurate results. However, even the most carefully planned study may have faulty results if the investigator doesn't consider the choice of instruments used to collect the experimental information. Usually there are many instruments or tests that a researcher may select that measure the same thing. Two important qualities of the research tool that need to be considered are its accuracy and consistency of measurement. Therefore it is not only important for an investigator to know how to use a measurement device but also to be knowledgeable about the quality of the data it generates. In this chapter we discuss the various factors of a research instrument or test related to its precision and reproducibility. Some other concerns relative to measurement procedures are presented as well.

## VALIDITY

Upon hearing a political candidate's remark in a debate, you may have challenged a statement by asking, "Well, how valid is that comment?" Essentially what you want to know is the accuracy of the statement. *Validity, from a research point of view, is the extent to which a test measures what it is supposed to measure.* For example, do pull-ups accurately measure upper body strength? Most of us would agree that they do. Do pull-ups measure lower body strength? The answer is obviously no.

Validity is a trait that is possessed by the test or instrument. That is, once the validity of an instrument is established, it does not need to be demonstrated again; it more or less "goes along" with the proper use of the instrument or test. When a new test or procedure is developed through research, the investigators will report some measures of validity in a journal article. The instrument should be accurate when used properly and under the conditions it was validated. For example, a skinfold test for body fat may be valid for women and not men, or a test for aerobic capacity may be accurate for adults and not children. In this regard validity is a highly specific trait.

There are several types of validity that are used to demonstrate test or instrument accuracy. In order to understand the nature of and make interpretations related to validity, one needs to become familiar with some of the common types of validity used in HPER.

### Logical Validity

Varieties of validity in this category are the weakest types because they are either taken at face value or are qualitatively rather than quantitatively determined. In other words, there are no statistics or numerical values that are used to express the degree of accuracy that a test or instrument has.

*Face Validity* Face validity is the weakest of all types of validity because all that can be said about the accuracy of the instrument is that it appears obvious that the test or device is measuring what it is supposed to. No statement can be made relative to the degree of precision of the data generated with its use.

The Bass Stick Test, to measure balance, is performed standing and balancing on the ball of one foot on a small square stick. Its validity is taken at face value because it is obvious that it measures balance, but one just doesn't know how accurately. The 40-yard dash for speed is another test where validity is taken at face value.

*Content Validity*  Content validity usually relates to written tests in educational settings, questionnaires, or other written instruments where a comparison to a standard is not possible. The primary concern with content validity is the extent to which the items or questions are capable of accurately measuring the desired information.

One way to approach the development of such an instrument is to construct a table of specifications. Table 13-1 contains such a table for a written knowledge test. Basically, it is a blueprint that allows the researcher to quantify the number, type, and proportion of the questions or items on the instrument. Once the instrument is completed a number of authorities or "jury of experts" in that research area may examine it and provide comments and critique on how it may be improved. They may also make a qualitative judgment on the instrument's validity (e.g., fair, good, excellent). Thus, someone wanting to conduct a survey may develop a questionnaire and have some experts in survey research critique the instrument and establish its content validity prior to initiating data collection.

Again, there is no statistical value related to content validity. It is a bit stronger than face validity because it employs both logic and authority opinion.

## Statistical Validity

Statistical measures of validity are considered stronger than logical types for two reasons. One is because there is some type of numerical or statistical index of the accuracy of the instrument, such as a correlation coefficient. This makes statistical validity quantitative in nature. The other is that usually some type of com-

**TABLE 13-1**  Table of specifications for a 50-item test for knowledge of measurement and evaluation in physical education

| Content | Knowledge (50%) | TYPE OF COGNITION | |
| --- | --- | --- | --- |
| | | Application (25%) | Analysis (25%) |
| Test administration (15%) $N = 8$ | 4 | 2 | 2 |
| Test selection (15%) $N = 8$ | 4 | 2 | 2 |
| Health-fitness tests (45%) $N = 22$ | 11 | 6 | 5 |
| Motor-fitness tests (25%) $N = 12$ | 6 | 3 | 3 |

parison is made to a standard that is thought to be a good measure of the variable in question.

*Criterion-based Validity*    Measures of criterion-based validity are established when the results of one test are compared to the results obtained when using an accepted standard or criterion. The criterion or standard—often referred to as the "gold standard"—usually is the most accurate measure available of the variable in question, and its selection is perhaps the most critical point to consider with this type of validity. Measurements of some variables in exercise physiology, for example, have gold standards associated with them. Underwater weighing determinations of body composition or laboratory assessments of maximal oxygen uptake are the methods that all other similar, but less accurate tests are compared to. In other instances there is no clear-cut gold standard for a variable.

Let's say that you have developed an instrument that is supposed to measure sportsmanship and you want to determine its accuracy. Sport psychologists may argue at length about what criterion or standard would be acceptable to validate a sportsmanship test against because there is no definitive measure of this trait. Therefore, when judging an index of criterion-based validity, it is important to know something about the model test or instrument used in the validation process. A test that has a high validity index generated from a poor criterion is, in fact, not accurate at all.

There are two types of criterion-based validity: concurrent and predictive.

CONCURRENT VALIDITY    A measure of concurrent validity is made when two measures of the same variable are obtained within a close period (e.g., minutes, hours, or a few days apart). One of the tests applied is the criterion and the other is the test or instrument to be validated. The accuracy of the test is determined by the degree of statistical relationship between the two measures. An example of concurrent validity would be to correlate the results of underwater weighing determinations of percent body fat and those from a skinfold test on a large group of subjects. A correlational analysis will provide an index of accuracy of the skinfold test as a measure of percent body fat.

PREDICTIVE VALIDITY    The purpose of predictive validity is to show the accuracy of estimating the occurrence of some future event through the present use of a test or instrument. In this case, the event to be predicted is considered the criterion measure and the present test is the one to be validated. Perhaps a health educator is interested in determining if an inventory that she developed is capable of predicting if a person is likely to become a regular cigarette smoker or not. This inventory may be composed of questions relative to age, gender, education, job type, exercise habits, income, and the like. The responses on the inventory would be summed to yield a type of composite score. She then administers the inventory to a representative sample of subjects that vary in terms of smoking habits. The level of smoking is also quantified by a score and is considered the criterion.

Once again, a correlational and prediction analysis is performed to examine the degree of relationship between the two sets of scores. The statistical analysis will provide an index of the validity of the health educator's inventory as a predictor of smoking habits. Assuming that a large enough and representative sample was used and the validity statistics were judged satisfactory, future predictions could be made on subjects similar to those used in the validation procedure. Remember, one of the critical factors in this type of validity is an acceptable criterion measure, in this example the health educator's definitions of smokers and nonsmokers.

*Construct Validity*   Construct validity is used when the variable of interest has no definitive criterion, is difficult to measure, or cannot be directly observed. The variable of interest is referred to as the construct. For example, we know that sportsmanship exists, but how is it measured? There are many tests of anaerobic power, but there is no acceptable criterion. What do we do if we want to establish a statistical measure of validity for these constructs?

One approach is to establish two distinct groups: one that is thought to possess a high degree of the construct and the other a low amount. The test in question is applied to each group and the results are analyzed, usually with an independent *t*. If there is a marked difference in the results between the two groups, favoring the group that has a high degree of the construct, the test is said to have construct validity. An example of this would be if a recreator has developed an instrument for the purpose of determining if someone has an inclination to participate in high-risk recreational activities or not. This particular construct may not be easily observed or is arguably difficult to measure. After the instrument is developed, it is administered to a group of high-risk recreators (sky divers, bungee-cord jumpers, fire eaters) thought to possess this trait and a group of low-risk recreators (bowlers, gardeners, quilt makers) thought not to. If the high-risk group's scores are judged significantly higher than those of the low-risk group, the instrument is considered to have construct validity.

## RELIABILITY

When we refer to someone as being a reliable worker, we typically mean that the person is dependable and is capable of producing at an expected level of consistency. In research, the concept of reliability means much the same thing: *Reliability measures refer to the consistency or repeatability of test scores or data.* For example, if someone's grip strength was measured on the hour over 6 hours, we would expect the scores to be very similar, but not exactly the same. This would typify a good measure of test score reliability. High levels of reliability are critical in research because they inform us about the dependability of test results.

It is important to point out that a measure of reliability refers to the scores or data and not to the instrument itself. Also, if two different people use the same instrument they may obtain different results, meaning that the test and the tester are different components. Reliability is not a generalizable trait of a test or instrument and thus needs to be established when it is important to consider or report reliability values, which is not all the time. Like measures of validity, investigators who have developed a new test or procedure will provide measures of reliability in an article to give the consumer a general idea of the level of consistency of scores they obtained during the study. Remember, this doesn't mean that if you were to use the test that you would get the same result, but it should probably be close. *Reliability measures should be considered for use any time a question may be raised about the agreement of test performances.* For instance, if cholesterol levels were a key variable in a study it would be important to demonstrate the repeatability of these measurements.

As with validity, there are several types of reliability measures. Each measures the repeatability of scores but is used under different conditions. The following discussion explains some characteristics of each.

## Stability

A measure of stability reliability is determined when the *same* test is administered on two or more separate occasions and the results are correlated. The purpose is to determine how closely a test performance can be repeated on a second, third, or more occasions. The size of the correlation between the trials is evaluated to determine if an acceptable level of consistency was achieved. This approach is known as the *test-retest method* and probably best defines the concept of reliability.

Although applying a test more than one time is a relatively easy (but time consuming) thing to do, there are several points to consider about this particular method. Because the same test is administered more than once, recall of items is quite likely. Therefore stability measures should not be used for knowledge or "paper and pencil" tests. It is better suited for variables like physical fitness and motor performance tests. Also, the time between administrations should not be so long that factors such as growth, learning, or maturation may affect test performance or too short where fatigue may be a concern.

An example of when it would be appropriate to use a stability measure would be in a study that involved obtaining blood pressure measures. It is very important to demonstrate the repeatability of assessments of this type. Therefore, the test-retest correlation of the researcher's measurements should be high.

## Equivalence

A measure of equivalence reliability is made when test scores from two *different* tests that measure the same variable are correlated. The purpose is to see if test performance can be repeated using a similar but distinct test or instrument (thus the term "equivalence"). Once again, the size of the correlation between the two sets of scores is evaluated to determine if an acceptable level of consistency between the two sets of test scores was achieved. This particular approach is known as a *parallel* or *alternate forms method* (e.g., forms A and B). Because different tests that measure the same thing are used, recall of items is not as much of a concern. Therefore this method is better suited for knowledge-type tests and is used in establishing reliability indices for standardized tests such as the ACT or SAT.

As you might imagine, one of the major drawbacks of this method is the difficulty in developing two good tests that have different items and that measure the same thing. It's hard enough to compose and develop one good test.

## Internal Consistency

The two methods of determining reliability just described are based on the administration of a test on two occasions. Measures of internal consistency may be established from *one single test administration*. Basically, this measure of reliability is used to show how consistent the scores of a test are within itself. This approach is commonly used with written tests and performance tests that incorporate many test trials. The most common means of determining this type of reliability is to use the *split-half method*.

Essentially the test is divided in half (usually the odd items are compared to the even items) and the scores from each half of the test are correlated. If the correlation between the halves of the test are judged satisfactory, then the test scores are deemed internally consistent. For example, let's say that a physical educator is interested in determining the reliability of scores from an archery test consisting of ten trials of shooting five arrows. A score is generated for each of the five arrows shot. The composite scores from trials 1, 3, 5, 7, and 9 would be correlated with the scores from trials 2, 4, 6, 8, and 10 for all of the subjects. If there was good internal consistency, we would expect a suitable correlation between the odd and even trials for the group.

One additional point about the split-half method: The reliability of test scores is roughly proportionate to the number of items or trials on a test. That is, the more items or trials a test has, the higher its reliability will be. In the split-half approach a test is divided in half and the halves are correlated. This basically reduces the original number of items by 50%, which will make the resulting correlation smaller than it would have been if the number of items were unchanged. Can we simply double the size of the correlation between the test halves to compensate?

An equation called the *Spearman-Brown prophecy* is used to "boost" the half-test correlation to what it would be if the test were its original length. This equation appears as:

$$\text{Whole test } r = \frac{2 \times r}{1 + r}$$

where *r* is the half-test reliability coefficient. It's not exactly doubling the half-test correlation, but the equation does correct it appropriately. For example, if a Pearson *r* = .60 was calculated for the odd and even trials on the archery test then the corrected correlation would be

$$\text{Whole test } r = \frac{2 \times .60}{1 + .60} = .75$$

The $r = .75$ indicates good consistency in performance between the odd and even trials of the test.

### Interrater Reliability or Objectivity

This is a special type of reliability that is used to determine the consistency of scores obtained by more than one tester. Sometimes this is referred to as a measure of objectivity. For example, if two researchers were hand-timing 40-yard dash times as part of a study, it would be important to show that they were capable of producing measurements that were in very close agreement with one another. The same would hold true if two individuals were involved in rating children's playground behavior, because with subjective assessments it is difficult for just a single evaluator to be consistent. The statistical correlation between or among the evaluators' scores is used to determine the level of consistency.

## THE RELATIONSHIP BETWEEN VALIDITY AND RELIABILITY

Both validity and reliability are important aspects of an instrument or test scores, but are different traits. Is there any connection between the two? The answer is yes. Consider the explanation of this concept, which is similar to one presented by Best (1981). Imagine an archer shooting 10 arrows at a target. If all 10 hit the bull's-eye we would say that the archer is very accurate, which is an illustration of validity. Because all of the arrows hit the target close together, we could also say that the archer was consistent, which is the definition of reliability. Now let's say that the archer shot 10 arrows at the target and none of them hit the bull's-eye. In fact, all of them missed by 12 inches, but they were all clustered on the outer edge of the target within a 3-inch circle. Because the archer was aiming at the bull's-eye and missed all 10 times, he was not very accurate, which is an example of poor validity. However, all of the arrows were grouped nicely together, so he was consistent or reliable. So what do we conclude about the relationship between validity and reliability? Quite simply, if a test is valid, its scores will be reliable and test scores may be reliable without being valid. Moreover, test scores need to be reproducible if a test is to be deemed valid. Consequently, these two traits need to be evaluated independently.

An example from the body composition field will help further illustrate this idea. There is a method for measuring body composition that is called bioelectrical impedance analysis, or BIA. BIA has been researched fairly thoroughly and has been shown to have questionable validity (McArdle, Katch, & Katch, 1991). However, the test-retest reliability of the measurements is almost perfect ($r = .99$). What this means is that when using this method one would get the

"Well Jeff, I'd say your shooting is highly reliable, but not valid!"

wrong values, consistently. If the device was off by 3% body fat, there is an excellent chance that it would be off by that much every time. So having excellent reliability does not ensure the accuracy of an instrument or test. Although, if a test has a high degree of validity and is used correctly, the scores should be highly reproducible.

## INTERPRETING VALIDITY AND RELIABILITY COEFFICIENTS

Table 13-2 contains some of the statistics used for assessing validity and reliability. Almost all of them are based on some type of correlational procedure (discussed in Chapter 10). As with any correlation, the size and the sign of the coefficient allow for a strict interpretation of the value. However, the interpretation, as has been said before, must go beyond that. Here is where knowledge of research in the field is invaluable. For instance, a validity coefficient of $r=.60$ may be quite acceptable for a health-lifestyle inventory predicting longevity but would be very low for a skinfold test to predict percent body fat. There is no question that reading research in your discipline will assist you in making interpretations relative to these measurement characteristics.

Safrit (1986) suggests that, in general, validity coefficients of $r = .90$ or higher are desirable, but values of above $r = .80$ are acceptable. She further advises that for tests used to make predictions, lower validity coefficients ($r = .50$ to $r = .60$) are acceptable if no better prediction method exists. On the issue of reliability, Safrit indicates that for maximal physical effort tests and precise laboratory tests, reliability coefficients should be $r = .85$ or higher. However, with performance tests that require the replication of accuracy (e.g., serving tennis balls

**TABLE 13-2**    Commonly used statistics for validity and reliability

| Measure | Statistics |
| --- | --- |
| Face validity | None |
| Content validity | None |
| Concurrent validity and predictive validity | Pearson $r$ <br> Spearman $r$ <br> Multiple $R$ <br> Standard error estimate <br> Coefficient of determination <br> Omega squared |
| Construct validity | Independent $t$ <br> Omega squared |
| Stability reliability and equivalence reliability | Pearson $r$ <br> Spearman $r$ <br> Multiple $R$, intraclass <br> Coefficient of determination <br> Omega squared |
| Internal consistency | Pearson $r$ (half-test) <br> Spearman-Brown prophecy <br> (whole-test correction) |
| Objectivity | Pearson $r$ <br> Spearman $r$ <br> Multiple $R$ <br> Coefficient of determination <br> Omega squared |

or chipping in golf) reliability coefficients will be lower. In any case, she recommends that any reliability coefficient below $r = .70$ is unacceptable.

In addition to a correlational method, other statistics may be used or reported to assess validity and reliability. Error statistics such as the standard error of estimate commonly accompany some type of correlation coefficient. Statistics like the coefficient of determination ($r^2 \times 100$) and omega squared are also helpful. These statistics and their interpretation were discussed previously, so just keep in mind what they are being used to measure when interpreting them. Researchers will routinely report several statistics to support validity. The more statistics that are provided, the better the overall ability to make good judgments. For example, validity statistics for a skinfold body fat test compared to underwater weighing may appear as $r = .90$, $r^2 \times 100 = 81.0\%$, and $SEE = 2.0\%$ fat. Here are many pieces of information to help draw a conclusion about that test's validity. These particular statistics indicate a strong positive relationship between the skinfold test and underwater weighing, that 81% of the variance in underwater weighing scores can be explained by the skinfold scores, and that a 68% confidence interval around a predicted score would be $\pm 2.0\%$ fat. Overall, it could be concluded that the skinfold test has excellent validity.

## VALIDITY: IS THERE REALLY SUCH A THING?

Some philosophers argue that the concept of validity can't be justified through logic. Perhaps the following example can show why they think this way: Say a scale in a lab needs to be calibrated prior to a study. The researcher goes to the physics department and borrows some calibration weights that are supposed to be very exact. You may wonder: How was the accuracy of the calibration weights determined? Maybe it was with some weights that are used by the U.S. Bureau of Standards. But how was the accuracy of the Bureau's calibration weights established? This line of reasoning can obviously go on and on. Technically, one could challenge any criterion standard, no matter how precise it may be, and ask how accurate it really is. So, can the concept of validity truly be justified if one can dispute the accuracy of any measurement? Obviously, at a certain point one must accept the given level of precision of a test, otherwise there could be no measurements made or research conducted. Without research our world would be a very dark and cold place.

## MEASUREMENT ERROR

When a measurement is made on a subject, the result is called an *observed score*. The observed score is a combination of what one really wants to assess, which is the *true score*, and any mistake that was made in the process, which is *measurement error*. Mathematically, then, the observed score = true score ± measurement error. The true score is one that is free of measurement error. Unfortunately a true score may never be known because it is more or less a theoretical construct since measurement error always exists to some degree. One of the basic parts of conducting sound research is to minimize measurement error so that you can increase the level of confidence that you are accurately measuring the variables of interest. In this manner the researcher is also more certain that any observed changes in an experimental variable are attributed to the treatment and not errors in measurement.

### Sources of Measurement Error

Anything that can contaminate a true score could be regarded as measurement error. Some of the sources of this error may be traced to the *test instrument*, to the *testing procedures*, or to the *performance of the subject*.

The instrument used should be in proper working order, calibrated, and the right tool for the job. The testing procedures should be clearly defined and executed in the same manner for all subjects. This means that the researcher should probably go through several mock trials or pilot tests to work out any bugs or kinks, which also allows the researcher to practice and review testing skills. Some attention should be given to how the test will be scored and the development of data collection forms. Finally, the subject needs to be properly instructed in and familiarized with the testing procedures. The subject's level of motivation, health, fatigue, and previous testing experience will all affect the quality of test performance and may contribute to measurement error.

Although it is difficult to control the psychological and behavioral aspects of subjects, many other sources of measurement error can be reduced by the researcher. Research testing needs to be conducted in a careful, attentive, and professional manner. When collecting research data, the end result is usually a mass of numbers, and only the researcher ultimately knows exactly how good those numbers really are. The phrase "garbage in, garbage out," or GIGO, comes to mind. Succinctly stated, a large amount of measurement error detracts from quality research. Working with or observing an experienced investigator is a good way for the novice to learn how to avoid some the common sources of measurement error related to particular types of research.

Can measurement error be quantified to some degree? Well, sort of. There are correlational methods such as the intraclass correlation that are based on estimates of true score, observed score, and error variance. With this technique measurement error can be estimated and its influence removed from the observed score. The reliability coefficient is actually a statistical expression of how free the test scores are of measurement error. Even though this statistical technique exists and can help buffer the presence of some measurement error, researchers still need to be meticulous in their testing techniques.

## SUMMARY

In this chapter we have focused on concepts that are related to measurement and data collection. Validity is considered to be the accuracy of an instrument or test that can be determined logically or statistically. Reliability relates to the consistency or reproducibility of test scores, which may be classified as a measure of stability, equivalence, internal consistency, or objectivity. The validity and reliability of a test or its scores need to be evaluated prior to its selection or use. Finally, recognize that measurement error always exists but can be minimized through careful, methodical, and professional testing procedures.

# CHAPTER 14

# EXPERIMENTAL VALIDITY AND CONTROL

---

**KEY CONCEPTS**

Internal validity
Threats to internal
    validity
External validity

Threats to external
    validity
Controlling for threats to
    experimental validity

**AFTER READING THIS CHAPTER, YOU SHOULD BE ABLE TO**

- Define and give examples of internal and external validity.
- Identify and provide examples of threats to internal and external validity.
- Describe several methods that might improve the internal or external validity of a study.
- Explain when internal or external validity is more important.

---

$R$esearchers must design experiments in such a way that they have a high degree of confidence in the results. This may be accomplished in part by just logically considering things that may possibly go wrong and flaw the experiment. Some contaminating factors may be unique to a particular type of study; others may be generic to virtually any type of research. Also, some of these conditions may be easily controlled for and others are not. Another consideration for investigators is to what extent it is possible to apply the results of their research to other subjects, conditions, and situations. Several elements need to be examined in this regard. In Chapter 13, the validity or accuracy of an instrument or test was discussed. In Chapter 1, other types of validity were presented briefly that are quite different, however, that pertain to the outcome of an experiment or study. In this chapter we address many of the factors related to these research concepts.

## INTERNAL VALIDITY

The independent and dependent variables have been discussed. For quick review: The independent variable is the one that the researcher manipulates. It is the variable that is referred to as the treatment, the one that is tested to determine if it caused an effect. The dependent variable is the one that is affected or is the one that the investigator is observing a change in. *Internal validity*, then, is the extent to which the research condition is controlled so that the independent variable causes an effect or change in the dependent variable. The stronger the control over an experimental condition the higher the degree of internal validity. Unfortunately there is no statistical value associated with internal validity for the researcher or consumer to judge. So one must carefully examine how the research was conducted and draw one's own qualitative conclusion.

Many factors have been identified as key threats to the internal validity of a study. Campbell and Stanley reported on these factors in their classic 1963 book, which has been presented in virtually every research textbook since then. A discussion and illustration of some of these threats follow. As each of the factors is discussed, it will be helpful to recall exactly what is of concern. These threats are conditions or things that may cause a change in the dependent variable other than the independent variable. These threats are summarized in Table 14-1.

### Maturation

Subjects change in many ways over time. They may become heavier, less anxious, smarter, more coordinated, leaner, and so on. Any time growth, learning, or maturation processes occur during the conduct of a study that influence the dependent variable, it raises the uncertainty of the effect that the independent variable may have had. Maturation effects are probably of the most concern when children are subjects because of their rapid and unpredictable growth rates. This is also a problem in studies that last for many years, regardless of the age of the subject.

**TABLE 14-1** Primary threats to internal and external validity

| Internal Validity | External Validity |
| --- | --- |
| Maturation | Reactive effects of pretesting |
| History | Subject–treatment interaction |
| Testing | Artificialness of experimental condition |
| Instrument accuracy | Multiple treatment interference |
| Statistical regression | |
| Experimental mortality | |
| Selection bias | |
| Selection maturation | |
| Placebo effect | |
| Hawthorne effect | |
| Halo effect | |

## History

History relates to all of the things that occur outside of a study to the subject that may influence the dependent variable. Typically these factors are recognized as possibilities but can't be controlled for. For instance, perhaps a health educator is interested in examining the effects of a smoking cessation program that uses a nicotine-type gum. Several subjects in the study may work for the same company that instituted a no-smoking policy in the workplace during the time the research was occurring. This may have created a condition of increased peer pressure to quit smoking. At the end of the study it would be difficult to conclude if the nicotine gum or the peer pressure may have caused an effect. Of course, there could be many other such outside influences. Controlling the effects of history can be very difficult.

## Testing

The process of testing provides a subject with some experience about the test that may influence subsequent test performance. This is called a practice or learning effect and is a confounding problem with many physical performance tests that are done the first time. The testing experience may also provide an increased incentive to improve in some manner that is independent of the experimental treatment.

## Instrument Accuracy

As was emphasized in Chapter 13, it is critical that tests and instruments be valid, reliable, in good working order, and the right tools for the job. It is possible that we could show a change or no change in a dependent variable because of faulty instrumentation. Instrument inaccuracies can occur due to inappropriate use or other violations in sound measurement. Sloppy measurement technique not only affects the accuracy of what we want to assess but also weakens the internal validity of a study—a double whammy!

Also, the question of instrument accuracy is confounded when more than one person is involved in the data collection. When this circumstance occurs it would be critical to demonstrate a high degree of interrater reliability between or among the evaluators.

## Statistical Regression

The phenomenon of statistical regression occurs when an individual scores high in an initial testing situation, then tends to score lower in a subsequent one. The reverse holds true for the initial low scorer, who tends to score higher on the next test. Why the term "statistical regression"? Because the tendency of extreme test scores is to "regress" or revert toward the mean or the more typical on a retest. This characteristic is often seen in the sports world with any "streak" performance. If a baseball player's batting average is .525 for the month of May and he is a lifetime .300 hitter (and is probably making $5 million a season), his average will assuredly regress toward the .300 level as the season goes on. Statistical regression may operate in the same fashion on group performance as well, if the group was formed on the basis of extreme pretest performance. So for the individual or group that had a low pretest score, a legitimate question becomes: Did the posttest or retest score improve because of the independent variable or be-

cause of statistical regression? This is an important point for the researcher to consider. Further, statistical regression is usually more of a problem with small groups.

## Selection Bias

Any time groups are formed in a nonrandom fashion, the possible effects of selection bias need to be considered. This is most likely to occur when volunteers are free to select one group or treatment. The basis of their option may indicate a stronger sense of motivation or predisposition than that of someone who didn't select that group. This is especially confounding when subjects are asked to volunteer to be in a control group (no treatment) versus an experimental group (treatment). Using intact groups such as teams or classes also represents a form of bias. The major drawback with selection bias is that the researcher doesn't know if a poststudy difference between the groups was due to any original discrepancies or was due to the independent variable.

## Experimental Mortality

No, this does not mean that our subjects pass into the great beyond! Strictly speaking, experimental mortality refers to the loss or dropout of subjects in a study. This happens for many obvious reasons: boredom, sickness, inconvenience, injury, discomfort. What types of problems does mortality cause? Assuming that groups were formed in an unbiased manner at the beginning of a study, it may be concluded that by and large they are similar to one another. After subject attrition occurs, the remaining subjects may be unique from the standpoint of motivation, health, interest, and the like. What then remains may be dissimilar groups. So this creates essentially the same problem that selection biases caused. The researcher doesn't know if poststudy differences can be attributed to the unique attributes of the remaining subjects or because of the independent variable.

## Selection Maturation

Selection maturation occurs when a subject or group has a characteristic that is being studied that will improve naturally over the passage of time (e.g., a physical injury, a psychological condition). In this case it would be difficult to know whether the independent variable caused the change or the condition improved by itself. This threat is compounded when groups are formed on the basis of this characteristic, which is a form of selection bias, and results in nonequivalent groups. Because the groups were not equal and the condition that distinguishes the groups may resolve itself over time, strict comparisons between the groups are difficult to make.

The threats to validity just described are the classic ones presented by Campbell and Stanley. Three other points should be considered, however. A description of them follows.

## Placebo Effect

It has long been observed that mere participation in a study may elicit an effect that is separate from the independent variable. In medicine, control subjects who participate in a drug study are given a placebo, which is simply an inactive substance. To avoid tipping off the subjects, drugs and placebos are usually administered in what is called a *blind* fashion, which prevents subjects from knowing what treatment they are receiving. Sometimes subjects in the placebo group show an improvement due to *expectation*, which is called the *placebo effect*. The true effectiveness of a drug, then, is the difference between what is observed in the experimental group and the placebo group. So without a placebo group it would be difficult to know what effect was attributed to the treatment and what amount the placebo was responsible for. Actually, there may be a placebo effect for any type of research treatment.

## Hawthorne Effect

A similar phenomenon is observed in behavioral research, which was highlighted by studies done of workers at the Hawthorne Plant of the Western Electric Company in Chicago years ago. Basically, the investigators were interested in studying the relationship between brightness of light and work output. It seemed that as the lights were made brighter, work output increased. After a certain point, the investigators reduced the lighting intensity to see if the relationship continued. To their surprise, as the illumination decreased, the workers' productivity continued to increase. What did they conclude? The increase in work output was probably because of the attention the subjects received—that is, *observation* by the researchers and/or management. Therefore, because subjects know they are being studied, they try harder.

The placebo effect is induced by expectation, whereas the Hawthorne effect is produced by observation. They are similar in nature. You can see how each may affect the dependent variable and, therefore, make it complicated to know the true effect of the independent variable.

## The Halo Effect

The halo effect usually is introduced when the researcher has some expectation about the performance of a subject and is assessing the experimental variable. This awareness creates a certain aura that may bias the researcher's judgment. Also, it may lead to the investigator having undue influence on a subject (e.g., providing encouragement or no encouragement, leading the subject to respond a certain way). The more subjectively assessed the experimental variable is, the greater the influence the halo effect becomes. An example of this sort of problem may be seen if an exercise physiologist knows that a subject is an athlete and provides encouragement toward the end of a maximal fitness test because of the belief that the athlete should do well and doesn't provide it for the nonathlete. Another illustration might be if a recreator was observing playground activity levels of children from two different economic strata. If the researcher expected children from the lower stratum to be more active for whatever reason, she may "look" for more signs of activity in that group, thus biasing the observations and assessments.

Hopefully, you can see why it is important for the researcher to be as objective as possible and avoid affecting the performance status of the subject or him- or herself. Halos of any type may cloud the investigator's impartiality or may lead to coercion of the subject in a manner that unfairly affects the dependent variable.

One way to reduce the halo threat would be to have someone skilled in the area being studied but not involved in the research make the experimental measurements. This, of course, is assuming also that the person is not familiar with the subjects. Another approach is to use what is called a *double-blind* method. With the double-blind method neither the researcher nor the subject knows what group the subject is in or what treatment (if any) the subject is getting. This approach may remove any expectations the researcher has about the subject, as he or she is not biased to how the participant should respond or behave.

## EXTERNAL VALIDITY

*External validity* refers to the ability to use the results of a study in other conditions or settings. If the results of a study showed that a type of aerobic training lowered cholesterol for men, can it work the same for women? If a method for teaching health education is effective for elementary school children, will it be so for college students? The ability to extend the results of a study into other situations is called *generalizability*. The greater the ability to generalize the results of a study, the higher the degree of external validity it has.

Like internal validity, external validity has no statistical reference and is qualitatively determined by the producer or consumer of research. Also, there are points to consider that threaten the external validity of an investigation. Campbell and Stanley presented these factors in their famous treatise as well (see Table 14-1). Let's examine each of these.

### Reactive Effects of Pretesting

We saw that pretesting a subject may enhance performance on a retest. Pretesting may also alter subjects' perception about the experimental treatment. Their perception may be changed in such a way that they are motivated to perform better than they would have had they not been pretested. When this occurs it is said that there is a reactive or interactive effect that the testing experience has with the experimental treatment. Why is this a threat to external validity? Essentially, because the treatment may only have an effect if preceded by the pretest, making the treatment generalizable only under those conditions.

### Subject–Treatment Interaction

Sometimes there is a unique characteristic about the subjects in a study that makes the treatment effective only for them or others possessing that same trait. For instance, if a sports psychologist was interested in examining the effect of a program designed to improve exercise adherence, he might find quite different results with a group of college freshmen who are nonathletes versus a group of varsity athletes. Therefore, if there is a group selection bias, the effectiveness of a treatment and generalizability of a study are limited to those with that trait.

### The Artificial Nature of the Experimental Condition

At the heart of this threat to validity is the question of whether a subject will perform in the same manner under experimental conditions as he or she would in the real world. Seldom are the conditions the same in a laboratory as they are in the field. So should one expect the subject to perform or behave differently, particularly when the subject knows that he or she is participating in a study? The Hawthorne effect also enters into this condition as well. The more artificial and constrained a research setting becomes, the less the ability to generalize from it.

### Multiple Treatment Interference

When a researcher is interested in studying more than one experimental variable or more than one level of one variable on the same subjects, there is a risk of the treatments interfering with one another. The performance of one task may inhibit or enhance the performance of an opposing one. Fatigue, learning effects, and so on may interact with test performance in such a way that the ability to generalize study results is reduced. For instance, perhaps performing a motor skill test for balance will allow someone to do better on a subsequent balance test.

## CONTROLLING FOR THREATS TO INTERNAL VALIDITY

By now you may be feeling that with all of the threats to experimental validity, it must be impossible to conduct research at all. That certainly is not true, but it does support what has been said before: *There are limitations and weaknesses in every study.* A producer of research needs to be aware of these factors so that methods can be used and designs implemented that minimize their effects. The consumer of research needs to be just as attentive so that informed judgments can be made about the quality of published and presented work. There are many methods and techniques that may be used to reduce threats to internal validity. In fact we have already referred to the blind and double-blind methods to control for the placebo effect and the halo effect, respectively. A discussion of some of the other strategies follows.

### Making Equivalent Groups

One of the key ways to reduce threats to internal validity is to form equivalent groups at the onset of a study. This is most commonly achieved by developing a list of qualifications for the subjects and then using *randomization* or chance assignment when placing them into groups. The premise behind randomization is that the only differences between groups will be those that are produced by chance or sampling error. Remember that the statistical estimate of sampling error is called error variance. How does randomization reduce threats to validity?

When groups are equivalent at the beginning of a study, it can be assumed that the effects of maturation and history will be similar across groups. It may also be argued that exposure to all of the possible events that may occur outside the study during its conduct, which may affect its outcome, is equally probable. However, the researcher must be aware of some of these events and be creative in a way to reduce the subjects' contact with them. Selection bias is automatically removed with randomization because subjects are not allowed to self-select their own group. This is also true with selection maturation problems because the primary factor that causes it is when groups are formed on the basis of a differential trait, which is a form of selection bias and results in nonequivalent groups. If groups were formed on the basis of extreme scores, statistical regression may be minimized by randomizing the subjects into groups instead. Randomization is not the only way to make groups equivalent, although is probably the easiest and most time-honored approach.

### Using Control Groups

Some types of research designs are based on making a comparison between the effects of treatment versus nontreatment. The group that is used to measure the effects of nontreatment is called the *control group*. The control group is similar in characteristics to the treatment or experimental group, with the only difference being they don't receive the independent variable. What is the best way to develop a sound and representative control group? The method of choice would be to randomize the subjects into groups, of course! Theoretically the subjects in the control group have an equivalent probability of being exposed to or demonstrating the effects of maturation, history, and testing. So any effects that these factors may exert may be assessed in the control group.

As was stated earlier, the use of blind and double-blind methods controls for the placebo and halo effects, respectively. In order to demonstrate the effect of participation without treatment, a placebo group must be used. Therefore the placebo group is a special type of control group because the subjects actually participate in the study but receive a bogus treatment. A true control group goes through the testing procedures but receives no treatment. The double-blind method is also based on the use of a control group, as, by definition, neither the subject nor the researcher knows who received the treatment. Control groups may also be used to assess the Hawthorne effect as well. Control groups are not required all the time, but they are important when considering means of reducing threats to validity.

### Other Control Methods

Instrument accuracy is under the control and responsibility of the researcher. It is imperative that the instrument is thoughtfully selected, calibrated, and used appropriately by the investigator; no research design or other method can minimize problems here. Experimental mortality is typically beyond the direct control of the researcher. If a subject wants to drop out of a study it is his or her prerogative to do so at any time, without fear of reprisals. Sometimes investigators will provide an incentive such as cash for the subject to complete the study. A researcher who resorts to begging or pleading with a subject is walking a fine line that borders on violating the subject's ethical rights. Threatening a subject who wants to withdraw from a study is a clear violation of research ethics. Finally, the effects of testing can be measured with the use of a control group or eliminated if it is possible not to pretest the subject. The primary means of controlling threats to internal validity are summarized in Table 14-2.

## CONTROLLING FOR THREATS TO EXTERNAL VALIDITY

Controlling for threats to external validity is another issue. Basically, the researcher must make decisions on the value of being able to generalize the study. A most fundamental question on this topic might be: What good is any research that can't be used or generalized to other conditions? It's an excellent question that we will try to answer a little later.

When conducting research where a high degree of external validity is desirable, it is important that the subjects in the study are representative of the population to be generalized to. For example, if an investigator wanted to develop a body fat prediction equation for older women, it would be important to obtain a large number of subjects through a random sampling procedure. This would be the best way to ensure that the sample was a good representation of this group, which would increase the power to accurately generalize the results.

The reactive effects of pretesting can be assessed through the use of a control group or groups. In the most ideal case one group would receive the pretest only, another would receive the treatment only, and a third would receive both the pretest and the treatment. A comparison would be made across the groups to measure the influence of each of the conditions. Other research designs that are based on this premise may also be used.

**TABLE 14-2**  Controlling for threats to internal validity

---

Maturation: Randomization, control group
History: Randomization, control group
Testing: Control group, no pretest
Instrument accuracy: Researcher
Statistical regression: Randomization
Selection bias: Randomization
Experimental mortality: Researcher hopes subjects stay in the study!
Selection maturation: Randomization
Placebo effect: Control group, blind or double-blind design
Hawthorne effect: Control group, blind or double-blind design
Halo effect: Blind or double-blind design

---

The effects of subject–treatment interaction have to be appraised by the researcher. He or she will have to analyze the nature of the subjects and contemplate if the treatment in question may work only on them. Also, there is a need to decide on the extent of external validity that is desired. If the researcher would like to be able to generalize the results of a study to college students, then a large, representative sample obtained through random sampling is needed. The use of intact groups or classes as a study sample would be inappropriate. That seems logical enough.

External validity may not be a major issue with some types of research. For instance, after concluding that a treatment might only be effective on a certain type of subject, a researcher might say, "That's O.K., I'm only concerned with this type of subject." This investigator may not be concerned about generalizing results to various populations and to be sure, not all researchers are. That's fine, too, as we will soon explain.

The artificial nature of the testing condition is another consideration because there is no technique to control for it. Moreover, some measurements can only be made under controlled laboratory conditions, so there isn't much that can be done in this regard. In other instances the investigator may think of creative ways to make the testing condition more like the real world, but this is only effective if the subject performs in a real-world manner.

Minimizing the effects of multiple treatment interference is also under the control of the researcher. Attention must be given to whether or not the treatments may affect one another. If they might, the investigator may need to consider arranging treatments in a unique manner, randomizing the treatment order, or having several experimental groups with each group receiving only one treatment.

Recall that there are instances when a researcher *is* interested in how treatments may interact with one another. This is the basis for factorial ANOVAs, where not only the main effect of each independent variable is assessed but any possible interaction between the variables is studied as well. The basic ways to control for threats to external validity are presented in Table 14-3.

## INTERNAL VERSUS EXTERNAL VALIDITY: WHICH ONE?

Now that both internal and external validity and possible methods to diminish their threats have been discussed, we turn our attention to the issue of which one is more significant. It would seem that both types of validity are important, but

**TABLE 14-3** Controlling for threats to external validity

| |
|---|
| Reactive effects of pretesting: Control group or design |
| Subject–treatment interaction: Researcher appraisal |
| Artificialness of experimental condition: Researcher, if possible |
| Multiple treatment interference: Randomization of treatments, design, or researcher appraisal |
| Overall: Have a representative sample |

is it possible to have a high degree of each? The answer is no. One may consider the relationship between internal and external validity to be a strong, inverse one. That is, the higher the degree of one, the less the degree of the other.

The best way to control for most threats to internal validity is to conduct research under very sterile, tightly controlled laboratory conditions. When research is done in this manner, plus using the other suggested techniques, a high degree of internal validity is assured. However, research carried out this way is not at all like the real world, so some generalizability of the results is reduced. This is typical of pure or basic research. On the other hand, if research is conducted in real-world settings or in the field, some element of control over the experimental condition is lost. So, in the process of making the study more externally valid, internal validity may be weakened. This is indicative of applied research.

Although it is not possible to have a high degree of both, it is conceivable to have a reasonable amount of each. When both of these experimental validities are desirable, research can still be done without compromising the known effect of the independent variable or the ability to generalize the study results.

Which type of validity is more important depends largely on the type and purpose of the research. If an investigator is conducting a basic research experiment that is predicated on theory development and requires a high degree of control, internal validity is more critical. When it is desirable to generalize research results, as it is with much of the research that is done in HPER, external validity is more essential. That does not mean the applied researcher is not interested in internal validity, because every investigator must be. An investigator has to feel at least reasonably confident that the independent variable in the study was responsible for the effect on the dependent variable. Without this assurance no viable research can be done. With applied research some element of internal validity is lost when gaining external validity. For applied research, striking an acceptable balance between the two varieties is the key.

## SUMMARY

In this chapter we have examined experimental validity and methods that can be used to minimize the threats to validity. Internal validity is the extent to which the research condition is controlled so that the independent variable causes an effect or change in the dependent variable. External validity refers to the ability to use the results of a study in other conditions or settings. The degree of these validity types is subjectively determined by the producer and consumer of research. Methods that may be used to minimize threats to validity include the use of control groups, the use of randomization, and the researcher's knowledge and logic in designing the study. Some degree of internal validity is important to every type of research. However, strong internal validity is more important in basic research, and in applied research good external validity is desirable. Most researchers in HPER should seek a reasonable balance between the two.

# CHAPTER 15

# EXPERIMENTAL RESEARCH AND DESIGNS

---

### KEY CONCEPTS

Cause and effect
relationship
Experimental control

Experimental research
designs: true, quasi-,
and pre-
Error and treatment variance

#### AFTER READING THIS CHAPTER, YOU SHOULD BE ABLE TO

- Explain the concept of cause and effect, especially as it relates to experimental research.
- Report why experimental research offers the greatest degree of experimental control.
- Describe the characteristics of the basic true, quasi-, and pre-experimental designs.
- Explain the concepts of treatment and error variance.
- Distinguish among the various experimental designs in terms of their ability to demonstrate a cause and effect relationship.

---

$T$hink about what most people's impression might be if you said you were going to conduct an experiment. They would probably conjure up visions of you in a white coat, in a laboratory with test tubes, beakers, and expensive electronic devices, and mixing chemicals and performing elaborate calculations. You know by now that much research, particularly the types usually done in HPER, doesn't fit that stereotype at all. However, many studies conducted in our disciplines are of the experimental variety. So what, exactly, is experimental research, and how is it done? We explore these and other related concepts in this chapter.

## EXPERIMENTATION AND THE CAUSE AND EFFECT RELATIONSHIP

The primary purpose for conducting research is to develop knowledge. The most organized, controlled, and powerful means of generating new facts is through experimentation. Research performed with experimental methods is typified by a careful and systematic approach to minimizing threats to validity and other factors that may contaminate the study. Needless to say, the researcher must be aware of these conditions if attempts to reduce their influence are to be successful. Along with a high degree of control come the introduction and manipulation of an independent variable. The experimental condition is such that there is a great degree of confidence that the independent variable caused an effect on the dependent variable.

When it is logically determined that one factor demonstrates a predictable influence on another, a *cause and effect relationship* is said to exist. Experimental research is the most robust way to demonstrate if such an association exists. If there is a true cause and effect relationship between two (or more) variables, then one of the more important purposes of research may be met. That aim is to be able to generalize the relationship to other conditions and situations outside the experiment. In this manner sound experimental research not only determines what happens in the present but also allows for the prediction of future events (i.e., given condition A, one is confident B will occur). In this regard, experimental research seeks to answer the basic question: What will be?

Experimental research also best embodies the scientific method of problem solving. It allows an investigator to propose a hypothesis, to design and conduct a study to test the hypothesis, and to draw a logical conclusion from the results. Although the scientific method may be used with other types of research, experimental methods remain the most important tool for discovering new information.

Because experimental research is typified by much control, it is probably better suited for laboratory conditions. This is true to a certain extent. However, a considerable amount of good experimental research in HPER is performed in nonlaboratory conditions. Regardless of the setting, conducting experimental research involves recognizing the main factors that may weaken the study, controlling for them the best way possible, and introducing and manipulating the independent variable.

## EXPERIMENTAL CONTROL REVISITED

As we have already mentioned, a high degree of control is characteristic of experimental research methods. In Chapter 14 we described several approaches to reducing threats to validity, thus increasing experimental control. The most common methods are randomization, control groups, and the researcher's ability to logically "troubleshoot" the situation. It is important to emphasize that although randomization and control groups are good procedures for restricting an experimental condition, they must accompany other means of diminishing the effects of variables that are extraneous to the study. To that extent we described the use of blind and double-blind techniques to minimize variables like the placebo and halo effects. Other contaminants to a study may be controlled for simply by removing them.

Sex, age, fitness level, health status, and race are examples of some factors whose influence may be diminished by using that element as a control variable. This may be accomplished by preparing a list of qualifying characteristics (delimitations) that may assist in eliminating extraneous variables between subjects. For instance, if it is perceived that cigarette smoking may produce a differential effect, require all of the subjects to be nonsmokers. Or if aging has a specific effect on the dependent variable, have all of the subjects be within a given age range. In order to be successful at understanding if variables may have undesirable effects on one another, there is no substitute for the researcher to be experienced in their field, read related literature, and be a logical thinker.

Sometimes the elimination of an extraneous variable may raise ethical questions. For example, the issue of sex differences as a confounding variable in biomedical research has been a long-standing problem. The wide fluctuations in female hormonal and biological cycles and their possible interactions with medications have been the focal point for using sex as a control variable. Women have also been restricted in participating in some types of research for the protection of their childbearing potential. The chronic effect of systematically eliminating women from biomedical research as an extraneous variable was brought to national attention recently by Bernardine Healy, director of the National Institutes of Health (NIH). She has reported that women's health concerns have been seriously neglected and understudied. Because of this issue, the NIH has developed policy statements regarding the future inclusion of women in biomedical research to help develop important knowledge in this area.

This problem wasn't caused by one investigator, but the effects of similar practices over time have had a significant cumulative impact. Discussion of this and other related research topics (e.g., bias for aging, or race) could lead to a spirited and enlightening debate. Why not try it in your class?

## EXPERIMENTAL RESEARCH DESIGNS

A research design is simply the blueprint for a study. It gives the study structure and direction and dictates the appropriate statistical analysis to test the researcher's hypothesis. Like an architect, the researcher must put ideas down on paper and sketch a draft of what is to be accomplished and how it will be done. This, of course, needs to occur prior to the actual conduct of the study. Sketching out the design before the study is done provides the researcher with an opportunity to consider many of the elements of the project, as well as a time for needed brainstorming. The goal of the study design is to allow the researcher to conduct the study and test the hypothesis with a minimum of contamination. This allows the investigator to make sound judgments about the relationship between the independent and dependent variables.

Experimental research designs are classified by their sophistication and degree of control they provide. The categories of these designs are called *true, quasi-, and pre-experimental. One thing all experimental designs have in common is the introduction and manipulation of an independent variable.* There are many possible research designs to choose from. The selection of the design is based on factors like the type of research problem, the number and variety of experimental variables, how groups will be formed, the threats to validity the researcher wants to control for, and so on. In the following sections are described a few of the more basic and common experimental designs used in HPER research. Those desiring more detail on this topic are referred to Kirk's (1968) authoritative text on experimental designs.

### Error and Treatment Variance

Before we examine the various experimental designs, it would be worthwhile to review a few concepts. Recall that the basis for the use of randomization for group equivalence is the premise that the only differences between experimental and control groups are those produced by chance or sampling error. The statistical estimate of sampling error is called *error variance.* A proper study design should optimize the effect the independent variable has on the dependent variable while reducing threats to experimental validity. The effect the independent variable has on the dependent variable will result in differences known as *experimental or treatment variance.* At the heart of any experiment is the desire to enhance the effect of the treatment while reducing sampling error. The most effective way of achieving this is through randomization, adequate sample size, and thoughtful selection and use of a sound design.

Upon completion of a study, an inspection and analysis of treatment and error variance are necessary. If there is considerably more treatment variance than error variance, the difference is judged to be the influence of the independent variable. Recall that the basis of statistics like $t$ and $F$ is the ratio of treatment to error variance.

### Symbols and a Helpful Hint

For the research designs and blueprints in the following sections, the following symbols or words will be used:

Random: Groups were formed by randomization
Nonrandom: Groups were formed in a nonrandom manner

IV: Introduction of the independent variable, the treatment

Test or retest: Measurement of the dependent variable

At this point it would be a good idea to review the threats to validity and ways to control them (Chapter 14) if these concepts are still vague. That way you may more fully appreciate how and why these designs work and why some are good and some are not so.

## True Experimental Designs

*True designs* are the strongest tools for experimental research. They offer a considerable degree of control and minimize threats to validity to the greatest extent. These designs incorporate the two key elements of experimental control: randomization of subjects into groups for equivalence and a control group. Randomization and control groups reduce most threats to experimental validity.

*Posttest-Only Design*    This design is based on randomizing subjects into either an experimental or control group for equivalence, introducing the independent variable into the experimental group, testing for the effects of treatment and nontreatment, and determining if any difference between the two groups is significant. If the groups were equivalent at the onset of the study, any difference between the two groups at the conclusion of the research is probably due to the independent variable. This particular design is the one of choice when there are significant concerns related to controlling the effects of testing. This design may be expanded to two or more experimental groups if there is more than one level of the independent variable to be examined. The appropriate statistical analysis would be an independent t for two groups and a one-way ANOVA for more than two groups.

A blueprint of the posttest-only design appears as:

Experimental: Random

Control: Random

| IV | Test |
|---|---|
| No treatment | Test |

Perhaps a health educator is interested in determining the effectiveness of a particular school-based drug education program. The researcher feels that exposing the subjects to a pretest on knowledge of drug use may adversely affect the experiment, so she elects to use the posttest-only design. Subjects are placed into groups by randomization (ideally, subjects were randomly sampled from a population, then randomized into groups), the drug education program is given to the experimental group only, the drug use knowledge test is given to both groups at the end of the study, and the test performances between the two groups are compared. This example could be extended to comparison of two or more different programs, with the logic of the design remaining the same.

*Pre–Posttest Design*    This design differs from the posttest only by the addition of a pretest. This approach may be used when the effects of testing are negligible or when pretest data are needed to initiate subject selection or group formation. The pre–posttest design allows the researcher to determine the amount of change in the dependent variable that was due to the independent variable. In other words, observing which group changes more is the basis of this design. The pre–posttest design, like the posttest-only, may be augmented to two or more experimental groups if there is more than one level of the independent variable. Appropriate statistical analyses include using the pretest as the covariate and an independent t or one-way ANOVA on gain scores. A gain score is simply the difference between the pre- and posttest performances. Although each of these approaches has advantages and disadvantages, they and other techniques are commonly seen in the literature.

Here is a blueprint of the pre–posttest design:

| Experimental: Random | Test | IV | Retest |
|---|---|---|---|
| Control: Random | Test | No treatment | Retest |

Maybe an exercise physiologist is interested in studying the effect of a 10-week aerobic exercise program on high blood cholesterol levels. The investigator wants only subjects with cholesterol levels above 250 mg/dl. Initially, each subject is given a pretest assessment of his or her cholesterol levels. The pretest data are used for two purposes in this case: to provide a baseline for change and as a subject selection criterion. After the pretest the subjects are randomly assigned into groups. The experimental group now participates in the exercise program, and the control group does not. The control group would also be instructed not to begin an exercise program during the study. The study would conclude with postassessments of cholesterol levels and the appropriate statistical comparisons.

*Other True Designs*    Technically, any time a study is designed with the use of randomization of subjects, a control group, and the introduction of an independent variable, it is a true experimental design. There are many other permutations of experimental and control groups that are possible, such as the two-way factorial ANOVA. This statistical analysis may be applied to some of the more elaborate experimental designs. See Chapter 11 for a review of factorial research problems.

## Quasi-Experimental Designs

Quasi means "to some degree or seemingly," so quasi-experimental designs are like true experimental ones, somewhat. One of the major differences is that randomization of subjects into groups is not used. The nonrandomization of subjects raises doubts about the equivalence of groups. Obviously, that causes some problems. Some quasi-experimental designs are based on observing a group of subjects over time and making repeated measurements on them. These types of designs are usually characterized by the subjects serving as their own control group. Some quasi-experimental research designs and methods are intended for studies conducted in "natural" settings, such as classrooms or other intact groups. The basic premise is to study the subject in a real-world setting, introduce the independent variable, and measure its effect. Overall, these designs are typified by good external validity, but suspect internal validity because of the absence of randomization. We present here a few of the more common quasi-experimental designs.

*Pre–Post Nonrandom Design*    This design is identical in form to the pre–post true experimental design for the exception of randomization of subjects into groups. It is used when the researcher does not have the ability to randomize subjects, desires to use groups that are intact for convenience, or wants to conduct a study in a real-world setting. The major drawback with this approach is the unlikeness of the equivalence of groups. As a check for group equivalence, an investigator may perform an independent t test or one-way ANOVA, if there are more than two groups, on the pretest results. If no significant difference is observed between or among the groups, a judgment of equivalence is made. This deduction may be faulty, for two reasons. One, a test of significance does not provide reliable information about the magnitude of a difference. It is possible to have a large difference that is not statistically significant. The other reason is that although there may be no significant difference between or among groups on the dependent variable, the subjects may be different on another or other factors that may influence the experiment. Therefore perhaps the most appropriate statistical analysis for this design is the ANCOVA using the pretest scores as the covariate. A blueprint of this design is as follows:

Experimental: Nonrandom

Control: Nonrandom

| Test | IV | Retest |
|------|--------------|--------|
| Test | No treatment | Retest |

Let's say that a recreator is interested in examining the effect of elders' participation in bingo games on socialization. For both convenience and to study the subjects in a real-world environment, the researcher decides to use two different retirement homes in her community. At one of the homes games of bingo (with cash prizes) will be instituted into the recreation program. This home will be used as the experimental group. The other home, which has a similar recreation program but no bingo, will be used as a control. Prior to and at the conclusion of the study, a socialization inventory will be administered to both groups. The ANCOVA could then be used to adjust for the initial socialization scores and the appropriate conclusions drawn. Obviously, the biggest problem with this study is not knowing what differences may have existed between the subjects of the two retirement homes. For instance, one home may have had a disproportionate number of well-to-do, widowed, or handicapped residents compared to the other. These factors or others like them may have adversely influenced the study's outcome. This is an example of why the interpretation of results of studies using this design needs to be done carefully.

*Repeated Measures Designs*    The repeated measures approach is a very commonly used method in HPER. Essentially, only an experimental group is exposed to more than one level of the independent variable. Usually, the effect of each level is measured on one dependent variable. Because the subjects have repeated measurements made on them, they technically serve as their own control group, making this actually a fairly sound design. This design works best when there is little interaction among the levels of the independent variable and not much time is required between the measurement sessions. To minimize any interaction or testing effect, the order of test administrations should be randomized for each subject. The appropriate statistical analyses for this design would be a correlated t test if comparing two levels or a one-way ANOVA for repeated measures for more than two levels, respectively. This is what a blueprint of the repeated measures design would look like if subjects were measured on three levels of an independent variable:

| Experimental: Nonrandom | $IV_1$ | Test | $IV_2$ | Test | $IV_3$ | Test |
|---|---|---|---|---|---|---|

Suppose a physical educator would like to compare the effect of three different seat heights on leg cycle power output. After careful consideration, the investigator thinks that there may be some testing or interactive effects, so he decides that the best approach would be to randomize the treatment order for each subject. Also, to minimize the effects that fatigue may have, he would test the subjects on three separate days. Each subject then reports to the testing facility three times to be assessed on a randomly selected seat height. The results are then compared with a one-way ANOVA for repeated measures and the appropriate conclusions are made.

A desirable aspect to this method is that fewer subjects are needed than if three separate groups were used for each test. (This would not be the correct approach if the levels of the independent variable were some type of long-term treatment, such as an educational program or a method of physical training that may take weeks or months to administer.) The most obvious concerns in this case would be the length of time it would take to expose the subjects to all of the treatment variables and the carry-over effect each treatment might have on the subsequent one. For long-term treatments it becomes necessary to use one of the other designs previously described.

Also, it should be pointed out that there are many possible repeated measures designs. For example, when repeated measures are made on the same subjects with more than one independent variable with more than one level of each, a factorial ANOVA for repeated measures is used.

*Time Series Design*    An approach that is fairly similar to the repeated measures is the time series design. A single experimental group, which serves as its own control, is assessed on a dependent variable several times over a specified time period. This is to establish a constant baseline for the variable. The independent variable is then introduced after which several more assessments of the dependent variable are made. Any departure from the baseline is thought to be attributed to the independent variable. A major weakness in this design is that without a control group it is difficult to know if the effects of history may have actually been responsible for the change. The blueprint for the time series design is:

Experimental: Nonrandom

| Test | Test | Test | IV | Test | Test | Test |
|------|------|------|----|------|------|------|

An example of the use of this design would be if a health educator is interested in examining the effect of a smoking cessation program. A group of smokers is identified and the smokers' blood levels of carbon monoxide are determined, to be used as an index of smoking quantity. These measurements are performed once a week for three weeks to establish a baseline. The researcher then introduces the smoking cessation program and repeats the carbon monoxide tests in the same fashion as before. Any reduction in group carbon monoxide level is thought to be attributed to the smoking cessation program. It is entirely possible, however, that an extraneous variable that presented itself simultaneously to the independent variable caused the change. For instance, what if there was a major news report that smoking significantly reduces sex drive. If many of the research subjects heard the news, that may have provided a strong stimulus to change despite the influence of the smoking cessation program. On the other hand, if there is no marked departure from the baseline, the program was probably ineffective.

## Pre-Experimental Designs

Pre-experimental designs have the weakest degree of experimental control and are characterized by nonrandomization, no control group, and no assurance of equivalence between groups if a control group was used. They are classified as experimental designs only because there is a manipulation of an independent variable. These designs offer such poor control that there is hardly any way an investigator could draw any meaningful conclusion about a cause and effect relationship. They are illustrated here only as *techniques not to use*. Anyone getting caught using a pre-experimental design will be summarily turned over to the experimental design division of the research police!

*One Group Pre–Post Design*   This approach is probably the best—the best of the worst that is—of all of the pre-experimental types. One experimental group is given a pretest, treated with the independent variable, and then given a posttest. A major flaw in this design is the lack of a control group. The change between the pre- and postscores is assumed to be attributed to the treatment. Of course, too many threats to internal validity are not controlled for, so one is not at all confident about why the change took place. The blueprint appears as:

Experimental: Nonrandom

| Test | IV | Retest |
|------|----|--------|

"Sorry professor, I have to cite you for using a pre-experimental design."

***Static Group Comparison Design***   This unsatisfactory design is based on non-randomization of subjects into groups. Basically, an intact experimental group receives the independent variable, and is compared with an intact, non-equivalent control group on the dependent variable. Because the groups were probably not comparable prior to the treatment, it would be difficult to conclude that any posttest differences between groups were due to the independent variable. Simply, the groups could have been different prior to the treatment. Here is what this design looks like.

| | | |
|---|---|---|
| Experimental: Nonrandom | IV | Test |
| Control:  Nonrandom | No treatment | Test |

***One-Shot Design***   Undoubtably, the one-shot design is the worst of the worst. With this technique an intact experimental group receives a treatment and is tested on its effect on the dependent variable. The results of the treatment are compared to what the researcher *expected to occur if the treatment was not given*. There is no pretest, no randomization, and no control group. Consequently, there is no way to statistically test for any possible effect that the independent variable might have had. Also, there is absolutely no control for threats to experimental validity. Any conclusions would be pure speculations that could not be supported logically or objectively. Here is a one-shot design:

| | | |
|---|---|---|
| Experimental: Nonrandom | IV | Test |

Imagine a sports psychologist interested in studying the effect of mental imagery on basketball free-throw shooting accuracy. He has the team use imagery for 10 minutes before each practice for one week prior to a game. After the game he examines the team's free-throw percentage and finds that it is higher than what he expected. He claims that this improvement was due to the mental imagery practice. Do you see problems with this? No wonder this is known as a one shot design. A study based on this method will have more holes in it than if it was shot one time with a shotgun.

## SUMMARY

Experimental designs are the best tools for establishing cause and effect relationships and to discover new knowledge. All of the designs are based on causing something to occur by introducing and manipulating an independent variable. These designs vary in terms of their ability to minimize threats to experimental validity. True designs are the foremost variety and are characterized by the use of control groups and randomization. Quasi-experimental designs are more real world oriented and are typified by nonrandomization of subjects or equivalence of groups. Pre-experimental methods are by far the weakest designs because of lack of randomization, equivalence of groups, and in some cases no control group. Professionals in HPER need to consider the type of design and its ability to reduce threats to validity when producing and consuming research. A summary of experimental designs appears in Table 15-1.

**TABLE 15-1**   Typical experimental designs used in HPER

| *True—Best* | *Quasi—Adequate* | *Pre—Worst* |
|---|---|---|
| Posttest only<br>Pre–posttest<br>Factorial | Same as true designs except nonrandom groups.<br>Repeated measures<br>Time series | One group pre–post<br>Static group<br>One shot |

# CHAPTER 16

# NONEXPERIMENTAL RESEARCH

**KEY CONCEPTS**

Nonexperimental research
  and cause and effect
Survey research
Correlational research
Developmental research

Epidemiological research
Observational research
Ex post facto research
Meta-analysis

**AFTER READING THIS CHAPTER, YOU SHOULD BE ABLE TO**

- Explain the relationship between nonexperimental research and cause and effect.
- Describe the basic steps in conducting a survey.
- Describe the characteristics of the various types of nonexperimental research commonly used in HPER.

Nonexperimental research methods are used when the introduction and manipulation of an independent variable are not practical, possible, or ethical. This technique of scientific inquiry is also known as descriptive research, which asks the basic question: What is? Nonexperimental research is typified by making observations or descriptions about the present status of a condition or situation. Investigators using this method do not manipulate variables or make things happen. They measure and record events that would have occurred had they not been there anyway.

Much of behavioral research is nonexperimental, because it would be impossible to replicate some elements of human conduct in a laboratory setting. For example, how could one study seat-belt usage or acts of sportsmanship in a laboratory environment? It is unethical to conduct experimental research on some aspects of human behavior. Even if a researcher lacked a certain moral conviction, no institutional review board would sanction a study that was based on the orchestration of something that was harmful or dangerous. For instance, a researcher could not deliberately inject athletes with megadoses of anabolic steroids to study their effects on strength or purposely cause athletic injuries in order to investigate the healing properties of a new type of therapy. Studies causing cancer, car accidents, and other such events would be profane to perform on humans in an experimental manner. However, these types of behaviors and conditions do exist and are important to examine. Therefore sometimes the only way to study certain situations or actions is through descriptive or nonexperimental methods.

Most nonexperimental studies are conducted using the basic elements of the scientific method—that is, a hypothesis is stated and tested and conclusions are made. In fact, the only distinction from experimental research in this respect is that the hypothesis is tested using nonexperimental procedures, and these methods characteristically do not have very good control over the experimental condition. Therefore it is important to emphasize that nonexperimental research is not as robust as experimentation when it comes to establishing cause and effect relationships. Still, it should not be thought of as second-rate research. In this chapter we examine the nature of several varieties of nonexperimental research that are frequently utilized in HPER.

## NONEXPERIMENTAL RESEARCH AND CAUSE AND EFFECT

There are a few basic reasons why nonexperimental research is not a rigorous means of verifying traditional cause–effect relationships. The primary reason is that the researcher does not introduce an independent variable and measure its effect. Rather, the investigator only records the presence of a certain variable as it occurs or after the fact. Let's say that a woman arrives on the scene of an auto accident and sees three cars with extensive damage. The only logical deduction that she can make is that an accident has occurred. She can't make any valid conclusions about the cause of the crash because she did not observe it directly, and even if she had, she wouldn't know for sure what caused it.

In nonexperimental research an independent variable is not introduced or extraneous variables may not be controlled, making it difficult to conclude that variable *A* caused *B* to occur. The most logical conclusion that may be drawn with this type of research is that variable *A* is present, but how it got to be that way is hard to say. We'll have more to say on this soon.

Another factor that reduces the ability to conclude cause and effect is that subjects typically are not randomized into groups. They are usually identified by some predetermined criteria and placed into groups in that fashion. However, it is significant to point out that that does not mean subjects are not or cannot be randomly selected from a population of subjects. This is an important procedure to use in any kind of research where it is desirable to make generalizations about a particular population of subjects and is commonly done with descriptive research. We already know that lack of randomization raises many threats to internal validity. Because the possible effects of extraneous variables haven't been controlled for, and the researcher didn't make something happen, serious questions may be raised about assuming cause and effect.

Nonexperimental research is based on making logical deductions about the connections that variables may have with one another. This type of association is referred to as a *causal relationship*. (No, this is not like friends dating!) Essentially, this means that variables are often observed with one another, but the true nature of the relationship may not be known or explained. Nevertheless, an association does not mean causation. We discussed this concern when interpreting correlation coefficients. These statistics depict mathematical relationships between variables, and only the producer or consumer of research may draw a cause and effect relationship from them.

Most large-scale epidemiological (research involved in the study of disease) studies are nonexperimental in nature. For instance, obesity is routinely identified as a secondary risk factor for heart disease. Does that mean that the more body fat one has the more likely having heart disease becomes? Maybe. Because variables are observed and not manipulated in this type of study, a careful interpretation might be that in large-scale studies high body fat levels are more typical in persons who have heart disease than those who do not. We all probably have known individuals who would be considered obese and lived long lives and didn't die from heart disease. Still, most people would agree that it would be prudent to reduce body fat for this and other health reasons. However, from the example cited here that decision is not based on a systematic cause and effect relationship.

See how cautious these statements are? Such is the nature of interpreting the results of research in general and nonexperimental research in particular. Producers and consumers of research need to use sound standards when making interpretations and speculations relative to nonexperimental research. Nonexperimental research is about discovering functional relationships between variables and using logic and knowledge to rationalize their association. Many possible explanations for the existence of variables and their causes must be entertained. A seemingly obvious relationship may be erroneously taken at face value, which would result in false conclusions. Now you can see why researchers are reluctant to use the term "cause and effect" when discussing relationships observed in nonexperimental research.

## SURVEYS

You probably could not have gotten to this point in your life without having participated in some type of survey. Someone more than likely has called you on the phone to ask your opinion about a politician, or mailed a questionnaire to you asking you to rate breakfast cereals, or stopped you in the shopping mall to ask questions regarding fast-food choices. We are constantly being bombarded by the media with statistics from surveys. Facts like 72% of dentists prefer this brand of toothpaste, 9 out of 10 kids like this brand of peanut butter, or less than 20% of Americans exercise regularly (sad, but true!) are the results of some type of survey research.

Surveys are abundant in our society and are used a great deal in HPER. Basically, a survey is a broad-based information gathering procedure that is designed to measure present practices, opinions, or other such variables. Typically, rather than a researcher observing a particular behavior, the subject reports it. With certain variables or behaviors this may represent a significant limitation. However, this drawback is a necessary one, because usually there may be no other means of obtaining such data. A routine assumption/limitation to self-reporting of information is if the subject is capable of making a valid assessment of the variable in question and/or if the subject is responding truthfully. Survey research should not be considered mere "bean counting" because it requires much skill to orchestrate, conduct, and draw conclusions. There are many steps and procedures that need to be attended to in order to carry out a successful survey. The most common type of survey is performed with a mailed questionnaire, so we will focus our discussion on that variety.

## STEPS IN CONDUCTING A SURVEY BY MAIL

Before survey research can be done, the investigator needs to develop a detailed plan of action. This "grocery list" should present all of the required steps in a logical, chronological order. Because so many things need to occur in order for the study to be successful, it is highly desirable to write them down. Even a veteran survey researcher can forget an essential item or two. Poor planning may result in meaningless data, at the expense of lost time and money.

### Step 1: Decide What You Want to Accomplish

As with any research project, the investigator must have a clear, defined purpose for why the study should be done and be able to state a testable hypothesis. The study must be designed in such a way that the hypothesis may be tested. This is nothing new, right? It is such an obvious characteristic of sound research that oftentimes it is not considered as seriously as it should be. In surveys, numerous details—type and number of questions, variables to be assessed, how to generate a representative sample, allocation of resources, preparation of the question-naire, scoring and analysis of data—need to be determined before the fact.

## Step 2: The Sample

One of the primary purposes of conducting a survey is to be able to make gener-alizations from a sample to a population. To accomplish this, two factors need to be considered. The researcher must decide on clear delimitations for subject in-clusion and have a systematic and unbiased means of establishing a representa-tive sample.

In some cases establishing subject delimitations is very easy. For exam-ple, in a broad-based public opinion poll, if you are a human who has a pulse and can communicate at the third grade level, you can be in the study. In other cases subject selection criteria need to be more precise. If a health researcher were interested in studying health behaviors between adults that exercise or don't exercise, many attributes would require distinct operational definitions. What is the criterion for an adult? That might be easy to define—maybe anyone over the age of 21. Is there an upper age limit? How are exerciser and nonexer-ciser defined? There are many possible definitions here. The point is that the re-searcher needs to identify carefully the characteristics of the type of subject he wants to study before he recruits them. A standard consideration, however, re-gardless of any other criteria, is whether the subject in question is capable of ac-curately providing the investigator with the desired information.

After deciding on the traits of the subjects, the investigator needs to de-termine how many subjects will be required and how they will be identified. The number of subjects to include will be dictated by several factors. From a statisti-cal standpoint, there needs to be a large enough sample in order to be consid-ered representative and to make reasonable generalizations. This is largely de-pendent on the potential size of the population in question. For example, if someone wanted to make generalizations to a population of 200 recreation lead-ers in a community park district, she would need a large percent (maybe 25% to 50% or so) of the 200 possible subjects in the sample to accomplish this. On the other hand, accurate generalizations and predictions are made in U.S. presiden-tial elections based on polling of much less than 1% of the voting population.

The last point to consider relative to sample size is cost. Envelopes, paper, copying, stamps—all cost money and have an insidious way of escalating quickly. For students or researchers on restricted budgets, compromises in sam-ple size and statistical power may need to be made in order to realistically con-duct the study. In some cases the restriction in sample size may be so great that it is not feasible to carry the study out at all. Needless to say, it is best from a time and money standpoint to figure this out beforehand!

Subject identification and the sampling procedure are other important steps to contemplate. We have discussed various random sampling procedures, such as the use of random numbers, counting off methods, and developing a stratified random sample. Any one of these may be appropriate, depending on the nature and diversity of the population and the size of the sample. You may find it helpful to review these procedures to determine which would be the best for your situation.

To simplify the sampling process, researchers sometimes use mailing lists from organizations. This is often desirable when the group has members who are the type of subjects that the researcher would like to study. For example, if someone was interested in studying the exercise habits of professionals in HPER, the quickest way to generate a sample of subjects would be to get a mailing list from AAHPERD. This would be easy, and practical. However, it would be an incorrect approach if the researcher used this list for convenience purposes and wanted to use it as a sample that would be representative of average Americans. Do you think there might be a difference in the exercise habits of HPER specialists and typical Americans? (Please say yes!)

## Step 3: Instrument Development

With surveys conducted by mail, the questionnaire is the instrument that is used to measure the experimental variables. The development of a valid questionnaire requires much time and skill. Many a survey has failed to yield any meaningful information because of a poorly prepared instrument. The type and number of questions, their format and wording, how they will be evaluated, and more—all of this needs to be considered in the planning process. Let's look at the major items in questionnaire construction.

Before preparing any questions or items, researchers should develop a list of the variables to be measured in the survey. There should be a clear understanding of exactly what is to be known or learned. Once these have been itemized, a table should be prepared. This table should include the areas or variables the researcher would like to assess and the number and type of items to be used. These procedures will reduce the likelihood of using a disorganized, "shotgun" approach to constructing the instrument.

The type of questions or items to be used has a large impact on the success of the survey. A concise, easy to answer survey instrument is much more likely to be completed and returned than one that takes considerable time or effort. Generally, questions or items may be classified as open- or closed-ended.

*Open-ended questions* allow the respondent an opportunity for free expression. An item like "Describe your attitude toward sex education in the public schools" is an example. Although they allow for free expression, these items have some undesirable aspects. One is that they are highly subjective to interpret, making them difficult to analyze and quantify. Another factor is that they take longer to complete and perhaps require the respondent to think too much about the answer. If faced with any or too many of these types of items, the respondent may throw the questionnaire in the circular file. Obviously, some kinds of information can only be provided by an open-ended item. Asking for an annual income or number of years lived in a city are open-ended items but are completely objective in nature. If subjective items are used, however, they should be kept to a minimum, with attention given to how they will be scored or analyzed.

*Closed-ended items* are objective, making them easier to analyze and quantify. One type of closed-ended item is a simple *ranking* process. For instance, from a list of 10 recreational activities the subject is asked to rank-order them according to preference with highest choice receiving a 1 and least favorite getting a 10. Another traditional approach is to use *scaled responses*. A *Likert scale* assigns point values to statements that indicate the degree of agreement or disagreement. Different words or terms may be applied to the scale, depending on the nature of the question. Here are two examples of Likert scale items:

During practices do you get mad at your teammates?

1 ......................2 ......................3 ..........................4 ..........................5

Never       Rarely       Sometimes       Often       All the time

High school students should be required to take a drug education class.

1 ......................2 ......................3 ..........................4 ..........................5

Strongly    Disagree    Not Sure       Agree       Strongly
Disagree                                                Agree

Incidentally, Likert scale responses are actually ordinal level measurements, thus requiring the use of nonparametric statistical analyses.

Some types of information can be provided very easily with a *categorical* response, such as yes/no, true/false, high/low, and female/male. Although binary responses are easy to quantify, they lack the ability to show the degree of association to an item. Take the two examples from the Likert scale and reduce them to yes/no questions. Doing this may present a limitation to certain items. Therefore categorical questions should be reserved for more binary or outright questions or opinions. Examples might be "Do you have a university degree? (yes/no)" or "Cigarette smoking is the number one preventable public health risk. (true/false)"

There is no magic number of items that should appear on a questionnaire, but a simple rule of thumb is "fewer are better." Only pertinent items should appear, in an attempt to minimize the length of the instrument, which increases the probability of a high rate of return. If an item can't provide the researcher with relevant information, it should be discarded. Borg and Gall (1983) report a negative relationship between the length of a questionnaire and a decrease in the rate of return. Wouldn't you have guessed that?

Regardless of the type of item selected, all items should have certain qualities. They should be concisely and unambiguously stated and convey only one question or idea. "Do you enjoy hiking and camping?" is a good example of a poor question because it is asking two things. A "yes" answer means that one enjoys *both* hiking and camping. A "no" response may mean that the subject

**TABLE 16-1**  Factors in the development of a survey instrument

The following factors need to be determined:
1. The variables to be studied
2. The types of questions to be asked, e.g.,
   open- vs. closed-ended
3. The number of questions
4. The order of questions
5. The scoring of the responses
6. The layout and appearance of the instrument
7. The exact instructions for completion of the instrumet
8. The instrument's content validity

doesn't like either activity or likes one and not the other. Verbiage that leads the subject to respond one way or another should be avoided. Finally, the items need to be written in such a manner that they are not too technical but are still stimulating and respective of the knowledge level of the subject.

The quality of the layout and appearance of the questionnaire is also a vital ingredient for a successful survey. The questions or items should follow a logical sequence and not hopscotch around to different topics. Also, the first several items need to be easily answered and be motivators so that the subject is more prone to completing it and is not immediately discouraged. Finally, the questionnaire should look neat and orderly, using easy to read type or lettering and quality paper. Erasures, fingerprints, blotch marks, cheap or torn paper, and other such detractors convey an unwanted and unprofessional message. By the way, did you think writing the questionnaire was going to be easy? A summary of the steps in the development of the instrument is given in Table 16-1.

**Step 4: The Cover Letter**

A well-developed questionnaire is functionally useless without an effective cover letter. As does the questionnaire, the cover letter needs to be concise, attractive, and professionally written. The letter should appear on the official letterhead stationery of the organization that is the home of the research. Perhaps the first thing that will catch the eye of the potential subject is the subject's name and how he or she is addressed. If a person's name is misspelled, or isn't addressed correctly, the survey could quickly be part of the recycling effort. In any type of professional correspondence, particularly when you do not know someone personally, the person should be respectfully addressed as Mr., Ms., Dr., Honorable, and so on.

The first few sentences should contain some information about the study, such as its purpose, and provide some brief background about the researcher and his or her affiliation. It helps to promote the study's credibility to state if it is being supported by a noted professional organization or individual. A letter of support or endorsement from a prominent officer in an organization to encourage the participation of its members would be invaluable in some cases.

Now one has to turn to the fine art of boosting and massaging egos. Within the letter you have to let the potential subjects know that they are part of a select group, are very special, and that you value their participation. Some people will participate in a study only if there is something of value in it for them. Therefore you need to tell them how they benefit (e.g., money, rewards, feedback), if at all. One can always let the subject know that only he or she can provide you with this information and it is needed for the advancement of knowledge. So, in that respect, the subject may feel good about contributing to a societal benefit and want to take part.

Exact instructions for completing the instrument should appear either in the letter or directly on the questionnaire. If the instructions are on the instrument, it would be a good idea to mention that fact in the letter. Also, it is helpful to provide an approximate amount of time that it will take to complete the questionnaire. A date of return should be indicated. Trying to determine an appropriate time for completing and returning the survey is a guessing game. If you give subjects too much time, they might forget about it or think that it's not important. On the other hand if you ask for it back within a few days and the subject is busy, or thinks that you're being too pushy, he or she simply won't complete it. The amount of time required should be based on the length of the instrument and the types of variables being measured. Seven to ten days for a short survey and two to three weeks for a longer one are good ballpark figures. Lastly, don't forget to include a stamped, self-addressed envelope.

Research subjects have the right to anonymity and confidentiality, and an assurance of those rights should be included in the letter. Of course, complete anonymity makes following up on subjects more costly or time consuming. More will be said on that shortly. A summary of the major considerations for writing a cover letter appears in Table 16-2.

**TABLE 16-2**   Factors in writing a cover letter

---

The following factors need to be considered:
 1. Use official letterhead stationery.
 2. Address subject properly: Mr., Ms., Dr.
 3. Check for spelling and other grammatical errors.
 4. Include letters of endorsement, if applicable.
 5. Encourage the subject's participation.
 6. Indicate any possible benefits to the subject or society.
 7. Include directions for completing the survey.
 8. Indicate the amount of time to complete the survey.
 9. Specify the return date.
10. Include a self-addressed stamped envelope.
11. Include a consent form, if applicable.
12. Assure confidentiality.

---

## Step 5: Checkout and Trial Run

After the hard work of developing the questionnaire and the cover letter is done, an assessment of their quality should be performed. This is best done by enlisting the help of a few individuals who have experience in this type and area of research. They should examine both documents for clarity, format, grammar, and appearance. The instrument and its items need to be evaluated for content validity. Any revisions in the letter or the instrument should be then incorporated. A pilot study of the survey to a few select subjects may also provide further feedback on the letter or the questionnaire and may give the investigator some concept of the time needed to complete the instrument and return it or what rate of return may be expected. The trial run may also furnish an opportunity to remedy oversights before the actual study takes place.

## Step 6: Send It

Now all you have to do is address the envelopes, stuff them, close them, lick the stamps, and mail them. Not so fast! If you want the best chance for a high rate of return, you need to consider when and where to mail the survey. If it is a professionally or occupationally related survey, the preferred place to mail it is to the subject's place of work. The season of the year may have some bearing on a good return rate. For instance, school-based surveys should be avoided during the weeks that schools are starting and finishing or during vacation times. A survey dealing with summer recreation choices might yield better results in July than in January. Trying to conduct any survey during holidays like Christmas and New Year most likely will not be successful.

## Step 7: Follow-up Procedures

A prime goal of any survey researcher is to obtain as high a rate of return as possible. Several strategies to increase the likelihood of subject participation have already been discussed. However, incorporating these methods into a study doesn't necessarily translate into a high return rate. Even well-meaning potential subjects may require some subtle "arm-twisting" to get involved. Sometimes people forget, get too busy, or just need a little extra encouragement to take part, and that is what follow-up tactics are all about.

Follow-up techniques will differ slightly if a study was conducted so that the respondents remained anonymous. If anonymously done, one approach is to send a new questionnaire to all of the participants about one week after the return date. This should be done under the guise that perhaps the survey didn't arrive or the subject lost it, or you're simply hoping that if you are persistent enough the subject will take part. This is an expensive approach. However, it is the price to pay for anonymity. If the respondents are known, then sending a new survey to the nonparticipants is all that is necessary. Another method is to send a post card to the subjects, either reminding them to complete and return the survey and/or if they have done so, thanking them. Of course if the nonrespondents are known, a reminder post card is all that is needed. This may be done once or twice after the return date. After two reminders it is fairly unlikely that the potential subject is going to take part. Some surveys are done with a few select subjects in mind and the inclusion of almost all of them is vital to the success of the study. If the respondents are known, placing a follow-up phone call or two may be the right personal touch to get the stragglers involved.

What rate of return is needed for a valid study? That really depends on the number of prospective participants and the size of the population that is to be generalized to. Generally, the smaller the sample the higher the rate of return; with a larger sample a smaller return rate can be tolerated. Overall, the higher the return rate the more representative the sample will be. Remember, statistical inferences can be accurately made from representative random samples with relatively low $N$ sizes. The key word here is "representative." Anytime there is a low rate of return, a fundamental question may be asked about how representative the sample is based on the subjects that responded. Is there something unique about them that is characteristically different than the nonrespondents? If so, this introduces a form of selection bias and reduces the experimental validity of the study in many respects. This is why both a proper random sampling procedure and a respectable return rate are crucial to valid survey research.

## Step 8: Results and Thanks

Recall that one of the rights of a research subject is to be provided with the results of a study. Therefore the final step in the survey is to provide the participants with a summary of the major findings of the investigation and to thank them for taking part. Not only is this a subject's right, it is also common courtesy on the part of the investigator. Also, it may increase the likelihood that the subject may participate in future studies. A summary of the major steps in conducting a mailed survey is presented in Table 16-3.

**TABLE 16-3**   Major steps in conducting a survey

1. Determine the research objectives for the study.
2. Determine the sample i.e., size, sampling procedure, subject characteristics.
3. Develop the instrument.
4. Develop the cover letter.
5. Establish the quality of the instrument and cover letter.
6. Get endorsements for the study, if applicable.
7. Conduct pilot survey, if applicable.
8. Conduct actual survey.
9. Use established follow-up procedures to get highest return rate possible.
10. Send results and thank-you letters.

## OTHER SURVEY METHODS

We have discussed in a fair amount of detail techniques to be used when conducting a survey by mail. Surveys are also conducted by personal interview. Interviews may be done over the telephone or face to face. These are usually more time costly and labor intensive than mail surveys. The basic tenets of carrying out a survey are similar no matter what the technique, particularly when it comes to developing the instrument. Typically, only the method of securing data is different. All survey procedures have distinct advantages and drawbacks. Factors such as time, cost, number of subjects, coding of responses, training and number of interviewers, sensitivity of questions, location of subjects, and sampling procedures need to be appraised when selecting the appropriate survey approach.

## INFORMED CONSENT AND SURVEYS

One of the ethical rights of a research subject is informed consent, and this right is *not* waived in survey research. How does a researcher get informed consent with a survey? One approach is the traditional way, with the subject reading and signing a written document. Informed consent documents may be included in a mailed survey and returned with the instrument or administered prior to a face-to-face interview or a survey that is completed by a subject in the presence of an investigator. Informed consent may be *implied* in the case of a mailed survey if the subject returns it. If the subject doesn't want to participate in the study, he or she simply need not send it back. If this approach is used, however, the subject should be provided with appropriate background information in the cover letter. Finally, informed consent may be obtained verbally, which would be the most appropriate for telephone interviews.

No matter what type of survey is used, subjects should have a clear understanding of the nature of the research and their role, so that they can make a knowledgeable decision about their participation. Failure to provide informed consent is a violation of the subject's rights and is considered unprofessional conduct on the part of the investigator.

## OTHER NONEXPERIMENTAL METHODS

Although survey research is a very commonly used and important technique, there are many other nonexperimental procedures. Some of these are quite complicated and difficult to conduct and usually require much skill and expertise. In fact, the core of entire texts, courses, and disciplines may be based on any one of these methods. Because of this, elaborate descriptions are beyond the scope of this text. In the following sections we would like to increase your awareness of some other types of nonexperimental research by presenting brief overviews of each.

## Correlational Research

The purpose of correlational research is to examine the relationships between or among variables. By using a variety of correlational statistics, the researcher may answer questions that pertain to the type and strength of relationships, prediction, or the accuracy of the prediction. Perhaps the most common approaches are the simple and multiple correlation techniques that examine relationships between two variables or more than two variables, respectively. Any or all of these procedures have applications in solving correlational research problems. (Refer to Chapter 10 for a review of correlational analyses and relevant examples.)

One of the most common errors made in correlational research is to readily assume a cause and effect relationship. Correlational statistics depict only mathematical relationships between or among variables. Knowledge and reason must be used by the producer or consumer of research to ultimately conclude cause and effect. Because no independent variable is introduced or manipulated, interpretations of correlational research are bound by the same limitations as other types of nonexperimental research.

## Case Studies

The case study is a widely used approach in fields like medicine, psychology, and the social sciences. Even in our disciplines case studies of unique situations appear in the literature. A case study is an in-depth analysis of a unique condition or situation. The subject in the case study may be one person, or it can be an intact class, an institution, or an entire community. The purpose of a study like this is to examine various aspects of the subject in question and to note how the case is unique or different from what is normal or expected. Usually, the event or situation in question is not well known or understood or rarely occurs, making experimental research not practical or possible.

Obviously, drawing any broad generalizations from a case study is not warranted. However, when many case studies have been performed on the same topic and similar results are reported, the basis of formulating a hypothesis or theory is made. Case study research may be the only way to provide a foundation of knowledge when examining exceptional circumstances or conditions. Also, in some instances, case studies may utilize experimental methods and designs.

## Developmental Research

The purpose of developmental research is to explain changes in factors such as behavior, growth, or knowledge throughout the life cycle or a specified time period. *Longitudinal* research is when the same subjects are studied over a long time period. Although this is a preferred method, any long-term study of variables in humans is very burdensome to carry out, for many reasons. The time needed to conduct the study, subject attrition, subject familiarity with testing procedures, and the Hawthorne effect are all factors that may negatively influence longitudinal research results.

Because of these concerns, sometimes developmental studies are performed using a *cross-sectional* approach. This involves generating a representative sample of subjects across several age group strata. For instance, in a study of the effects of aging on coordination, a stratified sample may consist of 25 subjects in each stratum for every decade of life. Although, the cross-sectional method reduces some of the limitations associated with longitudinal research, it has drawbacks. One question is how truly representative the subjects in each stratum are of the developmental process at that age. Another is the fact that the subjects are not the same in each stratum, so any differences across age groups may be because of individual variation in subjects and not necessarily to changes in maturation. Despite these concerns, the cross-sectional method is a very common and popular form of developmental research.

## Epidemiological Research

Research in epidemiology, the science concerned with studying diseases, may be experimental (both basic and applied) and nonexperimental. Nonexperimental investigations are usually large-scale descriptive studies that employ longitudinal or cross-sectional methods. The intent of such studies is to examine subjects in a "free living" environment and assess them on a periodic basis. More than 5000 residents of Framingham, Massachusetts, have participated in an ongoing heart disease study for more than 40 years. The Framingham study is a very famous epidemiological investigation and has provided extensive information about heart disease and cardiovascular risk factors.

The incidence rates of the disease in question are recorded, as well as the variables that are observed to be associated with the affliction. Causal relationships, but not cause and effect, may then be established between the disorder and variables that appear most frequently with it. Even though cause and effect relationships are not confirmed with this type of research, it doesn't mean the results are not of value. For instance, what if research has shown that of 100,000 confirmed cases of heart disease, 89% of the subjects had cholesterol levels above 240 mg/dl. This would be a very powerful finding, and it would be foolish to ignore it just because it may not demonstrate cause and effect.

It is considered unethical to introduce diseases into human subjects, so animal subjects are used. However, there are limitations to the ability to generalize the results of animal research to humans. So, in many instances, the only means to conduct human epidemiological research is in a nonexperimental manner.

## Observational Research

In observational research the investigator obtains data by examining or observing a behavior or trait and recording it rather than having the subject self-report it. This type of research is employed when there are serious questions about the subject's ability to provide accurate and honest information. Can you imagine the validity of the feedback if you asked an athlete how many acts of good or bad sportsmanship she or he displayed in a game? The athlete may be unaware of these actions at the time, may not be able to recall, or may not tell the truth. (Speaking about telling the truth, ask a runner what his or her weekly mileage is, then subtract about five miles from that total!)

Many observations of behavior may be contaminated or altered by the presence of an investigator or if performed in an artificial environment. Therefore it is important sometimes to observe behaviors or practices in an inconspicuous manner so that the subjects function normally. Observations may be made from a distance, through a one-way mirror, or other such unobtrusive means. Also, because it would be difficult to replicate most human behaviors in a laboratory, much observational research is performed in real-world settings. Observations can also be made with the assistance of a video camera. This enables the researcher to play back the video at a later time, allowing for a more accurate analysis. (In order for this approach to be effective, the camera needs to be positioned out of the view of the subjects.)

Observational studies require special attention to certain details. Before data collection can begin, the observational researcher needs to define specifically and functionally the behaviors and delimitations for the subjects to be studied. Careful consideration must be given to studying the subjects in the most natural setting and means possible. The investigator also needs to develop a means to measure and quantify the behavior in the most accurate and feasible way.

Sometimes ethical questions may be raised about the type of behavior studied and how observations are made. Let's say that a health researcher is interested in conducting an observational study to examine the use of illegal drugs by college students. To provide a setting for observation the researcher throws a party and invites students to come. During the party the investigator is covertly watching for (or videotaping) and recording the incidence of drug use, of course without the participants' knowledge. Would this be ethical? How would you feel if some aspect of your behavior, particularly if it was very personal, was being observed and chronicled without your knowledge or consent? There are no easy answers to these questions. Much of the rightness or wrongness of this type of practice centers around the sensitivity of the behavior and the amount of deception or concealment that is used to assess it. Try discussing this issue in your class. By the way, this example is similar to an actual study that went through our university research review board. After a rousing discussion by the board members the study was disapproved!

## "Descriptive" Research

Descriptive research attempts to describe selected meaningful characteristics of a distinctive group. The purpose may be to compare these traits to other groups, to develop normative information, or simply to profile the group for the sake of knowledge. Numerous studies have examined common physical fitness variables of athletes from different sports: football, soccer, rugby, karate, track, cycling. Once again, these studies do not involve the manipulation of an independent variable, making them purely nonexperimental or "descriptive" in nature.

### Ex Post Facto and Meta-Analysis Research

Ex post facto and meta-analysis research falls "between the cracks," because it is based on past data generated in an experimental or nonexperimental fashion. *Ex post facto* ("after the fact") or archival research uses past data to answer present questions or to test new hypotheses. For instance, a health researcher may examine public health records to investigate factors related to a particular illness or disorder. A recreator may inspect data on past park usage to estimate current or future participation patterns. Using appropriate past data eliminates the need for present information gathering and expedites the research process. Moreover, this method may represent the primary means in which some topics (e.g., deaths due to auto accidents, or factors related to deaths from a disease) are studied.

Data do not necessarily have to come from records or files. Results from published research may be used as a form of data to be analyzed and to test new hypotheses. This process is referred to as a *meta-analysis*. Essentially, studies examining the same variable may be inspected and relevant data extracted to calculate a statistic known as an *effect size*. The effect size statistic is then used as a form of raw data for further analysis and hypothesis testing. The meta-analysis procedure is technically a form of ex post facto research. More details on meta-analysis are presented in Chapter 18.

## SUMMARY

Nonexperimental research is typified by making observations or descriptions about the present status of a condition or situation. A primary feature of this type of research is that an independent variable is not introduced or manipulated. Because of this limitation, nonexperimental research is not as robust as experimentation when it comes to establishing cause and effect relationships. Still, it should not be thought of as second-rate research. Nonexperimental research may be conducted through the use of surveys and numerous other techniques. A summary of the major types of nonexperimental research appears in Table 16-4.

**TABLE 16-4**   Major types of nonexperimental research in HPER

Surveys (mailed, in person, telephone)
Correlational
Case studies
Developmental
Epidemiological
Observational
Descriptive
Ex post facto
Meta-analysis

# CHAPTER 17

# QUALITY CONTROL IN RESEARCH

**KEY CONCEPTS**

Internal quality control
External quality control
Peer review
Colloquia and defenses
Institutional review board
Review of journal articles

Blind review
Unblind review
Publish or perish
Research quality versus
   quantity

**AFTER READING THIS CHAPTER, YOU SHOULD BE ABLE TO**

- Distinguish between internal and external quality control measures.
- Describe the role of the institutional review board in regard to quality control.
- Discuss the journal review process, especially as it pertains to blind and unblind review of manuscripts.
- Understand the nature of publication demands and the potential impact on research quality and quantity.

$N$ow that we have discussed the nuts and bolts of the research process, you may wonder: Who watches over research to make sure that it is done correctly, safely, and honestly? This is not an easy question to answer, because there is no one person or process that assures or protects the quality of these factors. The individual researcher ultimately exerts the greatest influence over the quality of most facets of research. Consequently, the training, integrity, and work habits of the investigator are of vital importance. In this chapter some of the factors that affect research quality control are discussed.

## INTERNAL QUALITY CONTROL

Internal quality control in research may be regarded as any individual or group that exists within an institution that either approves research projects or protects the rights of research subjects. This measure affects research quality up to the point where the researcher attempts to publish or present the results of the study. Because much research in HPER is conducted in universities, we will consider some of the internal quality control mechanisms in place at these institutions. Most departments have some type of peer review of research proposals for faculty members, as well as colloquia and defenses for student theses and projects. Also, virtually every university has some type of institutional review board that approves research proposals. Let's look at each one of these and see how they work.

### Peer Review

Most departments have a person or committee that is responsible for reviewing research proposals prior to their submission to the institutional review board or before the research is conducted. Much of what is accomplished with this process is editing the proposal for content and methods and evaluating its scientific merit. One of the major problems with this process is related to one faculty member's ability to evaluate the work of another. For example if a recreation researcher is reviewing a proposal for a biomechanics study, it would be difficult for the recreator to pass reasonable judgment on the methods used or the scientific worthiness of the project. So the best outcome of the review may be only editorial suggestions or ethical questions related to the safety of subjects. Therefore peer review works best when someone with a similar level of expertise in the same area of study critiques the proposal. Unfortunately, in small departments this situation may not be possible.

Oftentimes peer review takes place at an informal level. That is, faculty members will approach a colleague and ask him or her to read a proposal and provide frank and sincere feedback. When faculty members respect each other's opinions and welcome constructive criticism, this approach works well. In this regard, successful researchers need to be open-minded and willing to accept and provide critique.

## Student Colloquia and Defenses

Students who elect to write a thesis or dissertation will have their work reviewed numerous times by their committee members. Perhaps the two most important reviews that take place are when the student formally presents the research proposal and the final thesis. The forum for presenting the proposal or final thesis is known as a colloquium or a defense. Typically, these are public presentations to which all faculty and students are invited. Contrary to popular belief, the purpose of these presentations is not to "roast the student" but to provide helpful critiques and suggestions in the attempt to have the best study possible. It is important to understand that this process is a learning experience for the student. Students are asked to answer questions that allow them to consider a problem and are guided toward a logical conclusion. Although this may seem intimidating, one should approach it with a positive frame of mind.

At our institution, students must successfully present their proposal and obtain the approval of their committee before they may submit the proposal to the institutional review board (IRB). These steps as well as IRB approval must be completed before any data collection can take place. Needless to say, students must also successfully defend the final thesis for their degree to be awarded. Approval of the final thesis must be obtained from the committee and usually the graduate dean for research. Some institutions have a thesis editor who gives final endorsement of the thesis. The thesis editor is concerned only for checking format, style, and grammar, not the content or merit of the study.

By its nature the thesis is a very structured and guided experience with many good quality control measures. Ultimately the goal of any research project is to publish or present the results and make a scholarly contribution to the discipline. This should also be the projected outcome of a thesis or dissertation. Publication or presentation of research is another benchmark of research quality and a type of control measure that we will discuss later.

## Institutional Review Boards

The institutional review board is the most important internal quality control mechanism, for many reasons. What exactly is an IRB, and what quality control functions does it serve? The following discussion explains.

The IRB exists primarily to assist researchers in the protection of research subjects. When scientifically sound and ethical studies are conducted, not only are the research subjects' rights upheld but, indirectly, the reputations of the institution and researcher are safeguarded to some extent. Research subjects may be categorized as human or animal, and there usually is a specific IRB that serves the needs of each. Because animal subjects are used only in a small number of highly specialized areas in HPER, we will limit our discussion to human subject IRBs.

U.S. government regulations (e.g., Code of Federal Regulations, 1983) specify that any institution that is receiving federal money to support research *must* have a committee that is competent to review research proposals that involve human subjects. Technically, any institution that is not receiving federal dollars is not *legally* required to have an IRB. However, it would seem logical that any organization that allows human subject research to be conducted has a moral and ethical charge to ensure subjects' welfare and, therefore, should have an IRB.

An IRB consists of members from a wide variety of academic specialties where human subject research is likely to be done. Depending on the size and needs of the institution, IRB membership may be quite large and diverse. Representatives may include physicians, psychologists, educators, lawyers, philosophers, sociologists, as well as community members such as clergy. Specialists in HPER often serve as well. This assorted membership is important so that experts from various areas may assist the IRB in competent review of research.

The material that an investigator usually submits to the IRB would be some form of a detailed written proposal and an informed consent document. The proposal would contain many of the components of a research paper that we have previously discussed, in addition to some others. The informed consent document (see Chapter 2) is examined for its clarity, simplicity, and completeness.

Not all research studies involving human subjects have the same element of risk. So it is not necessary for an entire IRB to deliberate over routine studies that pose no risk to the participant. Thus there are various levels of IRB review for proposals, depending on the risk to the subject.

Federal guidelines classify the review of proposals three ways: exempt, expedited, and full board. *Exempt* research studies typically have little or no risk and involve the collection of data from routine practices or procedures. Most educational research (e.g., research involving normal educational practices) would be classified as exempt. The chairperson of the IRB approves this type of proposal on behalf of the board. *Expedited* review is done on studies that involve no more than minimal risk. Examples of studies needing this level of review include the use of moderate exercise, noninvasive electronic monitoring of the subject, examination of pre-existing records, or obtaining small amounts of blood. Usually one expert board member is selected to review and approve the proposal for the IRB. Any study that does not qualify for exempt or expedited status must be reviewed by the *entire board*. These studies usually expose subjects to greater than minimal risk. An example is a study requiring subjects over age 40 to perform treadmill runs to exhaustion.

At the heart of every review is a basic question: What is the risk to the subject in relation to the possible benefit? This risk/benefit analysis must always favor more benefit, otherwise the proposal is unapprovable. There needs to be direct benefit to the subject or to society but not necessarily to both. Because the risk/benefit ratio is subjectively determined, IRB members may have lengthy debates on some studies. *The decisions of the IRB basically influence what human subject research can or cannot be done at that institution.* A thumbs up or down ruling on a controversial study may have lasting impact on, among other things, the research agenda of an investigator (which may alter a career) or the growth of a scientific discipline. For example, the IRB at the University of Utah debated at great length before allowing human research of the artificial heart. After the 1982 experiment headed by William deVries further human studies in this area were disapproved at that university.

Every proposal that involves the use of human subjects has to be approved by the IRB before it is initiated. The study then must be conducted in the manner in which it was approved and under full IRB guidelines. The IRB doesn't have a police force to ensure that investigators are in compliance with these guidelines. It is accepted in good faith that investigators will conduct research within this framework. Thus it is the researcher who has the primary responsibility for complying with all guidelines and regulations. Violations of this obligation could result in serious penalties for the institution as well as the investigator. Ask your professor for details regarding the IRB at your university.

## EXTERNAL QUALITY CONTROL

External quality control may be regarded as any process or procedure that exists outside an institution that regulates the publication or presentation of research results. After a research project has been completed and the results are determined, the investigator has the challenging task of presenting orally and/or publishing the study. Of the two media for transmitting research information, publication in a well-respected journal is considered the higher benchmark of research quality. Let's see how this aspect of quality control works.

### Publication of a Research Article

After the researcher completes the data collection phase of the study and performs the appropriate statistical analyses, he or she must try to determine if it is worth telling the scientific community. In other words will what is to be said make a contribution to a discipline's body of knowledge? Everyone who does research would like to think that his or her work is meaningful, but quite frankly, not all of it is. The same study may have been done elsewhere previously (although it is important to replicate studies), conducted with unacceptable methods or a faulty research design, all of which reduce the value of the outcome. Sometimes even a well-conducted study yields little of value because of incorrect interpretations or because it was poorly written. Obviously there are many things to consider and evaluate about a study to deem it worthy of publication. Who makes these decisions, and what is the process?

The investigator must decide on which journal to submit the study to and then write the manuscript according to that journal's style. The researcher then sends the article to the journal editor to initiate the review process. The editor will select two or three expert reviewers (sometimes called "referees" because of their impartiality), who volunteer their services to the journal, to provide a critique of the manuscript. In most instances these reviews are done in a "blind" fashion. A *blind review* means that there are no names or identifiers on the paper, so reviewers don't know who the authors are or their institutional affiliation, nor do the authors know the identity of the reviewers. This provides for an objective level of review because it removes any possible halo effect (both positive and negative) associated with the study. Most journals in HPER use the blind review method, but some journals don't. This *unblind* method does not provide the protection that blind review does. Most researchers tend to favor one approach over the other. Ask your professor's opinion regarding blind versus unblind reviews.

The reviewers submit their critiques to the journal editor, who ultimately makes a decision on its potential to be published. Usually there is one of three fates in store for an article on its initial submission: accepted (a very rare event for a first-time submission, $p < .0001$), resubmit with revisions for further consideration, and rejected. When a verdict of resubmit is reached, the researcher may have minor to major points to address. There is always the stipulation that even if these concerns are dealt with, there is no guarantee of acceptance. How long does the review process take? Each time a review takes place, it might take two to four months, so all together it takes about one year to have a manuscript that needed revisions accepted for publication. The original submission and acceptance dates are often printed with the article. It also takes about another six months for it to appear in print. Think about how "current" that research is the next time you read an article! What about the article that was rejected? When an article is rejected by one journal, the investigator usually will make some revisions and send it somewhere else. That "somewhere else" is typically a journal of lesser quality. Now the whole process starts all over. It should be obvious by now that perseverance is an essential element for publishing research. By the way, it is considered unethical to submit the same article to two journals simultaneously, just in case you were thinking of a way to speed up the publication process.

## Difficulties with the Review Process and Publication

The procedure just described sounds like it should provide pretty good external quality control, and for the most part it probably does. However, think for a moment about how important the judgments of the reviewers and the editor are. They are not only making a determination about what will be published in a journal but also what will be part of a discipline's body of knowledge. This decision has long-reaching effects: It influences what teachers teach, what students learn, what is printed in textbooks, and what professionals in a discipline practice. Needless to say, these are very important decisions. Let's assume that the reviewers and editors are highly qualified to make these decisions. What, then, may be difficulties with the process?

Perhaps the biggest limitation to this procedure is the inconsistency of the critiques of the reviewers. Recently, Morrow et al. (1992) reported on the interrater reliability of blind reviews done by independent evaluators on 363 manuscripts submitted to the *Research Quarterly for Exercise and Sport* (*RQES*). The *RQES* is considered one of the most respected HPER journals. Several reliability analyses were performed on the data, with not very impressive results. Overall, only 40% of the reviewers' ratings were in perfect agreement and with an intra-class reliability coefficient (consistency indicator) of $R = .37$. Although these results are similar to those reported in other disciplines, it indicates that the review process is not perfect. The authors concluded by suggesting that reviewers need increased orientation, experience, and better review guidelines to help improve the procedure. Anyone who has done research has probably experienced exactly what Morrow et al. studied. Ask your professor about his or her encounters with inconsistent review of research.

Another interesting study on this topic was done by Peters and Ceci (1982). They obtained 12 studies from different authors in highly respected psychology departments around the United States. These studies had been published 18 to 32 months before and were resubmitted to the same journal in which they were published. Three of the 12 were detected by the editorial staffs and prevented from review. Of the remaining nine studies reviewed, eight were rejected.

So what are we to gather from all of this? Due to the subjectivity of the review process, it is now and always will be less than perfect. Studies like that of Morrow et al. stress the continued need to improve the soundness and dependability of the process. In spite of the limitations surrounding it, the review process remains one of the most important and time-honored quality control measures of research.

Finally, it should be emphasized that just because a study is in print doesn't necessarily mean that it is of high quality. Consumers of research must be constantly aware that occasionally an inferior study may receive favorable evaluations from reviewers and be accepted for publication by the editor. Therefore, the reader must take an active role in assessing the quality of any study, whether it is published or orally presented. Consumers of research are the ultimate judge of its value.

## PUBLISH OR PERISH AND RESEARCH QUALITY

No doubt you have heard the term "publish or perish" used around the university before. What exactly does this mean, and what relationship does it have with research quality? Most universities have a research mission to some degree. Because of this mission, faculty are expected to conduct research and are evaluated accordingly.

Allow us to digress for a moment on the tenure process for a faculty member because it is intimately related to publish or perish. Typically a new faculty member with a Ph.D. starts off employment at the rank of assistant professor and strives to become tenured. Our university uses a seven-year tenure model, where at the end of six years a decision is made. If tenure is granted, for all practical purposes, the professor has a job at that university for the rest of his or her career. As you might imagine, receiving tenure is the ultimate in job security for a faculty member, making it very desirable.

If the university requires a high evaluation in the area of research for tenure, the faculty member is placed in a publish or perish situation. You know that it takes a long time to conduct and publish research, so this represents a challenge at most universities where much time is devoted to teaching and service. When the pressure to publish is considerable, there is an increased potential for research quality to be adversely affected.

### Quality versus Quantity

The mind-set of research as a numbers game is at the very root of this problem. Oftentimes you will hear professors talking about the number of studies they have published or how long their résumés are. University administrators often refer to the number of publications their faculty have. They toss these numbers around like baseball managers talking about their players' batting averages. This proclivity for research numbers is a prime reason for the dilution of quality.

Because the conduct of research is a mission of a university, there is an obligation to uphold its quality. In an attempt to address the quality versus quantity issue, some universities are trying interesting changes. One approach is to lengthen the time to a tenure decision from six or seven years to ten. That would allow a faculty member to develop a quality research agenda with less time pressure. Another strategy is to allow a faculty member to submit only a specified number of publications for a tenure decision. Say, for instance, the institution indicates that only four publications can be submitted. It wouldn't matter if the professor had 20 articles, because only the best four are presented. Therefore, the emphasis is placed on quality.

We would be remiss in not saying that the publish or perish problem is probably not that widespread. Institutions vary considerably on research and productivity standards for faculty. Publish or perish occurs at universities with unreasonable expectations of faculty or when there is a poor match between the professor's work output and the institution's demand. For example, some professors simply don't enjoy doing research and might think having to publish a requisite number of articles for tenure or promotion as asking too much. Hopefully, you can now see how the "publish or perish" situation may affect the quality of research.

## ONE LAST THING

Consider this: How would a reader of a research article really know if the investigators truly did what they said they did or if they falsified the results? No one knows the true incidence rates of research dishonesty. Our hope and guess is that it probably is not very widespread. Logically, when it does occur it affects the quality of published and presented research. Because there is no easy way to detect fraudulent work, we have to put our trust in those who conduct and publish research.

## SUMMARY

Research quality control has many aspects. Internal quality control relates to institutional guidelines on what type of research may be done and the protection of research subjects. This is accomplished by departmental peer review, colloquia and defenses of student research, and IRBs. External quality control relates to the publication or presentation of research results. This is best enforced by the blind review process.

Research quality control has many components, but the sources of control can be traced down to two individuals. One source is the producer of research. This person must be knowledgeable, diligent, and honest in order to support a major part of research quality. The other source is the consumer of research. This person must also possess knowledge of the research process and of the field. So even if one never takes part in the production of research, he or she still has an obligation as a professional in HPER to be active at the consumer level. Because the consumers of research ultimately decide either to use or not use research information, they are the foremost judge of research quality. A summary of the primary sources of research quality control appears in Table 17-1.

**TABLE 17-1**   Summary of quality control in research

Internal Quality Control
     Peer review
     Student colloquia and defenses
     Institutional review boards (IRBs)

External Quality Control
     Blind review of journal articles
     Unblind review of journal articles

Foremost Judge of Research Quality
     Consumers of research!

# CHAPTER 18

# ASSESSMENT AND APPLICATION OF RESEARCH

KEY CONCEPTS

Assessment
Internal validity
Sample size
Power
Level of significance
Treatment effect

Reputation
Post hoc error
Summarizing the results
  of research
Meta-analysis
Application

AFTER READING THIS CHAPTER, YOU SHOULD BE ABLE TO

- Assess the quality of research based on internal validity, limitations, and treatment effect.
- Discuss the importance of sample size and power in research.
- Describe factors affecting power.
- Discuss the merits of using significance levels lower and higher than .05.
- Distinguish between significance and treatment effect.
- Describe several ways of quantifying treatment effect.
- Explain why the reputation of people and publications should not be used to assess the quality of research.
- Describe post hoc error.
- Discuss several means of collating and interpreting the findings of many studies on a topic.
- Discuss several criteria to use in applying research.

$T$his chapter deals with several topics that are the main reasons for studying research in graduate school in the first place: to be able to interpret research, integrate the findings on a given topic, and determine what information can be applied to the real world. Progression within the disciplines of HPER will occur mostly because of the quality of work routinely performed by individual professionals. Unless we stay informed by reading professional literature and making modifications on the job stimulated by that reading, then the quality of work carried on by our disciplines is limited. This chapter highlights some strategies to use in interpreting research and making decisions about applying research findings to your professional life.

## ASSESSING THE QUALITY OF RESEARCH

A risk in reading published work is blind acceptance of the written word. Graduate work, however, should provide the knowledge and insight for soundly assessing the quality of research and the professional literature. Several assessment criteria are discussed here.

### Internal Validity

Every study must be judged on its academic merits, including its overall soundness or internal validity (e.g., adequate treatment, design, methods, and statistics) and limitations. A criterion for internal validity often overlooked in judging the quality of research is adequacy of sample size. A number of times, particularly in the statistics section of this text, we have emphasized that a large sample size facilitates achieving statistical significance. The capacity for a statistic to detect significance when the null hypothesis is false is termed *power*. Thus sample size and power are directly related. A large $N$ aids achieving significance because it reduces the error term or denominator of a statistic. Recall that

$$t \text{ or } F = \frac{\text{Treatment variance}}{\text{Error variance}}$$

The error term shrinks with a large $N$ because sampling error is reduced—that is, a large $N$ better represents a population than a small $N$. For example, compare a $t$ ratio with a constant treatment variance of 20 with an error variance of 10. The $t$ ratio = 20/10 = 2.00. With a larger $N$, which reduces the error variance to 5, the $t$ ratio = 20/5 = 4.00.

A very common limitation in many studies is a relatively small $N$. The limited power of any statistic used with a small $N$ tends to make acceptance of the null hypothesis more likely. This, unfortunately, may lead to the erroneous conclusion that no real difference or relationship exists when in reality there may be a difference with a larger sample. For every article published in which no difference is found, the tendency for other researchers to examine the problem diminishes. Thus research and the search for the truth suffer. Consequently, using an adequate $N$ behooves researchers in making sound conclusions. The development of knowledge to an extent depends on the quality of many published works. The higher the frequency that studies with major limitations are published, the more confusing it is to develop sound knowledge and principles.

Formulas exist to assist the reader in estimating appropriate sample size. No one threshold for $N$ exists because significance and power are dependent on several variables each of which varies from study to study. When comparing two groups, the following formula provides an estimate of the sample size needed to achieve significance at a specific level (Borg & Gall, 1979):

$$N = \frac{2\ SD(t)^2}{D^2}$$

where:

$SD$ = standard deviation in other similar studies

$t$ $\quad$ = $t$ ratio that is significant at .05 level in similar studies

$D$ $\quad$ = difference in the two variables, which is of practical significance

For example, let us estimate the number of subjects needed in a study where the $SD$ of other similar studies is 2, the $t$ ratio is 5, and the practical difference for the variable is 3. The number of subjects needed is 11: $N = 4(5)^2/3^2 = 100/9 = 11$. Selection of the appropriate values for each component of the equation is based on previously published work on the topic and an intuitive feel for practical difference. So the formula provides only an estimate rather than a definitive value. Cohen (1988) is an excellent reference with tables to facilitate the estimation of sample size.

"Aha! I will achieve significant results if I can just obtain 51,649 subjects!"

The authors contend that estimating sample size is well worth the effort if for no other reason than the study is far more likely to be accepted and published. Reviewers tend to critique nonsignificant findings harshly. But even more importantly, the purpose of research is to examine a condition carefully and test whether an occurrence of something is real or due to chance. Therefore, it is only fair to the principles of good research that an adequate sample size be used.

Christensen and Christensen (1977) determined the power for most of the studies appearing in the 1975 *Research Quarterly*. Studies were categorized into small, medium, and large effects, referring to the magnitude of change in the dependent variable. In studies with small and large effects, the chances of detecting significance were only 1 in 5 and 2 in 5, respectively. Thus, the average study was going against the odds of finding significance given the sample size used. They concluded that studies reporting no relationship or no significant effect be cautiously interpreted. Also, they urged researchers to examine more closely the importance of sample size and power.

Certain types of studies require a relatively large $N$. If comparing teaching techniques, for example, even teachers using the same technique will vary somewhat. When such a limitation is inherent in a study, the sample size must be large enough to overcome this source of error variance. When the expected difference is small, a larger sample size should be used. An example is comparing hamstring injuries in professional football players using two stretching programs. Most likely all of the players regularly stretch anyway, so any gain in flexibility would likely be small. Also, hamstring pulls may be caused by factors other than flexibility, such as strength, fatigue, and contact. Thus, a large $N$ would be needed to elicit a significant effect.

## Accuracy of Measurement

Accuracy is desirable in assessing the effect size or magnitude of the treatment. As measurement error increases, the numerator (treatment variance) decreases and the denominator (error variance) increases. Both changes reduce the size of the $t$ or $F$ ratio, thus reducing the likelihood of detecting significance.

## Variance

The variance of subjects also affects power. As $SD$ increases, note the effect on the formula to estimate sample size when comparing two groups ($N = 2SD(t)^2/D^2$). A large $SD$ increases the numerator, thereby increasing the number of subjects needed. Put another way, a large $SD$ increases the error variance for $t$ and $F$ ratios, thus denoting a reduction in $t$ and $F$. Therefore researchers should strive to select subjects with limited variance on the dependent variable. For example, if investigating the effects of walking on aerobic fitness, select subjects with similar levels of fitness and physical activity. This will reduce the sampling error. However, researchers often wish to use subjects with considerable dissimilarity because the results of the study can be more broadly applied to a larger segment of the population. In such cases, concern for external validity compromises the degree of internal validity and tends to reduce power.

## Significance Level

An interesting argument made by Franks and Huck (1986) contends that though increasing sample size to boost power is sound, it may be impractical for many researchers because of time and financial constraints. As an alternative they suggest changing the significance level from the commonly used .05 to a higher level, such as .10. The probability of making a Type I decision error is increased, but they contend that such an error in one study will not seriously undermine previous work in an area because scientists fully understand the hazard in making decisions based on a single study. Furthermore, they explain that increasing the probability of Type II error is not without problems. Remember that adjusting alpha to .10 reduces the probability of making a Type II decision error. For example, failure to find significant results may tend to steer other investigators away from a potentially meaningful area of study. Lastly, they recommend that significance levels be provided for all variables studied, which allows the reader to judge the potential for Type I error. Only indicating that a finding is significant or nonsignificant omits important information. An alpha level of .051 may be very differently interpreted than .60, yet they both fall into the nonsignificant category if $\alpha = .05$. The former narrowly misses meeting the common criterion for significance and the latter is well wide of the mark. This information should be available to the reader. However, more often than not, specific significance levels are not reported.

Feinstein (1983) reminds us that the .05 significance level was never meant by its originator, Sir Ronald Fisher, to be applied to all conditions but, rather, to serve as a guideline. The .05 level was suggested largely because of its mathematical advantages, including the fact that all but about 5% of scores will be within about two standard deviations of the mean. Through the years, however, the .05 level has become rigidly used and even demanded. Manuscripts failing to achieve significance at the .05 level are usually rejected regardless of the size of the treatment effect. Can you imagine a researcher finding that a new drug is 50% more effective than any other traditional treatment, yet having the manuscript rejected because the difference with a small sample size fails to meet the .05 standard? One wonders how many sound ideas and findings died because of lack of significance.

## Treatment Effect

As indicated, statistical significance and treatment effect are distinctly different characteristics of a study. Significance relates to the probability that a difference is real, whereas treatment effect refers to the magnitude of the differences between groups. Although nearly all studies report significance, few quantify the treatment effect. This is unfortunate because significant differences are not necessarily meaningfully different. This paradox may occur because of the effect of $N$ size in determining significance. With sample sizes exceeding 100, small differences of little practical consequence can be significant.

Obviously, treatment effect should be quantified wherever possible. There are several ways to do this. The simplest is reporting the percent difference between groups. Calculation and interpretation are easy. A second method is the calculation of omega squared ($\Omega^2$) or coefficient of determination ($r^2$). Recall that omega squared indicates the percent variance attributed to the independent variable, which is a different way of quantifying the treatment effect (see Chapter 11). The third method is to calculate what is termed the *effect size*.

$$\text{Effect size} = \frac{M_1 - M_2}{SD}$$

where:

$M_1$ = mean of first group
$M_2$ = mean of second group
$SD$ = standard deviation of control group

The calculation is simple, and usually is the most useful and interesting result from a study: How different are various treatments? Cohen (1969) proposed that in the behavioral sciences an effect size of .2 indicates small differences, .5 moderate differences, and .8 large differences. Comparison with other studies can directly be made if effect size is expressed directly or even indirectly, the latter by providing the *M* and *SD* of variables. It may be far more meaningful to analyze effect size than significance because the latter is so strongly affected by sample size and variance. This may aid the interpretation of new studies and hence the development of new knowledge, part of which would be expressed in principles and theory. J. R. Thomas, former editor of the *Research Quarterly for Exercise and Sport (RQES)*, for years has strongly advocated reporting either $\Omega^2$ or effect size. However, little or no change was noted in published articles in the *RQES* (Thomas, Salazar, & Landers, 1991). Obviously, both faculty and students should be encouraged to familiarize themselves with the merits of reporting magnitude of the treatment effect.

### Reputation and Quality

*Well-known names and prestigious journals do not guarantee sound research.* For example, Linus Pauling received a Nobel Prize in science years ago. Shortly thereafter, articles appeared in magazines and newspapers about his extolling the virtues of vitamin C in preventing and treating the common cold. His opinion was initially based on observations on himself and his wife. Although no research data were available to support his conclusion and recommendation, the American public assumed that the advice of an esteemed scientist must be sound. Thus was born the selling of vitamin C in every drugstore and grocery store in the land. The authors are familiar with several examples of misguided information from reputable scientists in our own disciplines.

Although the standards for publishing in most professional journals are high, not all that is printed is actually sound, and none of it is perfect. All manuscripts submitted to refereed publications are reviewed by expert reviewers.

However, that does not guarantee that every study appearing in a given volume used the best design, methods, or even statistical approach. All studies have their limitations, and readers should appreciate this.

In our disciplines we must be especially aware of the Madison Avenue approach to people's problems. Weight loss, health food, running shoes, and exercise clothing are multi-billion-dollar businesses. The approaches used to market products include star athletes and Hollywood personalities. They lend an excitement to a product or technique that, quite honestly, is not found in research. A widely used strategy is the "superclaim," that is, a benefit that is far larger than actually occurs. Some years ago 10 minutes of rope jumping was touted by one company as being equivalent to 30 minutes of jogging. New weight loss diets promise impossible results. Books such as *The 120 Year Diet and Nutrition Plan* tempt people because of their staggering implications. Pearson and Shaw, authors of *Life Extension: A Practical Scientific Approach,* claimed to be research scientists, but in fact both had no graduate degrees and neither had ever published a paper in a reputable research publication. Their book is filled with case histories that cannot be verified. The point emphasized here is that the expertise and claims of any author should be carefully examined, particularly if the claims seem extravagant. Unbelievable claims usually should not be believed.

## Post Hoc Error

Every beneficial change in behavior during and after an experimental period cannot be attributed to the independent variable. The tendency to do this is called *post hoc error*. If a woman started a running program and six months later was divorced, is it valid to conclude that running caused the divorce? If a person starts taking vitamin supplements and three weeks later has a cholesterol reading lower than ever, did the vitamins cause the low reading? Common sense makes each of the examples illogical, but when put in a more professional context logic can easily be swayed.

A business begins a health promotion program and hires a health educator or exercise scientist to administer it. To justify the merits of the program and its continuation, the administrator compares job absenteeism of those who regularly attend various activities of the health promotion program, such as exercise, blood pressure screening, and health fairs, with those who never attend any of these activities. The absenteeism rate is found to be significantly higher in those who never attend, much to the delight of the administrator, who proclaims that the program reduced absenteeism. Is this a valid conclusion? To demonstrate cause and effect, an experimental research design is needed. Groups would need to be randomly assigned to participant and nonparticipant groups and then compared. The participants may have been initially different in terms of job absenteeism as well as a variety of health habits. Unless these differences are controlled experimentally or statistically, no sound conclusion can be drawn. Believe it or not, many of the early studies in the 1980s that attempted to study the value of health promotion programs in the workplace made conclusions based on post hoc error. The more one wishes to see good things happen, the more good things will be found. Being enthusiastic about a program or treatment is fine, but be aware of the possibility of post hoc error.

Table 18-1 is a checklist to evaluate research. It includes research design, methods, threats to internal and external validity, and so on. It may be useful in assessing the many aspects of a research paper.

## INTERPRETING AND SUMMARIZING THE RESULTS OF RESEARCH

A difficult task for most of us when reading research is trying to present a fair analysis of the state of knowledge. Typically, many things studied are somewhat controversial by nature, which results in a variety of findings and conclusions. Furthermore, subject characteristics differ as do methods, treatment, research de-

**TABLE 18-1**  Checklist for evaluating research

| *Yes or No* | | *Comments* |
|---|---|---|
| _____ | 1. Purpose for research clearly stated | |
| _____ | 2. Need for study substantiated | |
| | 3. Methods | |
| _____ | a. Subjects described | |
| _____ | b. Measurements described adequately for replication | |
| _____ | c. Measures are valid and reliable | |
| _____ | d. Appropriate statistical procedures | |
| | 4. Results | |
| _____ | a. Clearly stated | |
| _____ | b. Tables/figures aid comprehension | |
| _____ | c. Significance levels given | |
| | 5. Discussion/Conclusions | |
| _____ | a. Results compared with other studies | |
| _____ | b. Effect size or magnitude quantified | |
| _____ | c. Limitations mentioned | |
| _____ | d. Plausible speculations made | |
| _____ | e. Conclusions based on data | |
| _____ | f. Discussion of application sound | |
| | 6. Internal Validity | |
| _____ | a. Adequate treatment | |
| _____ | b. Adequate sample size and power | |
| _____ | c. If some comparisons not significant, is sample size mentioned? | |
| _____ | d. Confounding variables | |
| | 7. External Validity | |
| | a. To whom can the results of this study be applied? | |
| | b. Were subjects volunteers? | |

sign, and statistics. How can one read about a topic and have a sense of confidence in integrating the mass of information? Several approaches are presented here.

## Read Current Reviews of the Literature

Most research journals regularly include review articles. In addition, some professional associations annually sponsor a review publication. For instance, the American College of Sports Medicine annually sponsors the publishing of the book *Exercise and Sport Science Reviews*, which includes about a dozen review articles. These are written by experts on a specific topic. Reviews typically include a discussion of the points of disagreement, possible causes of the disagreement, and recommendations for research in the area.

An interesting question is how these experts actually synthesize and weigh the literature. Probably their involvement as active researchers and readers over many years develops a level of familiarity that few could achieve without spending equivalent time and undergoing similar training. Thus they know the subject matter so well that every study that adds something new to the knowledge is fitted in at a logical conceptual point in their frame of reference. So take advantage of their expertise.

## Construct a Summary Table of Studies

Summary tables were discussed in Chapter 4, in the section on review of literature. A table with column headings of authors, date, subject characteristics, results, and comments is helpful in tallying the characteristics and results of a number of studies. Several pages of such tables roughed out on paper could be used to categorize the major findings. For example, one or two pages might summarize the studies having one finding (e.g., that technique A is superior) and several other pages would summarize studies with a different finding (e.g., technique B is superior), and so on. Then one can look for common factors among studies reporting the same result (e.g., technique A is superior mostly or only in children 6 to 12 years old). This should help to make generalizations that cut across many studies.

## Tally Studies Showing Significant and Nonsignificant Results

This method is limited because studies not finding significance may have methodological and statistical flaws. For example, measurement error and small sample size may have prevented significant findings although the treatment effect was strong. Furthermore, a mere counting does not include such factors as subject characteristics, magnitude of the treatment, and sample size.

## Use Meta-Analysis

Meta-analysis statistically treats the result of each study as one data point. The value used from each study is the *effect size*, which is the difference in the mean of the experimental group(s) and the control group divided by the standard deviation of the control group.

$$\text{Effect size } = \frac{\text{Experimental } M - \text{ Control } M}{SD \text{ of control}}$$

The effect size is expressed in units of *SD* and is therefore fairly easy to interpret. For example, .73 means the experimental mean was .73 standard deviations unit greater than the mean of the control group. The effect size of each study is calculated and used to determine the *M* and *SD* of all the effect sizes. Thus the mean effect of an independent variable across a number of studies can be quantified. The significance of the difference in effect size can be determined by using the *M* and *SD* of categories compared in an independent *t* test, if there are two means to compare, or an ANOVA if there are more than two means.

Meta-analysis has been performed by researchers only recently. Examples in HPER are Sparling's work comparing maximum oxygen uptake in males and females (1980), effect of exercise on blood lipids and lipoproteins by Tran, Weltman, Glass, and Mood (1983), and sex differences in motor performance by Thomas and French (1985). The technique offers great potential for quantitatively comparing the results of many studies, which in turn facilitates making sound conclusions about the literature. The advantages are too strong to ignore, and the technique will undoubtedly be refined and used far more commonly in the future.

## APPLICATION OF RESEARCH

Recall that the potential for applying the results of a study is called external validity. Most research in the disciplines of HPER is applied, so the potential for application is usually quite good. However, several precautions should be considered.

Technically, the only fully justified application of the results of a single study is to the subjects of that particular investigation. However, it is logical that people outside the study with similar traits as those of the original subjects may also be considered "fair game" for application. If this was not the case, applied research would be a misnomer and much of research would be done without a purpose. For example, if a new medication to reduce blood pressure in hypertensive patients is found superior to current medications, then the medication could be used in hypertensive patients in general as long as they met certain criteria for similarity such as age, sex, and absence or presence of other medical characteristics. Application to other patients is justified from random sampling. The study probably used a random sample of hypertensive patients. If they adequately represent all other hypertensive patients, then it is assumed that their response portrays the expected response of the entire population of hypertensives.

Good science includes a concern for appropriate application of results. The point is emphasized here because it is common to see results applied with little or no concern for matching the traits of research subjects with those of people outside the study. A group of weight lifters at a gym might read about a novel program used by the current Mr. America to build huge biceps. An article might go into great detail about the number of sets, repetitions, length of recovery, exercises, and so on. Is it scientifically defensible to assume that what worked for Mr. America will work for the readers of the magazine? (One of the authors knows it won't because he tried it: his arm circumference remained 12.5 firm inches!) Obviously not. Mr. America may possess some unique traits that allowed his biceps to grow massively with the program described. Unless others possess similar traits such as previous years of training experience, a lifestyle in which weight training is the main task each day of the week, and a high responsiveness to training, they will most likely not experience the same results.

Advertisements are largely based on not understanding or failing to admit the principle of trait similarity. Advertisements depict remarkable changes as a result of using a certain drink, food, perfume, hair spray, or toothpaste. The assumption of such advertising is that we will purchase the product with the hope that the same effect will happen to us.

A study shows that oatmeal lowers cholesterol 13%. Are you ready to buy some? First, the informed reader should know something about the subjects in the study. What if the subjects were men in their 50s and 60s all with cholesterol levels above 300 mg% at the start of the study? Are you still ready to head out the door? If you like oatmeal, fine. Buy some, because it is a wholesome food regardless of its impact on cholesterol levels. If you do not like oatmeal and you are in your 20s with a cholesterol of 156 mg%, you certainly should not expect the same effect as was found in the study.

Examples in a text rarely fool anyone, but we all probably have been hoodwinked into making decisions that violate common sense. However, when we make decisions on the job, more pressure may exist to make a sound decision. Unfortunately, there is no statistic or quantitative criterion available to help determine when results of a study can be applied in a given situation. One must use good judgment in analyzing the similarity of subjects and those people who may experience the treatment.

Several factors make the results that occur in a study less likely to occur when applied to the clinical setting or work environment. The effects of being a volunteer, history, pretest, and selection bias are discussed in Chapter 14. These factors do not preclude making applications from research. They merely indicate that the expected results may be a bit different.

Last, realize that the results of a single study are only observations of a sample. Until the study is replicated one or more times and similar results found, one is not dealing with facts. Replication is a basic part of science and application before replication is unscientific.

## SUMMARY

The quality of a study should always be considered when reading and assessing research. Quality is largely determined by the internal validity and limitations. In addressing internal validity, the treatment, design, methods, data analysis, and sample size should be assessed. The results should be interpreted not only in terms of significance but also magnitude. The latter is often omitted, but the insightful reader should at least estimate the effect size as it is basic to interpreting the results of a study. Assessment should not be swayed by reputation and prestige.

Summarizing a vast number of studies is difficult but greatly enhanced by reading recent reviews of the literature. Meta-analysis is a means of quantifying the results of many separate studies and will likely be used more frequently in the future to assess the state of knowledge in various topics. Making application from research to the real world requires judging the similarity of the subjects and conditions of a study to people and conditions outside the study. No statistical technique exists to aid the process of application, so common sense of both the practitioner and researcher must prevail.

# APPENDIX I
# STATISTICS TABLES

**TABLE A**  Critical Values of Chi Square

| df | .20 | .10 | .05 | .02 | .01 | .001 |
|----|-----|-----|-----|-----|-----|------|
| 1  | 1.64  | 2.71  | 3.84  | 5.41  | 6.64  | 10.83 |
| 2  | 3.22  | 4.60  | 5.99  | 7.82  | 9.21  | 13.82 |
| 3  | 4.64  | 6.25  | 7.82  | 9.84  | 11.34 | 16.27 |
| 4  | 5.99  | 7.78  | 9.49  | 11.67 | 13.28 | 18.46 |
| 5  | 7.29  | 9.24  | 11.07 | 13.39 | 15.09 | 20.52 |
| 6  | 8.56  | 10.64 | 12.59 | 15.03 | 16.81 | 22.46 |
| 7  | 9.80  | 12.02 | 14.07 | 16.62 | 18.48 | 24.32 |
| 8  | 11.03 | 13.36 | 15.51 | 18.17 | 20.09 | 26.12 |
| 9  | 12.24 | 14.68 | 16.92 | 19.68 | 21.67 | 27.88 |
| 10 | 13.44 | 15.99 | 18.31 | 21.16 | 23.21 | 29.59 |
| 11 | 14.63 | 17.28 | 19.68 | 22.62 | 24.72 | 31.26 |
| 12 | 15.81 | 18.55 | 21.03 | 24.05 | 26.22 | 32.91 |
| 13 | 16.98 | 19.81 | 22.36 | 25.47 | 27.69 | 34.53 |
| 14 | 18.15 | 21.06 | 23.68 | 26.87 | 29.14 | 36.12 |
| 15 | 19.31 | 22.31 | 25.00 | 28.26 | 30.58 | 37.70 |
| 16 | 20.46 | 23.54 | 26.30 | 29.63 | 32.00 | 39.29 |
| 17 | 21.62 | 24.77 | 27.59 | 31.00 | 33.41 | 40.75 |
| 18 | 22.76 | 25.99 | 28.87 | 32.35 | 34.80 | 42.31 |
| 19 | 23.90 | 27.20 | 30.14 | 33.69 | 36.19 | 43.82 |
| 20 | 25.04 | 28.41 | 31.41 | 35.02 | 37.57 | 45.32 |
| 21 | 26.17 | 29.62 | 32.67 | 36.34 | 38.93 | 46.80 |
| 22 | 27.30 | 30.81 | 33.92 | 37.66 | 40.29 | 48.27 |
| 23 | 28.43 | 32.01 | 35.17 | 38.97 | 41.64 | 49.73 |
| 24 | 29.55 | 33.20 | 36.42 | 40.27 | 42.98 | 51.18 |
| 25 | 30.68 | 34.38 | 37.65 | 41.57 | 44.31 | 52.62 |
| 26 | 31.80 | 35.56 | 38.88 | 42.86 | 45.64 | 54.05 |
| 27 | 32.91 | 36.74 | 40.11 | 44.14 | 46.96 | 55.48 |
| 28 | 34.03 | 37.92 | 41.34 | 45.42 | 48.28 | 56.89 |
| 29 | 35.14 | 39.09 | 42.56 | 46.69 | 49.59 | 58.30 |
| 30 | 36.25 | 40.26 | 43.77 | 47.96 | 50.89 | 59.70 |

*Source*: Abridged from Table IV of R. A. Fisher and F. Yates: *Statistical tables for biological, agricultural, and medical research*, published by Oliver & Boyd, Ltd., Edinburgh, by permission of the authors and publishers.

**TABLE B**  Critical Values of Spearman $r_s$ for the .05 and .01 Levels of Significance

| N | .05 | .01 | N | .05 | .01 |
|---|-----|-----|---|-----|-----|
| 6 | .886 | — | 19 | .462 | .608 |
| 7 | .786 | — | 20 | .450 | .591 |
| 8 | .738 | .881 | 21 | .438 | .576 |
| 9 | .683 | .833 | 22 | .428 | .562 |
| 10 | .648 | .818 | 23 | .418 | .549 |
| 11 | .623 | .794 | 24 | .409 | .537 |
| 12 | .591 | .780 | 25 | .400 | .526 |
| 13 | .566 | .745 | 26 | .392 | .515 |
| 14 | .545 | .716 | 27 | .385 | .505 |
| 15 | .525 | .689 | 28 | .377 | .496 |
| 16 | .507 | .666 | 29 | .370 | .487 |
| 17 | .490 | .645 | 30 | .364 | .478 |
| 18 | .476 | .625 | | | |

*Source*: Adapted from E. G. Olds, Distribution of sums of squares of rank differences for small numbers of individuals, *Annals of Mathematical Statistics 9*: 133–48 (1938), and E. G. Olds, The 5% significance levels for sums of squares of rank differences and a correction, *Annals of Mathematical Statistics 20*: 117–18 (1949). Copyright 1938 and Copyright 1949 by the Institute of Mathematical Statistics, Hayward, Calif. Reprinted by permission of the publisher.

**TABLE C**   Critical Values of the Pearson Correlation Coefficient

| df | LEVEL OF SIGNIFICANCE FOR ONE-TAILED TEST | | | |
|---|---|---|---|---|
| | *.05* | *.025* | *.01* | *.005* |
| | LEVEL OF SIGNIFICANCE FOR TWO-TAILED TEST | | | |
| | *.10* | *.05* | *.02* | *.01* |
| 1 | .988 | .997 | .9995 | .9999 |
| 2 | .900 | .950 | .980 | .990 |
| 3 | .805 | .878 | .934 | .959 |
| 4 | .729 | .811 | .882 | .917 |
| 5 | .669 | .754 | .833 | .874 |
| 6 | .622 | .707 | .789 | .834 |
| 7 | .582 | .666 | .750 | .798 |
| 8 | .549 | .632 | .716 | .765 |
| 9 | .521 | .602 | .685 | .735 |
| 10 | .497 | .576 | .658 | .708 |
| 11 | .476 | .553 | .634 | .684 |
| 12 | .458 | .532 | .612 | .661 |
| 13 | .441 | .514 | .592 | .641 |
| 14 | .426 | .497 | .574 | .623 |
| 15 | .412 | .482 | .558 | .606 |
| 16 | .400 | .468 | .542 | .590 |
| 17 | .389 | .456 | .528 | .575 |
| 18 | .378 | .444 | .516 | .561 |
| 19 | .369 | .433 | .503 | .549 |
| 20 | .360 | .423 | .492 | .537 |
| 21 | .352 | .413 | .482 | .526 |
| 22 | .344 | .404 | .472 | .515 |
| 23 | .337 | .396 | .462 | .505 |
| 24 | .330 | .388 | .453 | .496 |
| 25 | .323 | .381 | .445 | .487 |
| 26 | .317 | .374 | .437 | .479 |
| 27 | .311 | .367 | .430 | .471 |
| 28 | .306 | .361 | .423 | .463 |
| 29 | .301 | .355 | .416 | .456 |
| 30 | .296 | .349 | .409 | .449 |
| 35 | .275 | .325 | .381 | .418 |
| 40 | .257 | .304 | .358 | .393 |
| 45 | .243 | .288 | .338 | .372 |
| 50 | .231 | .273 | .322 | .354 |
| 60 | .211 | .250 | .295 | .325 |
| 70 | .195 | .232 | .274 | .303 |
| 80 | .183 | .217 | .256 | .283 |
| 90 | .173 | .205 | .242 | .267 |
| 100 | .164 | .195 | .230 | .254 |

*Source:* Abridged from R. A. Fisher and F. Yates, *Statistical tables for biological, agricultural, and medical research*, Oliver & Boyd, Ltd., Edinburgh, by permission of the authors and publishers.

**TABLE D**   Critical Values of *t*

| df | LEVEL OF SIGNIFICANCE FOR ONE-TAILED TEST | | | | | |
|---|---|---|---|---|---|---|
| | .10 | .05 | .025 | .01 | .005 | .0005 |
| | LEVEL OF SIGNIFICANCE FOR TWO-TAILED TEST | | | | | |
| | .20 | .10 | .05 | .02 | .01 | .001 |
| 1 | 3.078 | 6.314 | 12.706 | 31.821 | 63.657 | 636.619 |
| 2 | 1.886 | 2.920 | 4.303 | 6.965 | 9.925 | 31.598 |
| 3 | 1.638 | 2.353 | 3.182 | 4.541 | 5.841 | 12.941 |
| 4 | 1.533 | 2.132 | 2.776 | 3.747 | 4.604 | 8.610 |
| 5 | 1.476 | 2.015 | 2.571 | 3.365 | 4.032 | 6.859 |
| 6 | 1.440 | 1.943 | 2.447 | 3.143 | 3.707 | 5.959 |
| 7 | 1.415 | 1.895 | 2.365 | 2.998 | 3.499 | 5.405 |
| 8 | 1.397 | 1.860 | 2.306 | 2.896 | 3.355 | 5.041 |
| 9 | 1.383 | 1.833 | 2.262 | 2.821 | 3.250 | 4.781 |
| 10 | 1.372 | 1.812 | 2.228 | 2.764 | 3.169 | 4.587 |
| 11 | 1.363 | 1.796 | 2.201 | 2.718 | 3.106 | 4.437 |
| 12 | 1.356 | 1.782 | 2.179 | 2.681 | 3.055 | 4.318 |
| 13 | 1.350 | 1.771 | 2.160 | 2.650 | 3.012 | 4.221 |
| 14 | 1.345 | 1.761 | 2.145 | 2.624 | 2.977 | 4.140 |
| 15 | 1.341 | 1.753 | 2.131 | 2.602 | 2.947 | 4.073 |
| 16 | 1.337 | 1.746 | 2.120 | 2.583 | 2.921 | 4.015 |
| 17 | 1.333 | 1.740 | 2.110 | 2.567 | 2.898 | 3.965 |
| 18 | 1.330 | 1.734 | 2.101 | 2.552 | 2.878 | 3.922 |
| 19 | 1.328 | 1.729 | 2.093 | 2.539 | 2.861 | 3.883 |
| 20 | 1.325 | 1.725 | 2.086 | 2.528 | 2.845 | 3.850 |
| 21 | 1.323 | 1.721 | 2.080 | 2.518 | 2.831 | 3.819 |
| 22 | 1.321 | 1.717 | 2.074 | 2.508 | 2.819 | 3.792 |
| 23 | 1.319 | 1.714 | 2.069 | 2.500 | 2.807 | 3.767 |
| 24 | 1.318 | 1.711 | 2.064 | 2.492 | 2.797 | 3.745 |
| 25 | 1.316 | 1.708 | 2.060 | 2.485 | 2.787 | 3.725 |
| 26 | 1.315 | 1.706 | 2.056 | 2.479 | 2.779 | 3.707 |
| 27 | 1.314 | 1.703 | 2.052 | 2.473 | 2.771 | 3.690 |
| 28 | 1.313 | 1.701 | 2.048 | 2.467 | 2.763 | 3.674 |
| 29 | 1.311 | 1.699 | 2.045 | 2.462 | 2.756 | 3.659 |
| 30 | 1.310 | 1.697 | 2.042 | 2.457 | 2.750 | 3.646 |
| 40 | 1.303 | 1.684 | 2.021 | 2.423 | 2.704 | 3.551 |
| 60 | 1.296 | 1.671 | 2.000 | 2.390 | 2.660 | 3.460 |
| 120 | 1.289 | 1.658 | 1.980 | 2.358 | 2.617 | 3.373 |
| ∞ | 1.282 | 1.645 | 1.960 | 2.326 | 2.576 | 3.291 |

*Source:* Abridged from Table III of R. A. Fisher and F. Yates, *Statistical tables for biological, agricultural, and medical research*, published by Oliver & Boyd, Ltd., Edinburgh, by permission of the authors and publishers.

**TABLE E**  Critical Values of *F*

5 percent (roman type) and 1 percent (boldface type) points for the distribution of *F*

*DEGREES OF FREEDOM FOR GREATER MEAN SQUARE*

| Degrees of freedom for lesser mean square | 1 | 2 | 3 | 4 | 5 | 6 | 7 | 8 | 9 | 10 | 11 | 12 | 14 | 16 | 20 | 24 | 30 | 40 | 50 | 75 | 100 | 200 | 500 | ∞ |
|---|---|---|---|---|---|---|---|---|---|---|---|---|---|---|---|---|---|---|---|---|---|---|---|---|
| 1 | 161 **4052** | 200 **4999** | 216 **5403** | 225 **5625** | 230 **5764** | 234 **5859** | 237 **5928** | 239 **5981** | 241 **6022** | 242 **6056** | 243 **6082** | 244 **6106** | 245 **6142** | 246 **6169** | 248 **6208** | 249 **6234** | 250 **6258** | 251 **6286** | 252 **6302** | 253 **6323** | 253 **6334** | 254 **6352** | 254 **6361** | 254 **6366** |
| 2 | 18.51 **98.49** | 19.00 **99.01** | 19.16 **99.17** | 19.25 **99.25** | 19.30 **99.30** | 19.33 **99.33** | 19.36 **99.34** | 19.37 **99.36** | 19.38 **99.38** | 19.39 **99.40** | 19.40 **99.41** | 19.41 **99.42** | 19.42 **99.43** | 19.43 **99.44** | 19.44 **99.45** | 19.45 **99.46** | 19.46 **99.47** | 19.47 **99.48** | 19.47 **99.48** | 19.48 **99.49** | 19.49 **99.49** | 19.49 **99.49** | 19.50 **99.50** | 19.50 **99.50** |
| 3 | 10.13 **34.12** | 9.55 **30.81** | 9.28 **29.46** | 9.12 **28.71** | 9.01 **28.24** | 8.94 **27.91** | 8.88 **27.67** | 8.84 **27.49** | 8.81 **27.34** | 8.78 **27.23** | 8.76 **27.13** | 8.74 **27.05** | 8.71 **26.92** | 8.69 **26.83** | 8.66 **26.69** | 8.64 **26.60** | 8.62 **26.50** | 8.60 **26.41** | 8.58 **26.35** | 8.57 **26.27** | 8.56 **26.23** | 8.54 **26.18** | 8.54 **26.14** | 8.53 **26.12** |
| 4 | 7.71 **21.20** | 6.94 **18.00** | 6.59 **16.69** | 6.39 **15.98** | 6.26 **15.52** | 6.16 **15.21** | 6.09 **14.98** | 6.04 **14.80** | 6.00 **14.66** | 5.96 **14.54** | 5.93 **14.45** | 5.91 **14.37** | 5.87 **14.24** | 5.84 **14.15** | 5.80 **14.02** | 5.77 **13.93** | 5.74 **13.83** | 5.71 **13.74** | 5.70 **13.69** | 5.68 **13.61** | 5.66 **13.57** | 5.65 **13.52** | 5.64 **13.48** | 5.63 **13.46** |
| 5 | 6.61 **16.26** | 5.79 **13.27** | 5.41 **12.06** | 5.19 **11.39** | 5.05 **10.97** | 4.95 **10.67** | 4.88 **10.45** | 4.82 **10.27** | 4.78 **10.15** | 4.74 **10.05** | 4.70 **9.96** | 4.68 **9.89** | 4.64 **9.77** | 4.60 **9.68** | 4.56 **9.55** | 4.53 **9.47** | 4.50 **9.38** | 4.46 **9.29** | 4.44 **9.24** | 4.42 **9.17** | 4.40 **9.13** | 4.38 **9.07** | 4.37 **9.04** | 4.36 **9.02** |
| 6 | 5.99 **13.74** | 5.14 **10.92** | 4.76 **9.78** | 4.53 **9.15** | 4.39 **8.75** | 4.28 **8.47** | 4.21 **8.26** | 4.15 **8.10** | 4.10 **7.98** | 4.06 **7.87** | 4.03 **7.79** | 4.00 **7.72** | 3.96 **7.60** | 3.92 **7.52** | 3.87 **7.39** | 3.84 **7.31** | 3.81 **7.23** | 3.77 **7.14** | 3.75 **7.09** | 3.72 **7.02** | 3.71 **6.99** | 3.69 **6.94** | 3.68 **6.90** | 3.67 **6.88** |
| 7 | 5.59 **12.25** | 4.74 **9.55** | 4.35 **8.45** | 4.12 **7.85** | 3.97 **7.46** | 3.87 **7.19** | 3.79 **7.00** | 3.73 **6.84** | 3.68 **6.71** | 3.63 **6.62** | 3.60 **6.54** | 3.57 **6.47** | 3.52 **6.35** | 3.49 **6.27** | 3.44 **6.15** | 3.41 **6.07** | 3.38 **5.98** | 3.34 **5.90** | 3.32 **5.85** | 3.29 **5.78** | 3.28 **5.75** | 3.25 **5.70** | 3.24 **5.67** | 3.23 **5.65** |
| 8 | 5.32 **11.26** | 4.46 **8.65** | 4.07 **7.59** | 3.84 **7.01** | 3.69 **6.63** | 3.58 **6.37** | 3.50 **6.19** | 3.44 **6.03** | 3.39 **5.91** | 3.34 **5.82** | 3.31 **5.74** | 3.28 **5.67** | 3.23 **5.56** | 3.20 **5.48** | 3.15 **5.36** | 3.12 **5.28** | 3.08 **5.20** | 3.05 **5.11** | 3.03 **5.06** | 3.00 **5.00** | 2.98 **4.96** | 2.96 **4.91** | 2.94 **4.88** | 2.93 **4.86** |
| 9 | 5.12 **10.56** | 4.26 **8.02** | 3.86 **6.99** | 3.63 **6.42** | 3.48 **6.06** | 3.37 **5.80** | 3.29 **5.62** | 3.23 **5.47** | 3.18 **5.35** | 3.13 **5.26** | 3.10 **5.18** | 3.07 **5.11** | 3.02 **5.00** | 2.98 **4.92** | 2.93 **4.80** | 2.90 **4.73** | 2.86 **4.64** | 2.82 **4.56** | 2.80 **4.51** | 2.77 **4.45** | 2.76 **4.41** | 2.73 **4.36** | 2.72 **4.33** | 2.71 **4.31** |
| 10 | 4.96 **10.04** | 4.10 **7.56** | 3.71 **6.55** | 3.48 **5.99** | 3.33 **5.64** | 3.22 **5.39** | 3.14 **5.21** | 3.07 **5.06** | 3.02 **4.95** | 2.97 **4.85** | 2.94 **4.78** | 2.91 **4.71** | 2.86 **4.60** | 2.82 **4.52** | 2.77 **4.41** | 2.74 **4.33** | 2.70 **4.25** | 2.67 **4.17** | 2.64 **4.12** | 2.61 **4.05** | 2.59 **4.01** | 2.56 **3.96** | 2.55 **3.93** | 2.54 **3.91** |
| 11 | 4.84 **9.65** | 3.98 **7.20** | 3.59 **6.22** | 3.36 **5.67** | 3.20 **5.32** | 3.09 **5.07** | 3.01 **4.88** | 2.95 **4.74** | 2.90 **4.63** | 2.86 **4.54** | 2.82 **4.46** | 2.79 **4.40** | 2.74 **4.29** | 2.70 **4.21** | 2.65 **4.10** | 2.61 **4.02** | 2.57 **3.94** | 2.53 **3.86** | 2.50 **3.80** | 2.47 **3.74** | 2.45 **3.70** | 2.42 **3.66** | 2.41 **3.62** | 2.40 **3.60** |
| 12 | 4.75 **9.33** | 3.88 **6.93** | 3.49 **5.95** | 3.26 **5.41** | 3.11 **5.06** | 3.00 **4.82** | 2.92 **4.65** | 2.85 **4.50** | 2.80 **4.39** | 2.76 **4.30** | 2.72 **4.22** | 2.69 **4.16** | 2.64 **4.05** | 2.60 **3.98** | 2.54 **3.86** | 2.50 **3.78** | 2.46 **3.70** | 2.42 **3.61** | 2.40 **3.56** | 2.36 **3.49** | 2.35 **3.46** | 2.32 **3.41** | 2.31 **3.38** | 2.30 **3.36** |
| 13 | 4.67 **9.07** | 3.80 **6.70** | 3.41 **5.74** | 3.18 **5.20** | 3.02 **4.86** | 2.92 **4.62** | 2.84 **4.44** | 2.77 **4.30** | 2.72 **4.19** | 2.67 **4.10** | 2.63 **4.02** | 2.60 **3.96** | 2.55 **3.85** | 2.51 **3.78** | 2.46 **3.67** | 2.42 **3.59** | 2.38 **3.51** | 2.34 **3.42** | 2.32 **3.37** | 2.28 **3.30** | 2.26 **3.27** | 2.24 **3.21** | 2.22 **3.18** | 2.21 **3.16** |
| 14 | 4.60 **8.86** | 3.74 **6.51** | 3.34 **5.56** | 3.11 **5.03** | 2.96 **4.69** | 2.85 **4.46** | 2.77 **4.28** | 2.70 **4.14** | 2.65 **4.03** | 2.60 **3.94** | 2.56 **3.86** | 2.53 **3.80** | 2.48 **3.70** | 2.44 **3.62** | 2.39 **3.51** | 2.35 **3.43** | 2.31 **3.34** | 2.27 **3.26** | 2.24 **3.21** | 2.21 **3.14** | 2.19 **3.11** | 2.16 **3.06** | 2.14 **3.02** | 2.13 **3.00** |
| 15 | 4.54 **8.68** | 3.68 **6.36** | 3.29 **5.42** | 3.06 **4.89** | 2.90 **4.56** | 2.79 **4.32** | 2.70 **4.14** | 2.64 **4.00** | 2.59 **3.89** | 2.55 **3.80** | 2.51 **3.73** | 2.48 **3.67** | 2.43 **3.56** | 2.39 **3.48** | 2.33 **3.36** | 2.29 **3.29** | 2.25 **3.20** | 2.21 **3.12** | 2.18 **3.07** | 2.15 **3.00** | 2.12 **2.97** | 2.10 **2.92** | 2.08 **2.89** | 2.07 **2.87** |

*(continued)*

227

**TABLE E** *(continued)*
5 percent (roman type) and 1 percent (boldface type) points for the distribution of $F$

DEGREES OF FREEDOM FOR GREATER MEAN SQUARE

Each cell shows the 5 percent (roman) value over the 1 percent (boldface) value.

| Degrees of freedom for lesser mean square | 1 | 2 | 3 | 4 | 5 | 6 | 7 | 8 | 9 | 10 | 11 | 12 | 14 | 16 | 20 | 24 | 30 | 40 | 50 | 75 | 100 | 200 | 500 | ∞ |
|---|---|---|---|---|---|---|---|---|---|---|---|---|---|---|---|---|---|---|---|---|---|---|---|---|
| 16 | 4.49 **8.53** | 3.63 **6.23** | 3.24 **5.29** | 3.01 **4.77** | 2.85 **4.44** | 2.74 **4.20** | 2.66 **4.03** | 2.59 **3.89** | 2.54 **3.78** | 2.49 **3.69** | 2.45 **3.61** | 2.42 **3.55** | 2.37 **3.45** | 2.33 **3.37** | 2.28 **3.25** | 2.24 **3.18** | 2.20 **3.10** | 2.16 **3.01** | 2.13 **2.96** | 2.09 **2.89** | 2.07 **2.86** | 2.04 **2.80** | 2.02 **2.77** | 2.01 **2.75** |
| 17 | 4.45 **8.40** | 3.59 **6.11** | 3.20 **5.18** | 2.96 **4.67** | 2.81 **4.34** | 2.70 **4.10** | 2.62 **3.93** | 2.55 **3.79** | 2.50 **3.68** | 2.45 **3.59** | 2.41 **3.52** | 2.38 **3.45** | 2.33 **3.35** | 2.29 **3.27** | 2.23 **3.16** | 2.19 **3.08** | 2.15 **3.00** | 2.11 **2.92** | 2.08 **2.86** | 2.04 **2.79** | 2.02 **2.76** | 1.99 **2.70** | 1.97 **2.67** | 1.96 **2.65** |
| 18 | 4.41 **8.28** | 3.55 **6.01** | 3.16 **5.09** | 2.93 **4.58** | 2.77 **4.25** | 2.66 **4.01** | 2.58 **3.85** | 2.51 **3.71** | 2.46 **3.60** | 2.41 **3.51** | 2.37 **3.44** | 2.34 **3.37** | 2.29 **3.27** | 2.25 **3.19** | 2.19 **3.07** | 2.15 **3.00** | 2.11 **2.91** | 2.07 **2.83** | 2.04 **2.78** | 2.00 **2.71** | 1.98 **2.68** | 1.95 **2.62** | 1.93 **2.59** | 1.92 **2.57** |
| 19 | 4.38 **8.18** | 3.52 **5.93** | 3.13 **5.01** | 2.90 **4.50** | 2.74 **4.17** | 2.63 **3.94** | 2.55 **3.77** | 2.48 **3.63** | 2.43 **3.52** | 2.38 **3.43** | 2.34 **3.36** | 2.31 **3.30** | 2.26 **3.19** | 2.21 **3.12** | 2.15 **3.00** | 2.11 **2.92** | 2.07 **2.84** | 2.02 **2.76** | 2.00 **2.70** | 1.96 **2.63** | 1.94 **2.60** | 1.91 **2.54** | 1.90 **2.51** | 1.88 **2.49** |
| 20 | 4.35 **8.10** | 3.49 **5.85** | 3.10 **4.94** | 2.87 **4.43** | 2.71 **4.10** | 2.60 **3.87** | 2.52 **3.71** | 2.45 **3.56** | 2.40 **3.45** | 2.35 **3.37** | 2.31 **3.30** | 2.28 **3.23** | 2.23 **3.13** | 2.18 **3.05** | 2.12 **2.94** | 2.08 **2.86** | 2.04 **2.77** | 1.99 **2.69** | 1.96 **2.63** | 1.92 **2.56** | 1.90 **2.53** | 1.87 **2.47** | 1.85 **2.44** | 1.84 **2.42** |
| 21 | 4.32 **8.02** | 3.47 **5.78** | 3.07 **4.87** | 2.84 **4.37** | 2.68 **4.04** | 2.57 **3.81** | 2.49 **3.65** | 2.42 **3.51** | 2.37 **3.40** | 2.32 **3.31** | 2.28 **3.24** | 2.25 **3.17** | 2.20 **3.07** | 2.15 **2.99** | 2.09 **2.88** | 2.05 **2.80** | 2.00 **2.72** | 1.96 **2.63** | 1.93 **2.58** | 1.89 **2.51** | 1.87 **2.47** | 1.84 **2.42** | 1.82 **2.38** | 1.81 **2.36** |
| 22 | 4.30 **7.94** | 3.44 **5.72** | 3.05 **4.82** | 2.82 **4.31** | 2.66 **3.99** | 2.55 **3.76** | 2.47 **3.59** | 2.40 **3.45** | 2.35 **3.35** | 2.30 **3.26** | 2.26 **3.18** | 2.23 **3.12** | 2.18 **3.02** | 2.13 **2.94** | 2.07 **2.83** | 2.03 **2.75** | 1.98 **2.67** | 1.93 **2.58** | 1.91 **2.53** | 1.87 **2.46** | 1.84 **2.42** | 1.81 **2.37** | 1.80 **2.33** | 1.78 **2.31** |
| 23 | 4.28 **7.88** | 3.42 **5.66** | 3.03 **4.76** | 2.80 **4.26** | 2.64 **3.94** | 2.53 **3.71** | 2.45 **3.54** | 2.38 **3.41** | 2.32 **3.30** | 2.28 **3.21** | 2.24 **3.14** | 2.20 **3.07** | 2.14 **2.97** | 2.10 **2.89** | 2.04 **2.78** | 2.00 **2.70** | 1.96 **2.62** | 1.91 **2.53** | 1.88 **2.48** | 1.84 **2.41** | 1.82 **2.37** | 1.79 **2.32** | 1.77 **2.28** | 1.76 **2.26** |
| 24 | 4.26 **7.82** | 3.40 **5.61** | 3.01 **4.72** | 2.78 **4.22** | 2.62 **3.90** | 2.51 **3.67** | 2.43 **3.50** | 2.36 **3.36** | 2.30 **3.25** | 2.26 **3.17** | 2.22 **3.09** | 2.18 **3.03** | 2.13 **2.93** | 2.09 **2.85** | 2.02 **2.74** | 1.98 **2.66** | 1.94 **2.58** | 1.89 **2.49** | 1.86 **2.44** | 1.82 **2.36** | 1.80 **2.33** | 1.76 **2.27** | 1.74 **2.23** | 1.73 **2.21** |
| 25 | 4.24 **7.77** | 3.38 **5.57** | 2.99 **4.68** | 2.76 **4.18** | 2.60 **3.86** | 2.49 **3.63** | 2.41 **3.46** | 2.34 **3.32** | 2.28 **3.21** | 2.24 **3.13** | 2.20 **3.05** | 2.16 **2.99** | 2.11 **2.89** | 2.06 **2.81** | 2.00 **2.70** | 1.96 **2.62** | 1.92 **2.54** | 1.87 **2.45** | 1.84 **2.40** | 1.80 **2.32** | 1.77 **2.29** | 1.74 **2.23** | 1.72 **2.19** | 1.71 **2.17** |
| 26 | 4.22 **7.72** | 3.37 **5.53** | 2.98 **4.64** | 2.74 **4.14** | 2.59 **3.82** | 2.47 **3.59** | 2.39 **3.42** | 2.32 **3.29** | 2.27 **3.17** | 2.22 **3.09** | 2.18 **3.02** | 2.15 **2.96** | 2.10 **2.86** | 2.05 **2.77** | 1.99 **2.66** | 1.95 **2.58** | 1.90 **2.50** | 1.85 **2.41** | 1.82 **2.36** | 1.78 **2.28** | 1.76 **2.25** | 1.72 **2.19** | 1.70 **2.15** | 1.69 **2.13** |
| 27 | 4.21 **7.68** | 3.35 **5.49** | 2.96 **4.60** | 2.73 **4.11** | 2.57 **3.79** | 2.46 **3.56** | 2.37 **3.39** | 2.30 **3.26** | 2.25 **3.14** | 2.20 **3.06** | 2.16 **2.98** | 2.13 **2.93** | 2.08 **2.83** | 2.03 **2.74** | 1.97 **2.63** | 1.93 **2.55** | 1.88 **2.47** | 1.84 **2.38** | 1.80 **2.33** | 1.76 **2.25** | 1.74 **2.21** | 1.71 **2.16** | 1.68 **2.12** | 1.67 **2.10** |
| 28 | 4.20 **7.64** | 3.34 **5.45** | 2.95 **4.57** | 2.71 **4.07** | 2.56 **3.76** | 2.44 **3.53** | 2.36 **3.36** | 2.29 **3.23** | 2.24 **3.11** | 2.19 **3.03** | 2.15 **2.95** | 2.12 **2.90** | 2.06 **2.80** | 2.02 **2.71** | 1.96 **2.60** | 1.91 **2.52** | 1.87 **2.44** | 1.81 **2.35** | 1.78 **2.30** | 1.75 **2.22** | 1.72 **2.18** | 1.69 **2.13** | 1.67 **2.09** | 1.65 **2.06** |
| 29 | 4.18 **7.60** | 3.33 **5.42** | 2.93 **4.54** | 2.70 **4.04** | 2.54 **3.73** | 2.43 **3.50** | 2.35 **3.33** | 2.28 **3.20** | 2.22 **3.08** | 2.18 **3.00** | 2.14 **2.92** | 2.10 **2.87** | 2.05 **2.77** | 2.00 **2.68** | 1.94 **2.57** | 1.90 **2.49** | 1.85 **2.41** | 1.80 **2.32** | 1.77 **2.27** | 1.73 **2.19** | 1.71 **2.15** | 1.68 **2.10** | 1.65 **2.06** | 1.64 **2.03** |
| 30 | 4.17 **7.56** | 3.32 **5.39** | 2.92 **4.51** | 2.69 **4.02** | 2.53 **3.70** | 2.42 **3.47** | 2.34 **3.30** | 2.27 **3.17** | 2.21 **3.06** | 2.16 **2.98** | 2.12 **2.90** | 2.09 **2.84** | 2.04 **2.74** | 1.99 **2.66** | 1.93 **2.55** | 1.89 **2.47** | 1.84 **2.38** | 1.79 **2.29** | 1.76 **2.24** | 1.72 **2.16** | 1.69 **2.13** | 1.66 **2.07** | 1.64 **2.03** | 1.62 **2.01** |

Table of $F$ values (5% points in roman type, 1% points in **bold** type). Degrees of freedom for numerator are the unlabeled columns; degrees of freedom for denominator are in the first column.

| df | | | | | | | | | | | | | | | | | | | | | | | | |
|---|---|---|---|---|---|---|---|---|---|---|---|---|---|---|---|---|---|---|---|---|---|---|---|---|
| 32 | 4.15 | 3.30 | 2.90 | 2.67 | 2.51 | 2.40 | 2.32 | 2.25 | 2.19 | 2.14 | 2.10 | 2.07 | 2.02 | 1.97 | 1.91 | 1.86 | 1.82 | 1.76 | 1.74 | 1.69 | 1.67 | 1.64 | 1.61 | 1.59 |
| | **7.50** | **5.34** | **4.46** | **3.97** | **3.66** | **3.42** | **3.25** | **3.12** | **3.01** | **2.94** | **2.86** | **2.80** | **2.70** | **2.62** | **2.51** | **2.42** | **2.34** | **2.25** | **2.20** | **2.12** | **2.08** | **2.02** | **1.98** | **1.96** |
| 34 | 4.13 | 3.28 | 2.88 | 2.65 | 2.49 | 2.38 | 2.30 | 2.23 | 2.17 | 2.12 | 2.08 | 2.05 | 2.00 | 1.95 | 1.89 | 1.84 | 1.80 | 1.74 | 1.71 | 1.67 | 1.64 | 1.61 | 1.59 | 1.57 |
| | **7.44** | **5.29** | **4.42** | **3.93** | **3.61** | **3.38** | **3.21** | **3.08** | **2.97** | **2.89** | **2.82** | **2.76** | **2.66** | **2.58** | **2.47** | **2.38** | **2.30** | **2.21** | **2.15** | **2.04** | **2.00** | **1.98** | **1.94** | **1.91** |
| 36 | 4.11 | 3.26 | 2.86 | 2.63 | 2.48 | 2.36 | 2.28 | 2.21 | 2.15 | 2.10 | 2.06 | 2.03 | 1.98 | 1.93 | 1.87 | 1.82 | 1.78 | 1.72 | 1.69 | 1.65 | 1.62 | 1.59 | 1.56 | 1.55 |
| | **7.39** | **5.25** | **4.38** | **3.89** | **3.58** | **3.35** | **3.18** | **3.04** | **2.94** | **2.86** | **2.78** | **2.72** | **2.62** | **2.54** | **2.43** | **2.35** | **2.26** | **2.17** | **2.12** | **2.04** | **2.00** | **1.94** | **1.90** | **1.87** |
| 38 | 4.10 | 3.25 | 2.85 | 2.62 | 2.46 | 2.35 | 2.26 | 2.19 | 2.14 | 2.09 | 2.05 | 2.02 | 1.96 | 1.92 | 1.85 | 1.80 | 1.76 | 1.71 | 1.67 | 1.63 | 1.60 | 1.57 | 1.54 | 1.53 |
| | **7.35** | **5.21** | **4.34** | **3.86** | **3.54** | **3.32** | **3.15** | **3.02** | **2.91** | **2.82** | **2.75** | **2.69** | **2.59** | **2.51** | **2.40** | **2.32** | **2.22** | **2.14** | **2.08** | **2.00** | **1.97** | **1.90** | **1.86** | **1.84** |
| 40 | 4.08 | 3.23 | 2.84 | 2.61 | 2.45 | 2.34 | 2.25 | 2.18 | 2.12 | 2.07 | 2.04 | 2.00 | 1.95 | 1.90 | 1.84 | 1.79 | 1.74 | 1.69 | 1.66 | 1.61 | 1.59 | 1.55 | 1.53 | 1.51 |
| | **7.31** | **5.18** | **4.31** | **3.83** | **3.51** | **3.29** | **3.12** | **2.99** | **2.88** | **2.80** | **2.73** | **2.66** | **2.56** | **2.49** | **2.37** | **2.29** | **2.20** | **2.11** | **2.05** | **1.97** | **1.94** | **1.88** | **1.84** | **1.81** |
| 42 | 4.07 | 3.22 | 2.83 | 2.59 | 2.44 | 2.32 | 2.24 | 2.17 | 2.11 | 2.06 | 2.02 | 1.99 | 1.94 | 1.89 | 1.82 | 1.78 | 1.73 | 1.68 | 1.64 | 1.60 | 1.57 | 1.54 | 1.51 | 1.49 |
| | **7.27** | **5.15** | **4.29** | **3.80** | **3.49** | **3.26** | **3.10** | **2.96** | **2.86** | **2.77** | **2.70** | **2.64** | **2.54** | **2.46** | **2.35** | **2.26** | **2.17** | **2.08** | **2.02** | **1.94** | **1.91** | **1.85** | **1.80** | **1.78** |
| 44 | 4.06 | 3.21 | 2.82 | 2.58 | 2.43 | 2.31 | 2.23 | 2.16 | 2.10 | 2.05 | 2.01 | 1.98 | 1.92 | 1.88 | 1.81 | 1.76 | 1.72 | 1.66 | 1.63 | 1.58 | 1.56 | 1.52 | 1.50 | 1.48 |
| | **7.24** | **5.12** | **4.26** | **3.78** | **3.46** | **3.24** | **3.07** | **2.94** | **2.84** | **2.75** | **2.68** | **2.62** | **2.52** | **2.44** | **2.32** | **2.24** | **2.15** | **2.06** | **2.00** | **1.92** | **1.88** | **1.82** | **1.78** | **1.75** |
| 46 | 4.05 | 3.20 | 2.81 | 2.57 | 2.42 | 2.30 | 2.22 | 2.14 | 2.09 | 2.04 | 2.00 | 1.97 | 1.91 | 1.87 | 1.80 | 1.75 | 1.71 | 1.65 | 1.62 | 1.57 | 1.54 | 1.51 | 1.48 | 1.46 |
| | **7.21** | **5.10** | **4.24** | **3.76** | **3.44** | **3.22** | **3.05** | **2.92** | **2.82** | **2.73** | **2.66** | **2.60** | **2.50** | **2.42** | **2.30** | **2.22** | **2.13** | **2.04** | **1.98** | **1.90** | **1.86** | **1.80** | **1.76** | **1.72** |
| 48 | 4.04 | 3.19 | 2.80 | 2.56 | 2.41 | 2.30 | 2.21 | 2.14 | 2.08 | 2.03 | 1.99 | 1.96 | 1.90 | 1.86 | 1.79 | 1.74 | 1.70 | 1.64 | 1.61 | 1.56 | 1.53 | 1.50 | 1.47 | 1.45 |
| | **7.19** | **5.08** | **4.22** | **3.74** | **3.42** | **3.20** | **3.04** | **2.90** | **2.80** | **2.71** | **2.64** | **2.58** | **2.48** | **2.40** | **2.28** | **2.20** | **2.11** | **2.02** | **1.96** | **1.88** | **1.84** | **1.78** | **1.73** | **1.70** |
| 50 | 4.03 | 3.18 | 2.79 | 2.56 | 2.40 | 2.29 | 2.20 | 2.13 | 2.07 | 2.02 | 1.98 | 1.95 | 1.90 | 1.85 | 1.78 | 1.74 | 1.69 | 1.63 | 1.60 | 1.55 | 1.52 | 1.48 | 1.46 | 1.44 |
| | **7.17** | **5.06** | **4.20** | **3.72** | **3.41** | **3.18** | **3.02** | **2.88** | **2.78** | **2.70** | **2.62** | **2.56** | **2.46** | **2.39** | **2.26** | **2.18** | **2.10** | **2.00** | **1.94** | **1.86** | **1.82** | **1.76** | **1.71** | **1.68** |
| 55 | 4.02 | 3.17 | 2.78 | 2.54 | 2.38 | 2.27 | 2.18 | 2.11 | 2.05 | 2.00 | 1.97 | 1.93 | 1.88 | 1.83 | 1.76 | 1.72 | 1.67 | 1.61 | 1.58 | 1.52 | 1.50 | 1.46 | 1.43 | 1.41 |
| | **7.12** | **5.01** | **4.16** | **3.68** | **3.37** | **3.15** | **2.98** | **2.85** | **2.75** | **2.66** | **2.59** | **2.53** | **2.43** | **2.35** | **2.23** | **2.15** | **2.06** | **1.96** | **1.90** | **1.82** | **1.78** | **1.71** | **1.66** | **1.64** |
| 60 | 4.00 | 3.15 | 2.76 | 2.52 | 2.37 | 2.25 | 2.17 | 2.10 | 2.04 | 1.99 | 1.95 | 1.92 | 1.86 | 1.81 | 1.75 | 1.70 | 1.65 | 1.59 | 1.56 | 1.50 | 1.48 | 1.44 | 1.41 | 1.39 |
| | **7.08** | **4.98** | **4.13** | **3.65** | **3.34** | **3.12** | **2.95** | **2.82** | **2.72** | **2.63** | **2.56** | **2.50** | **2.40** | **2.32** | **2.20** | **2.12** | **2.03** | **1.93** | **1.87** | **1.79** | **1.74** | **1.68** | **1.63** | **1.60** |
| 65 | 3.99 | 3.14 | 2.75 | 2.51 | 2.36 | 2.24 | 2.15 | 2.08 | 2.02 | 1.98 | 1.94 | 1.90 | 1.85 | 1.80 | 1.73 | 1.68 | 1.63 | 1.57 | 1.54 | 1.49 | 1.46 | 1.42 | 1.39 | 1.37 |
| | **7.04** | **4.95** | **4.10** | **3.62** | **3.31** | **3.09** | **2.93** | **2.79** | **2.70** | **2.61** | **2.54** | **2.47** | **2.37** | **2.30** | **2.18** | **2.09** | **2.00** | **1.90** | **1.84** | **1.76** | **1.71** | **1.64** | **1.60** | **1.56** |
| 70 | 3.98 | 3.13 | 2.74 | 2.50 | 2.35 | 2.23 | 2.14 | 2.07 | 2.01 | 1.97 | 1.93 | 1.89 | 1.84 | 1.79 | 1.72 | 1.67 | 1.62 | 1.56 | 1.53 | 1.47 | 1.45 | 1.40 | 1.37 | 1.35 |
| | **7.01** | **4.92** | **4.08** | **3.60** | **3.29** | **3.07** | **2.91** | **2.77** | **2.67** | **2.59** | **2.51** | **2.45** | **2.35** | **2.28** | **2.15** | **2.07** | **1.98** | **1.88** | **1.82** | **1.74** | **1.69** | **1.62** | **1.56** | **1.53** |
| 80 | 3.96 | 3.11 | 2.72 | 2.48 | 2.33 | 2.21 | 2.12 | 2.05 | 1.99 | 1.95 | 1.91 | 1.88 | 1.82 | 1.77 | 1.70 | 1.65 | 1.60 | 1.54 | 1.51 | 1.45 | 1.42 | 1.38 | 1.35 | 1.32 |
| | **6.96** | **4.88** | **4.04** | **3.56** | **3.25** | **3.04** | **2.87** | **2.74** | **2.64** | **2.55** | **2.48** | **2.41** | **2.32** | **2.24** | **2.11** | **2.03** | **1.94** | **1.84** | **1.78** | **1.70** | **1.65** | **1.57** | **1.52** | **1.49** |
| 100 | 3.94 | 3.09 | 2.70 | 2.46 | 2.30 | 2.19 | 2.10 | 2.03 | 1.97 | 1.92 | 1.88 | 1.85 | 1.79 | 1.75 | 1.68 | 1.63 | 1.57 | 1.51 | 1.48 | 1.42 | 1.39 | 1.34 | 1.30 | 1.28 |
| | **6.90** | **4.82** | **3.98** | **3.51** | **3.20** | **2.99** | **2.82** | **2.69** | **2.59** | **2.51** | **2.43** | **2.36** | **2.26** | **2.19** | **2.06** | **1.98** | **1.89** | **1.79** | **1.73** | **1.64** | **1.59** | **1.51** | **1.46** | **1.43** |
| 125 | 3.92 | 3.07 | 2.68 | 2.44 | 2.29 | 2.17 | 2.08 | 2.01 | 1.95 | 1.90 | 1.86 | 1.83 | 1.77 | 1.72 | 1.65 | 1.60 | 1.55 | 1.49 | 1.45 | 1.39 | 1.36 | 1.31 | 1.27 | 1.25 |
| | **6.84** | **4.78** | **3.94** | **3.47** | **3.17** | **2.95** | **2.79** | **2.65** | **2.56** | **2.47** | **2.40** | **2.33** | **2.23** | **2.15** | **2.03** | **1.94** | **1.85** | **1.75** | **1.68** | **1.59** | **1.54** | **1.46** | **1.40** | **1.37** |
| 150 | 3.91 | 3.06 | 2.67 | 2.43 | 2.27 | 2.16 | 2.07 | 2.00 | 1.94 | 1.89 | 1.85 | 1.82 | 1.76 | 1.71 | 1.64 | 1.59 | 1.54 | 1.47 | 1.44 | 1.37 | 1.34 | 1.29 | 1.25 | 1.22 |
| | **6.81** | **4.75** | **3.91** | **3.44** | **3.14** | **2.92** | **2.76** | **2.62** | **2.53** | **2.44** | **2.37** | **2.30** | **2.20** | **2.12** | **2.00** | **1.91** | **1.83** | **1.72** | **1.66** | **1.56** | **1.51** | **1.43** | **1.37** | **1.33** |
| 200 | 3.89 | 3.04 | 2.65 | 2.41 | 2.26 | 2.14 | 2.05 | 1.98 | 1.92 | 1.87 | 1.83 | 1.80 | 1.74 | 1.69 | 1.62 | 1.57 | 1.52 | 1.45 | 1.42 | 1.35 | 1.32 | 1.26 | 1.22 | 1.19 |
| | **6.76** | **4.71** | **3.88** | **3.41** | **3.11** | **2.90** | **2.73** | **2.60** | **2.50** | **2.41** | **2.34** | **2.28** | **2.17** | **2.09** | **1.97** | **1.88** | **1.79** | **1.69** | **1.62** | **1.53** | **1.48** | **1.39** | **1.33** | **1.28** |
| 400 | 3.86 | 3.02 | 2.62 | 2.39 | 2.23 | 2.12 | 2.03 | 1.96 | 1.90 | 1.85 | 1.81 | 1.78 | 1.72 | 1.67 | 1.60 | 1.54 | 1.49 | 1.42 | 1.38 | 1.32 | 1.28 | 1.22 | 1.16 | 1.13 |
| | **6.70** | **4.66** | **3.83** | **3.36** | **3.06** | **2.85** | **2.69** | **2.55** | **2.46** | **2.37** | **2.29** | **2.23** | **2.12** | **2.04** | **1.92** | **1.84** | **1.74** | **1.64** | **1.57** | **1.47** | **1.42** | **1.32** | **1.24** | **1.19** |
| 1000 | 3.85 | 3.00 | 2.61 | 2.38 | 2.22 | 2.10 | 2.02 | 1.95 | 1.89 | 1.84 | 1.80 | 1.76 | 1.70 | 1.65 | 1.58 | 1.53 | 1.47 | 1.41 | 1.36 | 1.30 | 1.26 | 1.19 | 1.13 | 1.08 |
| | **6.66** | **4.62** | **3.80** | **3.34** | **3.04** | **2.82** | **2.66** | **2.53** | **2.43** | **2.34** | **2.26** | **2.20** | **2.09** | **2.01** | **1.89** | **1.81** | **1.71** | **1.61** | **1.54** | **1.44** | **1.38** | **1.28** | **1.19** | **1.11** |
| ∞ | 3.84 | 2.99 | 2.60 | 2.37 | 2.21 | 2.09 | 2.01 | 1.94 | 1.88 | 1.83 | 1.79 | 1.75 | 1.69 | 1.64 | 1.57 | 1.52 | 1.46 | 1.40 | 1.35 | 1.28 | 1.24 | 1.17 | 1.11 | 1.00 |
| | **6.64** | **4.60** | **3.78** | **3.32** | **3.02** | **2.80** | **2.64** | **2.51** | **2.41** | **2.32** | **2.24** | **2.18** | **2.07** | **1.99** | **1.87** | **1.79** | **1.69** | **1.59** | **1.52** | **1.41** | **1.36** | **1.25** | **1.15** | **1.00** |

Reprinted, by permission, from G. W. Snedecor, *Statistical methods*, 5th ed., pp. 246–249, Iowa State College Press, Ames, Iowa, 1956.

**TABLE F**    Areas Under the Normal Curve Between the Mean and $z$

| $z$ | Area from Mean to $z$ | $z$ | Area from Mean to $z$ | $z$ | Area from Mean to $z$ |
|------|------|------|------|------|------|
| 0.00 | .0000 | 0.35 | .1368 | 0.70 | .2580 |
| 0.01 | .0040 | 0.36 | .1406 | 0.71 | .2611 |
| 0.02 | .0080 | 0.37 | .1443 | 0.72 | .2642 |
| 0.03 | .0120 | 0.38 | .1480 | 0.73 | .2673 |
| 0.04 | .0160 | 0.39 | .1517 | 0.74 | .2704 |
| 0.05 | .0199 | 0.40 | .1554 | 0.75 | .2734 |
| 0.06 | .0239 | 0.41 | .1591 | 0.76 | .2764 |
| 0.07 | .0279 | 0.42 | .1628 | 0.77 | .2794 |
| 0.08 | .0319 | 0.43 | .1664 | 0.78 | .2823 |
| 0.09 | .0359 | 0.44 | .1700 | 0.79 | .2852 |
| 0.10 | .0398 | 0.45 | .1736 | 0.80 | .2881 |
| 0.11 | .0438 | 0.46 | .1772 | 0.81 | .2910 |
| 0.12 | .0478 | 0.47 | .1808 | 0.82 | .2939 |
| 0.13 | .0517 | 0.48 | .1844 | 0.83 | .2967 |
| 0.14 | .0557 | 0.49 | .1879 | 0.84 | .2995 |
| 0.15 | .0596 | 0.50 | .1915 | 0.85 | .3023 |
| 0.16 | .0636 | 0.51 | .1950 | 0.86 | .3051 |
| 0.17 | .0675 | 0.52 | .1985 | 0.87 | .3078 |
| 0.18 | .0714 | 0.53 | .2019 | 0.88 | .3106 |
| 0.19 | .0753 | 0.54 | .2054 | 0.89 | .3133 |
| 0.20 | .0793 | 0.55 | .2088 | 0.90 | .3159 |
| 0.21 | .0832 | 0.56 | .2123 | 0.91 | .3186 |
| 0.22 | .0871 | 0.57 | .2157 | 0.92 | .3212 |
| 0.23 | .0910 | 0.58 | .2190 | 0.93 | .3238 |
| 0.24 | .0948 | 0.59 | .2224 | 0.94 | .3264 |
| 0.25 | .0987 | 0.60 | .2257 | 0.95 | .3289 |
| 0.26 | .1026 | 0.61 | .2291 | 0.96 | .3315 |
| 0.27 | .1064 | 0.62 | .2324 | 0.97 | .3340 |
| 0.28 | .1103 | 0.63 | .2357 | 0.98 | .3365 |
| 0.29 | .1141 | 0.64 | .2389 | 0.99 | .3389 |
| 0.30 | .1179 | 0.65 | .2422 | 1.00 | .3413 |
| 0.31 | .1217 | 0.66 | .2454 | 1.01 | .3438 |
| 0.32 | .1255 | 0.67 | .2486 | 1.02 | .3461 |
| 0.33 | .1293 | 0.68 | .2517 | 1.03 | .3485 |
| 0.34 | .1331 | 0.69 | .2549 | 1.04 | .3508 |

**TABLE F**  (*continued*)

| z | Area from Mean to z | z | Area from Mean to z | z | Area from Mean to z |
|------|------|------|------|------|------|
| 1.05 | .3531 | 1.40 | .4192 | 1.75 | .4599 |
| 1.06 | .3554 | 1.41 | .4207 | 1.76 | .4608 |
| 1.07 | .3577 | 1.42 | .4222 | 1.77 | .4616 |
| 1.08 | .3599 | 1.43 | .4236 | 1.78 | .4625 |
| 1.09 | .3621 | 1.44 | .4251 | 1.79 | .4633 |
| 1.10 | .3643 | 1.45 | .4265 | 1.80 | .4641 |
| 1.11 | .3665 | 1.46 | .4279 | 1.81 | .4649 |
| 1.12 | .3686 | 1.47 | .4292 | 1.82 | .4656 |
| 1.13 | .3708 | 1.48 | .4306 | 1.83 | .4664 |
| 1.14 | .3729 | 1.49 | .4319 | 1.84 | .4671 |
| 1.15 | .3749 | 1.50 | .4332 | 1.85 | .4678 |
| 1.16 | .3770 | 1.51 | .4345 | 1.86 | .4686 |
| 1.17 | .3790 | 1.52 | .4357 | 1.87 | .4693 |
| 1.18 | .3810 | 1.53 | .4370 | 1.88 | .4699 |
| 1.19 | .3830 | 1.54 | .4382 | 1.89 | .4706 |
| 1.20 | .3849 | 1.55 | .4394 | 1.90 | .4713 |
| 1.21 | .3869 | 1.56 | .4406 | 1.91 | .4719 |
| 1.22 | .3888 | 1.57 | .4418 | 1.92 | .4726 |
| 1.23 | .3907 | 1.58 | .4429 | 1.93 | .4732 |
| 1.24 | .3925 | 1.59 | .4441 | 1.94 | .4738 |
| 1.25 | .3944 | 1.60 | .4452 | 1.95 | .4744 |
| 1.26 | .3962 | 1.61 | .4463 | 1.96 | .4750 |
| 1.27 | .3980 | 1.62 | .4474 | 1.97 | .4756 |
| 1.28 | .3997 | 1.63 | .4484 | 1.98 | .4761 |
| 1.29 | .4015 | 1.64 | .4495 | 1.99 | .4767 |
| 1.30 | .4032 | 1.65 | .4505 | 2.00 | .4772 |
| 1.31 | .4049 | 1.66 | .4515 | 2.01 | .4778 |
| 1.32 | .4066 | 1.67 | .4525 | 2.02 | .4783 |
| 1.33 | .4082 | 1.68 | .4535 | 2.03 | .4788 |
| 1.34 | .4099 | 1.69 | .4545 | 2.04 | .4793 |
| 1.35 | .4115 | 1.70 | .4554 | 2.05 | .4798 |
| 1.36 | .4131 | 1.71 | .4564 | 2.06 | .4803 |
| 1.37 | .4147 | 1.72 | .4573 | 2.07 | .4808 |
| 1.38 | .4162 | 1.73 | .4582 | 2.08 | .4812 |
| 1.39 | .4177 | 1.74 | .4591 | 2.09 | .4817 |

(*continued*)

**TABLE F**   *(continued)*

| z | Area from Mean to z | z | Area from Mean to z | z | Area from Mean to z |
|---|---|---|---|---|---|
| 2.10 | .4821 | 2.45 | .4929 | 2.80 | .4974 |
| 2.11 | .4826 | 2.46 | .4931 | 2.81 | .4975 |
| 2.12 | .4830 | 2.47 | .4932 | 2.82 | .4976 |
| 2.13 | .4834 | 2.48 | .4934 | 2.83 | .4977 |
| 2.14 | .4838 | 2.49 | .4936 | 2.84 | .4977 |
| 2.15 | .4842 | 2.50 | .4938 | 2.85 | .4978 |
| 2.16 | .4846 | 2.51 | .4940 | 2.86 | .4979 |
| 2.17 | .4850 | 2.52 | .4941 | 2.87 | .4979 |
| 2.18 | .4854 | 2.53 | .4943 | 2.88 | .4980 |
| 2.19 | .4857 | 2.54 | .4945 | 2.89 | .4981 |
| 2.20 | .4861 | 2.55 | .4946 | 2.90 | .4981 |
| 2.21 | .4864 | 2.56 | .4948 | 2.91 | .4982 |
| 2.22 | .4868 | 2.57 | .4949 | 2.92 | .4982 |
| 2.23 | .4871 | 2.58 | .4951 | 2.93 | .4983 |
| 2.24 | .4875 | 2.59 | .4952 | 2.94 | .4984 |
| 2.25 | .4878 | 2.60 | .4953 | 2.95 | .4984 |
| 2.26 | .4881 | 2.61 | .4955 | 2.96 | .4985 |
| 2.27 | .4884 | 2.62 | .4956 | 2.97 | .4985 |
| 2.28 | .4887 | 2.63 | .4957 | 2.98 | .4986 |
| 2.29 | .4890 | 2.64 | .4959 | 2.99 | .4986 |
| 2.30 | .4893 | 2.65 | .4960 | 3.00 | .4987 |
| 2.31 | .4896 | 2.66 | .4961 | 3.01 | .4987 |
| 2.32 | .4898 | 2.67 | .4962 | 3.02 | .4987 |
| 2.33 | .4901 | 2.68 | .4963 | 3.03 | .4988 |
| 2.34 | .4904 | 2.69 | .4964 | 3.04 | .4988 |
| 2.35 | .4906 | 2.70 | .4965 | 3.05 | .4989 |
| 2.36 | .4909 | 2.71 | .4966 | 3.06 | .4989 |
| 2.37 | .4911 | 2.72 | .4967 | 3.07 | .4989 |
| 2.38 | .4913 | 2.73 | .4968 | 3.08 | .4990 |
| 2.39 | .4916 | 2.74 | .4969 | 3.09 | .4990 |
| 2.40 | .4918 | 2.75 | .4970 | 3.10 | .4990 |
| 2.41 | .4920 | 2.76 | .4971 | 3.11 | .4991 |
| 2.42 | .4922 | 2.77 | .4972 | 3.12 | .4991 |
| 2.43 | .4925 | 2.78 | .4973 | 3.13 | .4991 |
| 2.44 | .4927 | 2.79 | .4974 | 3.14 | .4992 |

**TABLE F**  (*continued*)

| z | Area from Mean to z | z | Area from Mean to z | z | Area from Mean to z |
|------|------|------|------|------|------|
| 3.15 | .4992 | 3.22 | .4994 | 3.29 | .4995 |
| 3.16 | .4992 | 3.23 | .4994 | 3.30 | .4995 |
| 3.17 | .4992 | 3.24 | .4994 | 3.40 | .4997 |
| 3.18 | .4993 | 3.25 | .4994 | 3.50 | .4998 |
| 3.19 | .4993 | 3.26 | .4994 | 3.60 | .4998 |
| 3.20 | .4993 | 3.27 | .4995 | 3.70 | .4999 |
| 3.21 | .4993 | 3.28 | .4995 |  |  |

# APPENDIX II
# ANSWERS TO STATISTICS EXERCISES

## Chapter 7

1. a. Nominal
   b. Ratio
   c. Ordinal
   d. Nominal
   e. Interval
   f. Nominal
   g. Ratio
   h. Interval
   i. Ratio
   j. Ordinal

2. 
| Group A | Group B | Group C |
|---|---|---|
| $\Sigma X = 29$ | $\Sigma X = 27$ | $\Sigma X = 21$ |
| $\Sigma X^2 = 175$ | $\Sigma X^2 = 155$ | $\Sigma X^2 = 99$ |
| $(\Sigma X)^2 = 841$ | $(\Sigma X)^2 = 729$ | $(\Sigma X)^2 = 441$ |

## Chapter 8

1. 
| Percent Body Fat | Percent Income for Recreation | Stress Index |
|---|---|---|
| $M = 8.4$ | $M = 12.5$ | $M = 9.7$ |
| MED = 8 | MED = 11.5 | MED = 9 |
| Range = 8 or 9 | Range = 11 or 12 | Range = 10 or 11 |
| $SD = 2.61$ | $SD = 3.35$ | $SD = 3.32$ |
| 68% = 5.8 – 11.0 | 68% = 9.2 – 15.9 | 68% = 6.4 – 13.0 |
| 95% = 3.3 – 13.6 | 95% = 5.9 – 19.1 | 95% = 3.2 – 16.2 |
| 99% = 1.7 – 15.2 | 99% = 3.9 – 21.1 | 99% = 1.1 – 18.3 |

2. a. 6.68%
   b. 40.13%
   c. 46.49%
   d. 8.57%
   e. 15.25%

**3.** Health Test          Recreation Test
  a. $z = .43$                $z = 1.25$
  b. $z = 1.43$             $z = 2.25$
  c. $z = .71$                $z = -.50$
  d. $z = -1.43$           $z = -1.25$
  e. $z = -.43$             $z = .50$

## Chapter 9

1. There was a significant difference ($p \le .05$) between the diet group and the diet and exercise group. Dieting and exercising were better at lowering blood cholesterol.
2. There was a significant difference ($p \le .05$) between Utahans and Nebraskans on the percent of income spent on leisure activities. The Utahans spent more. (This is probably due to the excellent skiing in Utah!)
3. There was no significant difference ($p > .05$) between running four and six days per week on the improvement of $VO_2$ max.
4. There was no significant difference ($p > .05$) between the two stress reduction techniques.
5. There was a significant difference ($p \le .01$) between body fat measures obtained by UWW and the skinfold method. The skinfold method is less accurate.

## Chapter 10

1. $r = .82$, which is significant at the .05 as well as .01 level. The percent common variance is 67.2 and the percent specific variance is 32.8.
2. $r = .76$
3. $r = -.85$, which is significant at the .05 as well as .01 level. The explained variance is 72.3%.
4. a. $Y' = .78X + 30.77$
   b. $SEE = 2.48$
   c. $Y' = 40.91$
5. a. $Y' = -1.13X + 58.60$
      $SEE = 2.11$
   b. $Y' = 46.1$. The 68% confidence interval $= 46.1 \pm 2.1$ or 44.0 to 48.2.
6. a. $Y' = 1.87X + 138.6$
      $SEE = 57.13$
   b. $Y' = 437.4$
      The 95% confidence interval $= 437.4 \pm 1.96\ (57.13)$ or 325 to 549.
      (Note that the interval is rounded to the nearest *whole person.*)

## Chapter 11

1. a. $t = -2.37$
   b. Yes
2. a. $t = -1.19$
   b. No

3. a. $t = -2.26$, which is significant at the .05 level.

   b. Women in this study were more flexible than men.

   c. $\Omega^2 = .186$, which means that 18.6% of the variance in flexibility between the groups is due to gender.

4. a. $\Omega^2 = .038$

   b. This means that 3.8% of the difference in salaries is due to the occupational group.

5. $t = 4.75$, which is significant at the .05 as well as .01 level.

6. a.

| Source | SS | df | MS | F |
|--------|-----|----|-------|-------|
| Between | 725 | 2 | 362.5 | 31.41 |
| Within | 150 | 13 | 11.54 | |
| Total | 875 | 15 | | |

   b. Yes

   c. It is 95% likely that a real difference in $VO_2$ max exists in the three groups of athletes.

   d. Perform a multiple comparison test to identify which groups are significantly different from each other.

   e. $\Omega_2 = .79$, which indicates that 79% of the variance in scores is due to being a track athlete, basketball player, or volleyball player.

7. a. Yes

   b. The difference is 95% likely to be real and only 5% likely to be due to chance.

   c. Perform a multiple comparison test to identify which groups are significantly different from each other.

   d. $\Omega_2 = .50$, which means that 50.0% of the variation among groups in bone mineral content can be attributed to estrogen replacement therapy and 50.0% is due to other factors.

## Chapter 12

1. Chi-square = 52.0, $p \le .001$.

2. Chi-square = 27.2, $p \le .001$.

3. Chi-square = 4.36, $p \le .05$.

4. Spearman $r = .786$, $p \le .05$.

5. Spearman $r = -.901$, $p \le .05$.

# APPENDIX III
# SAMPLE INFORMED CONSENT, SURVEY COVER LETTER, AND THANK-YOU LETTER

 University of
Nebraska at
Omaha

School of Health, Physical
Education and Recreation
Omaha, Nebraska 68182-0216
(402) 554-2670

### *SAMPLE INFORMED CONSENT*

IRB # 171-93
Adult Informed Consent Form

## Determinants Of The Oxygen Cost Of Cycle Ergometry

### Invitation To Participate

You are invited to participate in a research study that will determine the important factors that account for the oxygen cost of stationary cycling. Your participation in this study is completely voluntary.

### Basis For Subject Selection

You are being asked to participate in this study because you are a healthy male or female between the ages of 19 and 35. You may participate only if you are free from any cardiovascular, metabolic, and/or muscle or joint risk factors and you are a nonsmoker.

### Purpose Of The Study

The purpose of this study is to determine the important factors that account for how much oxygen someone uses when they pedal a stationary cycle. It has been recently shown that men and women differ on how much oxygen they use when exercising at the same workload. This study will help to explain what accounts for this difference.

### Explanation Of Procedures

You will be asked to come to the Exercise Physiology Laboratory at UNO for two test sessions. Each will last about one hour. Prior to any testing you will be required to complete a medical questionnaire and read and sign a consent form.

University of Nebraska at Omaha    University of Nebraska Medical Center    University of Nebraska—Lincoln    University of Nebraska at Kearney

237

During the first session measurements of your height, weight, leg and thigh length and inseam height will be made. The angle from your kneecap to your hip will be measured with a device that resembles a protractor. Inseam will be determined by measuring the height of a clipboard placed between your thighs at crotch level. This information will be used to establish an appropriate seat height. Next, you will be asked to perform an exercise test during which we will measure the amount of oxygen your body uses, and your heart rate. Measurement of your oxygen consumption will be done through a mouthpiece attached to an electronic instrument known as a metabolic cart. You may find the mouthpiece slightly uncomfortable. Your heart rate will be measured by an electronic wrist watch and electrode belt attached to your chest.

The exercise test you will perform is submaximal and will be done on a stationary cycle. The exercise will begin with five to ten minutes of rest on the cycle. If you are a male you will perform three exercise stages lasting about five minutes each. One stage will be performed against no resistance, with the other two at light to moderate resistance levels. After the test you will pedal for about five minutes to cool down.

If you are a female you will perform the same exercise tests as the males plus two additional stages at a light and moderate resistance.

In order to obtain accurate test results you will be asked to refrain from eating for at least four hours before testing, and not to exercise or perform strenuous activity 12 hours prior to participating.

During the second visit to the lab you will be asked to perform two strength tests on your dominant leg. One test will be performed at a moderate speed in which you will feel modest resistance. The other test will be done at a fast speed where the resistance will feel very light. Both tests together require only about five minutes to do.

Finally, you will be underwater weighed to determine your percent body fat. You will need to bring a swim suit for this test. You will sit in a plastic chair that is suspended from a scale in a tank of warm water. You will be asked to submerge yourself while blowing all of the air out of your lungs that you can. After this is done an underwater weight is taken. You will be asked to repeat this about 10 times. Afterwards you will be asked to breathe into a device known as a spirometer to measure a lung volume. You will repeat this test twice. Underwater weighing and lung volume testing will take about 20 to 30 minutes.

### Potential Risks And Discomforts

The following are the risks and discomforts you could potentially experience during this study:

*Cycle and Strength Tests*:

Possible risks include and are not limited to heart attack, abnormal heart rhythms, abnormal blood pressure, stroke, shortness of breath, dizziness, reduced coordination and muscle soreness.

*Underwater Weighing and Lung Volume Test*:

Possible risks include and are not limited to swallowing water and apprehension of the water. The lung volume test may make you light-headed.

The risks of these occurring in healthy, younger subjects is very low. Most of the discomforts are relatively short-lived.

## Potential Benefits To Subjects

You will benefit by obtaining a predicted measure of your aerobic capacity, which is an important index of cardiovascular fitness, and a measure of your percent body fat.

## Potential Benefits To Society

Society would benefit by determining the important factors that account for the oxygen cost of cycle ergometry.

## Financial Obligations

The tests will be provided to you free of charge.

## In Case Of Injury Compensation

In the unlikely event that you should suffer an injury as a direct consequence of the research procedures described above, the emergency medical care required to treat the injury will be provided at the University of Nebraska at no expense to you, providing that the cost of such medical care is not reimbursable through your health insurance. However, no additional compensation for physical care, hospitalization, loss of income, pain suffering, or any other compensation will be provided. None of the above shall be construed as a waiver of any legal rights or redress you may have.

## Assurance of Confidentiality

Information obtained from you in this study will be treated confidentially. Your name will not be used in the publishing of the results of this study. Only grouped data will be reported.

## Rights of Research Subjects

Your rights as a research subject have been explained to you. If you have any additional questions concerning the rights of research subjects you may contact the University of Nebraska Institutional Review Board (IRB), telephone (402) 559-6463.

## Voluntary Participation and Withdrawal

You are free to decide not to participate in this study or to withdraw at any time without adversely affecting relationship with the investigators or the University of Nebraska at Omaha. Your decision will not result in loss of benefits to which you are otherwise entitled.

If any information develops or changes occur during the course of this study that may affect your willingness to continue participating you will be informed immediately.

Documentation of Informed Consent

YOU ARE VOLUNTARILY MAKING A DECISION WHETHER OR NOT TO PARTICI-
PATE IN THIS RESEARCH STUDY. YOUR SIGNATURE CERTIFIES THAT THE CON-
TENT AND MEANING OF THE INFORMATION ON THIS CONSENT FORM HAVE
BEEN FULLY EXPLAINED TO YOU AND THAT YOU HAVE DECIDED TO PARTICI-
PATE HAVING READ AND UNDERSTOOD THE INFORMATION PRESENTED.
YOUR SIGNATURE ALSO CERTIFIES THAT YOU HAVE HAD ALL YOUR QUES-
TIONS ANSWERED TO YOUR SATISFACTION. IF YOU THINK OF ANY ADDITION-
AL QUESTIONS DURING THIS STUDY PLEASE CONTACT THE INVESTIGATORS.
YOU WILL BE GIVEN A COPY OF THIS CONSENT FORM TO KEEP.

_____       _____

Signature of Subject          Date

MY SIGNATURE AS WITNESS CERTIFIES THAT THE SUBJECT SIGNED THIS CON-
SENT FORM IN MY PRESENCE AS HIS/HER VOLUNTARY ACT AND DEED.

_____       _____

Signature of Witness          Date

IN MY JUDGMENT THE SUBJECT IS VOLUNTARILY AND KNOWINGLY GIVING
INFORMED CONSENT AND POSSESSES THE LEGAL CAPACITY TO GIVE
INFORMED CONSENT TO PARTICIPATE IN THIS RESEARCH STUDY.

_____       _____

Signature of Investigator     Date

(The investigators' names, titles, and phone numbers)

**University of
Nebraska at
Omaha**

School of Health, Physical
Education and Recreation
Omaha, Nebraska 68182-0216
(402) 554-2670

### SAMPLE SURVEY COVER LETTER

Dear Athletic Trainer/Conditioning Coach:

We are surveying all NCAA Division I men's basketball teams to describe the size, strength, speed, agility, etc. of the modern player. Surprisingly little information has been published on the topic despite the great interest it undoubtedly has for coaches, athletic trainers, players, and fans. Therefore, we ask for your help to spend about 15 minutes in completing the attached form.

Because our purpose in doing this study is in concert with the efforts of the National Strength and Conditioning Association (NSCA) to promote effective conditioning of athletes, the NSCA Executive Director has written a letter endorsing the study (see attached). We will send to every survey participant a summary report giving the average of all schools as well as the average scores for your own team. Thus, you can readily compare your players with those of the national average for each variable. We are sure you will find this most interesting and hopefully also useful.

Your assistance is greatly appreciated. Please return the survey in the enclosed self-addressed, stamped envelope by (specify the return date).

Sincerely,

(The investigators' names and titles)

 **University of Nebraska at Omaha**

School of Health, Physical
Education and Recreation
Omaha, Nebraska 68182-0216
(402) 554-2670

*SAMPLE THANK-YOU LETTER*

Dear Coach _____:

We are pleased to provide you with a copy of the results of the survey on NCAA
Division I basketball players. Attached are two printouts of the data. One presents the
mean, mode, median, standard deviation, etc. of your team while the second is the data
for all teams combined. The columns are keyed as follows:

1. height
2. weight
3. % fat
4. vertical jump
5. power clean
6. bench press
7. squat
8. 1 mile run in minutes
9. 1.5 mile run in minutes
10. 40 yard in seconds
11. 30 yard in seconds
12. agility run: T test in seconds
13. power clean divided by weight
14. bench press divided by weight
15. squat divided by weight
16. fat free weight or lean weight
17. power in vertical jump in kilograms per meter per second

Forty-five teams representing 437 players responded to the survey. Hopefully the information presented to you will be interesting as well as useful. You can compare how your
team's players compare to those across the country. The 400 plus players' data represent
a rather good cross-section of players in Division I.

We appreciate your assistance on the project and wish you and your team the best for
the next season. Thanks again!

Sincerely,


(The investigators' names and titles)

# Appendix IV
# Glossary of Terms

**absolute zero:** a zero representing the absence of a trait or characteristic.

**abstracts:** a source of reference information including a summary. Also, a summary appearing at the beginning of an article.

**alternative hypothesis:** a statistical hypothesis that is the logical alternative to the null hypothesis. It is written in such a way that if the null is not true the alternative must be.

**american psychological association (APA) style:** a guideline for writing research papers and reports published by the APA. It includes information regarding organization, expression of ideas, editorial style, and typing instructions.

**analysis of covariance (ANCOVA):** a statistic used to compare two or more mean scores that adjusts mean scores on the basis of the effects of a variable called a covariate.

**analysis of variance (ANOVA):** a statistic used to compare more than two mean scores.

**appendix:** supplementary nonessential information to a research paper.

**applied research:** research conducted with a specific application in mind.

**basic research:** research with no specific application in mind; research for knowledge's sake alone.

**bibliography:** a source of reference information from books, articles, and documents; also refers to sources not cited in a paper but related to the topic.

**blind method:** a research technique where subjects do not know if they are receiving the experimental treatment.

**blind review:** review of a research manuscript where the reviewer(s) does not know the identity of the author(s) or institution as well as the author not knowing the identity of the reviewers.

**cause and effect relationship:** occurs when it is logically determined that one factor has a predictable influence on another.

**central tendency:** statistics used to express a score that is the most representative of all scores in a distribution.

**chi-square:** a nonparametric statistic that compares frequency counts of what is theoretically expected to occur versus what is empirically observed.

**coefficient of determination:** a statistic used to determine the strength of a relationship by accounting for the variance shared by two variables (common variance).

**coefficient of nondetermination:** a statistic used to determine the variance unaccounted for by a second variable (specific variance).

**computerized information retrieval:** use of the computer to speed information retrieval.

**concurrent validity:** a type of statistical validity where a proposed test is compared to a criterion standard within a short time to establish its accuracy.

**confidence interval:** a range of statistical values in which there is a stated probability that another statistic will be within. Typical interval probabilities are .68, .95, and .99.

**construct validity:** a type of statistical validity where there is no definitive criterion. Typically, two groups that are distinctly different on the trait (construct) are compared with the use of the proposed test.

**content validity:** a type of logical validity that assumes that the components of an instrument accurately measure what it is supposed to measure.

**control group:** a group of subjects that is similar to the experimental group except that they do not receive the experimental treatment.

**correlated *t* test:** see dependent *t* test.

**correlation:** a statistic used to assess relationships between or among variables. There are several types, including Pearson and Spearman correlations.

**correlation matrix:** a table of correlation coefficients.

**correlational research:** a type of nonexperimental research where the relationship between or among variables is studied.

**criterion-based validity:** a category of statistical validity where a proposed test is compared to a criterion or "gold standard."

**critical statistic or value:** a value in a statistics table (sampling distribution) that a calculated statistic is compared to, the purpose of which is to test the null hypothesis.

**deductive reasoning:** a logical method of reasoning moving from a generalization to specific conditions.

**degrees of freedom:** the number of variables that are free to vary in size. Degrees of freedom must be known to determine the critical statistic from a statistics table.

**delimitations:** the scope of a study or a description of the subjects to be used, the location and duration of the study, and the variables studied.

**dependent *t* test:** a statistic used to compare two mean scores that are correlated with each other; also called a correlated *t* test.

**descriptive statistics:** statistics that only characterize the subjects being observed.

**dependent variable:** a variable that measures some form of behavior; the effect of the independent variable.

**developmental research:** a type of non-experimental research where growth or maturation of subjects is studied. This type of research may be cross sectional (different subjects) or longitudinal (same subjects).

**discussion:** section of a research paper that analyzes and interprets the results.

**double-blind method:** a research technique where subjects and researchers do not know who is receiving the experimental treatment.

**Educational Research Information Center (ERIC):** a data bank of indexed and abstracted reference information in the field of education.

**effect size:** a statistic used to assess the magnitude of the treatment effect or the effect of the independent variable on the dependent variable.

**empirical probability:** probability that is based on the occurrence of past events.

**epidemiological research:** research on the incidence and causes of diseases.

**equivalence reliability:** a type of reliability that is determined by repeated testing of the same subjects using alternate forms of a test that measures the same thing. The method is also known as parallel-forms reliability.

**error variance:** variation in a dependent variable due to chance or sampling error.

**ex post facto research:** a type of nonexperimental research where data collected in the past are used to solve present problems.

**experimental group:** a group of subjects that receives the experimental treatment.

**experimental mortality:** a threat to internal validity due to subjects' withdrawal from a study for nonrandom reasons.

**experimental research:** a type of research where the researcher introduces an independent variable. This type of research is the best way to establish a cause and effect relationship.

**external quality control:** research quality control measures for publishing or presenting research results.

**external validity:** a type of experimental validity that refers to the extent to which the results from a study may be applied to different conditions or subjects.

**face validity:** a type of logical validity that assumes an instrument accurately measures what it is supposed to measure.

**factor analysis:** a statistical procedure used to determine the commonality of a large number of measures or variables.

**field research:** research conducted outside the laboratory or in the setting of the practitioner.

**Friedman's ANOVA:** a nonparametric statistical test used to determine if a significant difference exists among more than two dependent groups.

**gain score:** the difference between pre- and posttest scores.

**general variance:** the variation in scores explained by a second variable.

**generalizability:** the ability to apply the results of a study to other conditions or situations.

**halo effect:** an effect introduced when a researcher has an expectation about the performance of a subject and influences his or her behavior.

**Hawthorne effect:** an effect that a subject demonstrates due to participating and being observed in a study.

**history:** a threat to internal validity due to all of the events that may occur to a subject outside the conditions of a study.

**hypothesis test:** a statistical procedure used to objectively test the truth of the null hypothesis.

**independent *t* test:** a statistic used to compare mean scores of two different or independent groups.

**independent variable:** a variable manipulated by the researcher to determine the effect on behavior.

**index:** a source of reference information limited to periodicals.

**inductive reasoning:** a logical method of reasoning based on making generalizations from specific observations.

**inferential statistics:** statistics determined on a representative sample for the purpose of generalizing or inferring a trait to a population.

**informed consent:** the process of clearly familiarizing a potential research subject about the purpose, risks, and benefits associated with a study. This is done so the subject may make an informed decision about participating in a study.

**institutional review board (IRB):** a committee of research experts that examines, approves, or disapproves research proposals at an institution. Its primary functions are to protect the rights of research subjects, the researcher, and the institution.

**internal consistency reliability:** a type of reliability that is determined by comparing one-half of items on a single test to the other items. The method is also known as split-half reliability.

**internal quality control:** research quality control measures up to the point of publishing or presenting research results.

**internal validity:** a type of experimental validity that refers to the extent to which an independent variable has an effect on a dependent variable.

**interrater reliability:** see objectivity.

**interval scale:** a level of measurement that allows distinguishing a difference and a direction of difference and has a scale of equal units.

**introduction:** chapter or section of a research report that provides a background and justification of a study; may also include statement of the problem, hypothesis, delimitations, limitations, definition of terms, and significance.

**Kruskal–Wallis ANOVA:** a nonparametric statistical test used to determine if a significant difference exists among more than two independent groups.

**laboratory research:** research in which the treatment and data collection are conducted in a laboratory or highly controlled environment.

**limitations:** events that may interfere with the results of a study.

**logical validity:** a type of validity that is qualitatively determined. Types include face and content.

**Mann–Whitney *U*:** a nonparametric statistical test used to determine if a significant difference exists between two independent groups.

**maturation:** a threat to internal validity due to the natural growth or development of subjects during a study.

**mean:** a measure of central tendency that is the arithmetic average of all scores in a distribution.

**measurement error:** an error that is made when measuring a variable. Measurement error is the difference between a score that is free from error and one that is actually measured. Measurement error always exists to some extent.

**median:** a measure of central tendency that is the midpoint in distribution of scores.

**meta-analysis:** a procedure using statistics to interpret the results of many studies by treating the results of each investigation as a discrete bit of data.

**methods:** section of a research paper that describes the subjects, data collection, research design, and data analysis.

**mode:** a measure of central tendency that is the most frequently occurring score in a distribution.

**multiple regression:** a statistical procedure used to predict one variable from knowledge about two or more variables.

**multiple treatment interference:** a threat to external validity. This occurs when treatments interact with one another making any effect dependent on that order of testing.

**negatively skewed distribution:** a nonnormal distribution with the majority of scores being high and few low scores.

**nominal scale:** a level of measurement that only allows comparisons distinguishing a difference.

**nonexperimental research:** a type of research that is typified by making observations or descriptions about present status of a given condition or situation. No independent variable is introduced or manipulated. This type of research is also known as descriptive research.

**nonparametric statistics:** a variety of statistics that are based on data that are nominal or ordinal level, with populations from which observations are made are thought to be nonnormally distributed.

**normal curve:** a model for statistical decision making. The unit normal curve has a mean equaling 0, a standard deviation equaling 1, and an area equaling 1.0 square unit. The normal curve is also referred to as the z distribution.

**null hypothesis:** a statistical hypothesis that states no difference or no relationship. It is always assumed to be true unless demonstrated otherwise.

**objectivity:** a type of reliability that is determined by correlating the results between or among more that one evaluator. This is also known as interrater reliability.

**observational research:** a type of nonexperimental research where the researcher observes and records certain behaviors of subjects.

**omega squared:** a statistic used to determine the strength of a treatment or independent variable. It indicates the percent variance explained by the independent variable on the dependent variable.

**one-tailed hypothesis test:** a statistical test where the probability region for rejecting the null hypothesis is on one end of a sampling distribution. This is used when the researcher can predict the direction of outcome.

**operational definition:** a definition that specifies the exact usage in a study. It should reflect common usage in the discipline.

**order effect:** a change in behavior due to the sequence of testing.

**ordinal scale:** a level of measurement that allows distinguishing a difference and a direction of difference.

**parallel-forms reliability:** see equivalence reliability.

**parameter:** a trait of a population.

**parametric statistics:** a variety of statistics based on data that are interval or ratio level with populations from which observations made are thought to be normally distributed.

**partial correlation:** a statistical procedure used to assess the relationship between two variables with the effects of a third variable removed.

**pedantic:** using uncommon terms to express oneself in hopes of being perceived as intellectual.

**placebo effect:** an effect that a subject demonstrates due to participating in a study when no treatment is actually given.

**plagiarism:** using the ideas, language, or thoughts of someone else and presenting them as your own.

**population:** an all-inclusive group defined by the researcher.

**positively skewed distribution:** a nonnormal distribution with the majority of scores being low and few high scores.

**post hoc error:** attributing any beneficial change in behavior to the influence of the independent variable when it is not known.

**post hoc tests:** statistics used to identify group differences after ANOVA indicates a main effect is significant; also known as follow-up, multiple comparison, and a posteriori tests. Examples are the Tukey and Scheffe tests.

**predictive validity:** a type of statistical validity where a proposed test is used to accurately predict the occurrence of a future event.

**pre-experimental research designs:** a type of experimental research design that is typified by using subjects in intact groups and introducing an independent variable. Control groups are typically not used.

**primary reference:** directly referencing an original work.

**quasi-experimental research designs:** a type of experimental research design that is typified by using subjects in intact groups and introducing an independent variable. Control groups are used in some cases.

**random sampling:** an unbiased method of forming a representative sample from a population. When used, every element in the population has an equal probability of being selected. Methods include random numbers, systematic counting, and stratified samples.

**randomization:** the chance placement of subjects into groups.

**range:** a measure of variability that is the difference between the highest and lowest scores in a distribution.

**ratio scale:** a level of measurement that allows distinguishing a difference, as well as the direction of difference; has scale of equal units, and has an absolute zero.

**reactive effects of pretesting:** a threat to external validity. This occurs when an independent variable is only effective when preceded by a particular pretest.

**regression line:** a line in a scattergram that allows prediction of a variable; commonly called the line of best fit.

**reliability:** the extent to which test scores are repeatable.

**research:** a logical, methodical procedure for solving problems and discovering knowledge.

**research hypothesis:** what the researcher thinks will occur in a study.

**research review:** analysis of the literature on a specific topic.

**results:** section of a research paper that reports the outcome.

**review of literature:** section of a research paper that analyzes and interprets the literature.

**sample:** a representative subset of a population.

**sampling distribution:** a probability table that provides values for the chance occurrence of a particular statistic. This may also be a data set obtained from a sampling procedure.

**sampling error:** occurs when chance or random effects cause an event to occur in a manner different than expected.

**scattergram:** a graph that depicts the relationship between two variables.

**scientific method:** a logical plan for solving problems and drawing conclusions. Components include the problem, hypothesis, methods, gathering and analysis of data, and conclusion.

**secondary reference:** a reference to an original work in another source.

**selection bias:** a threat to internal validity. This occurs when subjects may select being in an experimental group or control group.

**selection maturation:** a threat to internal validity. This occurs when a subject has a unique condition that will improve naturally over the time of a study.

**simple linear regression:** a statistical procedure to predict one variable from knowledge about a second variable.

**Spearman–Brown equation:** an equation that corrects a correlation calculated on halves of a test.

**Spearman r:** a nonparametric statistic that determines the relationship between two distributions of ranked data.

**specific variance:** the variation in scores not explained by a second variable.

**speculation:** a plausible explanation not directly supported by data.

**split-half reliability:** see internal consistency reliability.

**stability reliability:** a type of reliability that is determined by repeated testing of the same subjects using the same test. The method is also known as test-retest reliability.

**standard deviation:** a measure of variability that is the approximate deviation each score in a distribution is from the mean.

**standard error of estimate (SEE):** the error in a prediction equation or the standard deviation of scores around a regression line.

**statistical hypotheses:** the null and the alternative hypotheses. Statistical procedures are used to determine if they are true or not.

**statistical power:** the ability of a statistic to reject the null hypothesis when it is false.

**statistical regression:** a threat to internal validity. This occurs when an individual has an extreme pretest score the tendency is to regress toward a more average performance on a subsequent test.

**statistical significance:** the statistical reference point that is selected for the purpose of testing the null hypothesis. This is also called the alpha level. Traditional probability levels are .05 and .01.

**statistical validity:** a type of validity that is quantitatively determined. Types include concurrent, predictive, and construct.

**subject-treatment interaction:** a threat to external validity. This occurs when a treatment is only effective for a particular type of subject.

**survey research:** a type of nonexperimental research that is typified by broad-based data collection e.g., use of a questionnaire.

**test-retest reliability:** see stability reliability.

**testing:** a threat to internal validity. It is the effect of a pretest that may improve subsequent testing performance.

**theoretical probability:** probability that is expressed as the ratio of the number of ways an event can occur divided by the number of possible events. Probability statements are commonly symbolized with $p$ and are expressed in proportions of 1.0.

**theory:** integration of facts into a framework for explaining a phenomenon.

**thesaurus:** a list of synonyms.

**treatment:** the independent variable to which subjects in a study are exposed.

**treatment variance:** variation in a dependent variable due to the treatment or independent variable.

**true experimental designs:** a type of experimental research design that is typified by randomization of subjects into groups, use of control groups, and introducing an independent variable.

**two-tailed hypothesis test:** a statistical test where the probability regions for rejecting the null hypothesis are on both ends of a sampling distribution. This is used when the researcher cannot predict the direction of outcome.

**Type I error:** a decision error that occurs if a null hypothesis is rejected when it is actually true. The probability of making a Type I error is called the alpha level.

**Type II error:** a decision error that occurs if the null hypothesis is not rejected when it is actually false. The probability of making a Type II error is called the beta level.

**unblind review:** review of a research manuscript where the reviewer(s) knows the identity of the author(s) or institution.

**validity:** the extent to which an instrument accurately measures what it is supposed to measure.

**variability:** statistics that are used to express the dispersion of scores in a distribution.

**variance:** a measure of variability that is a squared standard deviation. Variance is the basis for calculating numerous inferential statistics.

**verbose:** using excessive words to convey a thought.

**Wilcoxon matched pairs test:** a nonparametric statistical test used to determine if a significant difference exists between two related groups.

**z score:** a standard score of the normal distribution expressed in standard deviation units. Most $z$ scores range from −3.0 to 3.0.

# APPENDIX V

# REFERENCES AND SELECTED
# READINGS

AMERICAN PSYCHOLOGICAL ASSOCIATION. (1973). *Ethical principles and the conduct of research with human participants.* Washington DC: Ad-Hoc Committee on Ethical Standards.

AMERICAN PSYCHOLOGICAL ASSOCIATION. (1983). *Publication manual of the American Psychological Association* (3rd ed.) Washington, DC: author.

BACKSTROM, C. H., & HURST, G. D. (1963). *Survey research.* Evanston, IL: Northwestern University Press.

BARTZ, A. E. (1988). *Basic statistical concepts.* New York: Macmillan.

BAUMGARTNER, T. A., & JACKSON, A. S. (1991). *Measurement and evaluation in physical education and exercise science.* Dubuque, IA: William C. Brown.

BEST, J. W. (1981). *Research in education.* Englewood Cliffs, NJ: Prentice Hall.

BORG, W. R., & GALL, M. D. (1979). *Educational research, an introduction* (3rd ed.). New York: Longman.

BORG, W. R., & GALL, M. D. (1983). *Educational research: An introduction.* New York: Longman.

BRADLEY, J. V. (1971). *Distribution-free statistical tests.* Englewood Cliffs, NJ: Prentice Hall.

CAMPBELL, D. T., & STANLEY, J. C. (1963). *Experimental and quasi-experimental designs for research.* Chicago: Rand McNally.

CECI, S. J., & PETERS, D. P. (1984). How blind is blind review? *American Psychologist, 39,* 1491–1494.

CHRISTENSEN, J. E., & CHRISTENSEN, C. E. (1977). Statistical power analysis of health, physical education, and recreation research. *Research Quarterly, 48,* 204–208.

CODE OF FEDERAL REGULATIONS 45 CFR 46. (1983). *Protection of human subjects.* Office of Protection from Research Risks (OPRR) Reports. Washington, DC.

COHEN, J. (1969). *Statistical power analysis for the behavioral sciences.* New York: Academic Press.

COHEN, J. (1988). *Statistical power analysis for the behavioral sciences* (3rd ed.). New York: Academic Press.

COOK, D. (1962). The Hawthorne effect in educational research. *Phi Delta Kappan, 44,* 116–122.

DANIEL, W. (1978). *Applied non-parametric statistics.* Boston: Houghton Mifflin.

DAY, R. A. (1983). *How to write and publish a scientific paper.* Philadelphia: Institute for Scientific Information.

EICHORN, P., & YANKAUER, A. (1987). Do authors check their references? A survey of accuracy of references in three public health journals. *American Journal of Public Health, 77,* 1011–1012.

FEINSTEIN, A. R. (1983). Science, sanity, and "statistical significance." *Infectious Diseases, 13,* 5–8.

FLEISHMAN, E. A. (1969). *The structure and measurement of physical fitness.* Englewood Cliffs, NJ: Prentice Hall.

FOX, D. J. (1969). *The research process in education.* New York: Holt, Rinehart, and Winston.

FRANKS, B. D., & HUCK, S. W. (1986). Why does everyone use the .05 level of significance? *Research Quarterly for Exercise and Sport, 57,* 245–249.

GLASS, G. V., McGAW, B., & SMITH, M. (1981). *Meta-analysis in social research.* Beverly Hills, CA: Sage.

GOODRICH, J. E., & ROLAND, C. G. (1977). Accuracy of published medical reference citations. *Journal of Technical Writing and Communication, 7,* 15–19.

GREEN, L. W., & LEWIS, F. M. (1986). *Measurement and evaluation in health education and health promotion.* Mountain View, CA: Mayfield.

HANSON, D. L. (1967). Influence of the Hawthorne effect upon physical education research. *Research Quarterly, 38,* 723–724.

HAYS, W. L. (1981). *Statistics.* New York: CBS College Publishing.

KACHIGAN, S. K. (1986). *Statistical analysis.* New York: Radius Press.

JACKSON, A., POLLOCK, M., & WARD, A. (1980). Generalized equations for predicting body density of women. *Medicine and Science for Sports and Exercise, 12,* 175–182.

KERLINGER, F. N. (1964). *Foundations of behavioral research* (pp. 258–259). New York: Holt, Rinehart, and Winston.

KERLINGER, F., & PEDHAZAR, E. (1973). *Multiple regression in behavioral research,* (pp. 446–447). New York: Holt, Rinehart, and Winston.

KILPATRICK, J. (1988). Negative constructions: What tangled prose we weave. *Omaha World-Herald,* January 27.

KIRK, R. E. (1968). *Experimental design: Procedures for the behavioral sciences.* Belmont, CA: Brooks/Cole.

MCARDLE, W., KATCH, F., & KATCH, V. (1991). *Exercise physiology.* Philadelphia: Lea & Febiger.

*MINITAB REFERENCE MANUAL.* (1989). State College, PA: Minitab, Inc.

MORROW, J. R., BRAY, M. S., FULTON, J. E., AND THOMAS, J. R. (1992). Interrater reliability of 1987–1991 Research Quarterly of Exercise and Sport Reviews. *Research Quarterly for Exercise and Sport, 63,* 200–204.

NATIONAL COMMISSION FOR THE PROTECTION OF HUMAN SUBJECTS OF BIOMEDICAL AND BEHAVIORAL RESEARCH. (1978). *The Belmont Report: Ethical principles for the protection of human subjects of research.* Washington, DC: U.S. Government Printing Office.

NORUSIS, M. J. (1986). *The SPSS guide to data analysis.* Chicago: SPSS, Inc.

THE NUREMBERG CODE. (1949). Reprinted in *Trials of war criminals before the Nuremberg military tribunals under control council law No. 10* (Vol. 12, pp. 81–82). Washington, DC: U.S. Government Printing Office.

PEARSON, D., & SHAW, S. (1982). *Life extension: A practical scientific approach.* New York: Warner Books.

PELEGRINO, D. A. (1979). *Research methods for recreation and leisure.* Dubuque, IA: William C. Brown.

PETERS, D. P., & CECI, S. J. (1982). Peer review practices of psychological journals: The fate of articles submitted again. *Behavioral and Brain Sciences, 5,* 187–255.

SAFRIT, M. J. (1986). *Introduction to measurement and evaluation in physical education and exercise science.* St. Louis: Times Mirror/Mosby College.

SAGE, G. E. (1989). A commentary on qualitative research in sport and physical education. *Research Quarterly for Exercise and Sport, 60,* 204–207.

SCHMIDT, M. J. (1975). *Understanding and using statistics.* Lexington, MA: D. C. Heath.

SPARLING, P. B. (1980). A meta-analysis of studies comparing maximal oxygen uptake in men and women. *Research Quarterly for Exercise and Sport, 51,* 542–552.

STRUNK, W., & WHITE, E. B. (1979). *The Elements of Style* (3rd ed.). New York: Macmillan.

STULL, G., CHRISTINA, R., & QUINN, S. (1991). Accuracy of references in Research Quarterly for Exercise and Sport. *Research Quarterly for Exercise and Sport, 62,* 245–248.

THOMAS, J. R., & FRENCH, K. E. (1986). The use of meta-analysis in exercise and sport: A tutorial. *Research Quarterly for Exercise and Sport, 57,* 196–204.

THOMAS, J. R., & NELSON, J. K. (1990). *Research methods in physical activity.* Champaign, IL: Human Kinetics Books.

THOMAS, J. R., SALAZAR, W., & LANDERS, D. M. (1991). What is missing in $p < .05$? Effect size. *Research Quarterly for Exercise and Sport, 62,* 344–348.

TOLSON, H. (1980). An adjustment to statistical significance: $\Omega^2$. *Research Quarterly for Exercise and Sport, 51,* 580–584.

TRAN, Z. V., WELTMAN, A., GLASS, G. V., & MOOD, D. P. (1983). The effects of exercise on blood lipids and lipoproteins: A meta-analysis. *Medicine and Science in Sports and Exercise, 15,* 393–402.

UNIVERSITY OF NEBRASKA INSTITUTIONAL REVIEW BOARD FOR THE PROTECTION OF HUMAN RESEARCH SUBJECTS. (1992). *IRB guidelines for the protection of human subjects in research studies.* Omaha: University of Nebraska.

WINER, B. J. (1962). *Statistical principles in experimental design* (p. 88). New York: McGraw-Hill.

WORLD MEDICAL ASSOCIATION. (1974) *Declaration of Helsinki.* World Medical Journal.

YANKAUER, A. (1991). The accuracy of medical journal references: A follow-up study. *CBE Views, 14,* 23–24.

# INDEX